The Bicameral Critic

COLIN WILSON

The Bicameral Critic

Edited and introduced by
HOWARD F. DOSSOR

Salem House
Salem, New Hampshire

First published in the United States
by Salem House, 1985. A member of the
Merrimack Publishers' Circle, 47 Pelham
Road, Salem NH 03079.

ISBN 0–88162–047–5

Library of Congress Catalog
Card Number
84–052305

Printed in Great Britain

CONTENTS

ACKNOWLEDGEMENTS

Association Press, New York, 1972: Otto, Herbert A. (Ed.), *Love Today: A New Exploration* (Love as an Adventure in Human Freedom)

Books and Bookmen, London, Feb–May 1975 (Ronald Duncan: A Self-revealing Poet)

Encounter, London, April 1960 (On the Bridge: A Memoir of the 'Fifties); June 1969 (Writer in Residence)

Hodder and Stoughton, London, 1979: Holroyd, M. (Ed.) *The Genius of Shaw* (George Bernard Shaw: A Personal View)

Malahat Review, University of Victoria, Canada, October 1972 ('Dual Value Response' . . . A New Key to Nietzsche?)

McGraw Hill Inc., New York, 1967: Bugental, J.F.T. *Challenges of Humanistic Psychology* (Existential Psychology: A Novelist's Approach)

Pan Books, London, 1965: Defoe, Daniel, *Moll Flanders*, Introduction by Colin Wilson (Daniel Defoe and *Moll Flanders*)

Rider-Hutchinson, London, 1980: Roberts, A. and Gilbertson, G. *The Dark Gods*, Introduction by Colin Wilson (Introduction to *The Dark Gods*)

Routledge and Kegan Paul, London, 1977: Hessing, S. (Ed.) *Speculum Spinozanum* (Spinoza – the outsider)

Shenandoah, Lexington, U.S.A., vol 13 no 2, 1962 (Some Notes on Graves's Prose)

Neville Spearman, London, 1975: Briussov, V. *The Fiery Angel*, Foreword by Colin Wilson (Valeri Briussov and *The Fiery Angel*)

Twentieth Century, London, Winter 1964–5 (Crimes of Freedom and Their Cure)

Twentieth Century Literature, New York, vol 22 no 3, 1976 (An Integrity Born of Hope: Notes on Christopher Isherwood)

Vision Press, London, 1976: Smith, Anne (Ed.) *The Art of Emily Bronte* (A Personal Response to *Wuthering Heights*)

Colin Wilson: the case for optimism

Gather together a random group of twenty people anywhere in the English-speaking world and it is likely that you have identified at least one individual who knows the work of Colin Wilson. Speak with those who do know of him and it may well be that you think each has a different Colin Wilson in mind. Some will refer to a science fiction writer; some will refer to the man who identified 'The Outsider'; some will speak of the writer on the psychology of murder; some will refer to the mystery writer; some will be thinking of the authority on the Occult; some may have in mind the psychologist who wrote penetrating studies of Maslow, Reich and Jung; others might refer to the Englishman who wrote an interesting book on music.

The fact is that they could all have the same person in mind, for such is the diversity of Wilson's writing that he has written on all the above topics. He has also written on film, literature, wine, time, witches, poetry, King Arthur, Rasputin, adult and teenage sexuality, and his own life.

Before we dismiss these people who know of Wilson, let us examine them a little more closely, for they may help us understand something of this prolific writer. It is very likely that certain characteristics inhabit each of them. If they are questioned closely they might reveal themselves to be particularly sensitive; somewhat introverted; concerned at depth, not only with their own lives but with the destiny of mankind and convinced that much of the intellectual evaluation of the human condition currently being undertaken is somehow out of touch with reality. Further, these individuals may believe that they see deeply into the soul of man themselves. They may be highly conscious of a pervasive frustration yet describe themselves as optimists. Most of them will not simple recognise Colin Wilson but will probably argue that in some manner he seems to understand something

1

within themselves that they cannot quite identify; a kind of secret need that cannot find full expression or satisfaction. In short, it is likely that most of these people will be what Wilson himself has called 'Outsiders'.

Perhaps the first assertion then, that we can make about Colin Wilson is that he is recognised by a distinct group within society while remaining largely unknown outside that group – or, if known, largely dismissed.

In his *Systematic Theology*, the theologian Paul Tillich warned that his work could be understood only by those who were within 'the theological circle'. In essence he meant by this that only committed Christians would be able to accept his argument since it rested on certain pre-suppositions which were held in common by Christians. Those outside the faith would simply have to disagree since they brought a different perspective to the argument. Much the same holds in regard to Colin Wilson. Outsiders, those who have struggled relentlessly with their own identity and spent their lives trying to make sense of social relations and cultural values, will know immediately what it is that Wilson is writing about. Others, those for whom life is a daily superficiality and an ostensibly meaningful interaction with their fellow man, will be inclined to dismiss him as arrogant, foolish and irrelevant. Interestingly, they will respond to this very paragraph precisely as they respond to Wilson but those people described above as Outsiders will know precisely what I am trying to say. They bring to their reading of these words a certain sensitivity that helps them identify a shared concern.

What has been described here is a basic dichotomy, perhaps as basic as C.P. Snow's 'two cultures'. Snow recognised the difference between the scientific and the artistic temperament: I am arguing that there are sensitive and insensitive temperaments. What the proportion between the two might be I have no way of knowing, but Wilson has persistently argued that it is precisely five per cent of the world's population. (Hence my one in each group of twenty, although this does not mean that all Outsiders know of Wilson or that only Outsiders have heard of him.)

This dichotomy goes a long way towards explaining the incredible reversal that met the publication of Wilson's second book. With the publication of *The Outsider*, in 1956, he was instantly feted as an important writer: a year later, with the appearance of *Religion and the Rebel*, he was dismissed as an impossible 'autodidact'. What really happened? In my view, what happened was that *The Outsider* was found first by a group of sensitives, including Edith Sitwell and Cyril Connolly, who immediately understood its importance. Over the next year the book found its way into the hands of the professional philosophers, such as A.J. Ayer, whose intellect has swamped intuition to the extent that the deepest feelings are denied and total obeisance is given to scientific methodology. The reversal by Connolly may be explained by social pressures, for in this case they were certainly powerful and constant.

Yet, as his Outsiders themselves know, Wilson was not trying to write a scientific statement. He was delving into the history of literature and ideas in an attempt to make some sense of his own perceptions. In doing so, he identified a long pattern of human discontent and individual struggle as men and women acknowledged in themselves a real potential and tried to direct themselves towards its realization amidst an environment that was largely opposed to their development.

We are fortunate that the bitter attack on Wilson did not deter him. Had it done so, we might never have seen the completion of the 'Outsider Cycle' with its final work, *Beyond the Outsider*. It is another mark against Wilson's detractors that they continue to see *The Outsider* as a single work on which they can heap derision. Together with *Religion and the Rebel*, *The Outsider* is an opening statement which defines a problem. That problem is explicated and examined through a further three books, *The Age of Defeat*, *The Strength to Dream*, and *The Origins of the Sexual Impulse* until it is finally resolved in *Beyond the Outsider*. In my own view, *An Introduction to the New Existentialism* properly belongs within the cycle as a second part of *Beyond the Outsider* but even if we leave it out, we are left with a seminal twentieth century document.

If Outsiders were thrilled that at last their identity had been recognised and placed within a human context in *The Outsider*, they were all the more thrilled to find a way forward for themselves in *Beyond the Outsider*. This was the end of a one hundred and fifty year old impasse. The pessimism that found its roots in Kierkegaard's dark theology and its full fruit in Sartre's notion of man as a useless passion, was pushed to one side by a tide of positive endeavour that had none of the demeaning self-delusion offered by an insipid, popular psychology and an indifferent culture.

With the completion of the Outsider Cycle, Wilson had accomplished one of the major tasks of this century. He had plunged into the dilemma of millions of people and had surfaced with an answer.

During his writing of the Outsider Cycle, Wilson gave an indication of his interest in the occult. He had written a study of Rasputin in which he had drawn attention to the mystery that surrounded the man. Now, with the cycle complete, Wilson began to assemble the material that would burst into print as *The Occult* in 1970.

What is the relationship between Wilson's study of the Outsider and his study of the occult? The former, which dealt with formal ideas (even though, according to the pundits, in an informal way) stands, at first glance, at a remove from his work on the occult which deals with raining fish and mysterious moving objects. Yet the relationship between the two is clear. In the resolution of the Outsider's problem, Wilson had advocated a new consciousness – a shifting of perception so that the real world could become more visible. Once the strictures of scientific methodology and 'respectable' thinking have been removed, intuition is allowed greater play and at once the previously hidden dimensions of life spring into view. Thus the world of the occult becomes available to examination.

For centuries, literature has dealt with events that defy the rational mind of man. Individuals from Paracelsus to Bishop James Pike have challenged the human imagination to admit flights and fancies that the academic philosopher had dismissed as absurd. Wilson, however, now free of the constraints of outsiderism, chose a new definition of philosophy – 'the pursuit of reality through intuition, aided by intellect'. Thus he was free, not only in a negative way (free from) but in a positive way (free to). The world opened itself to him and he began to explore its mysteries. The occult became a playground of potentialities.

The facility for penetrating into the mysteries of life has been called by Wilson, 'Faculty X'. Faculty X is latent in all of us.

Much of Wilson's solution to the problems of the Outsider were indebted to Husserl's notion of intentionality. Simply expressed, intentionality is a matter of purpose. When one does something with a purpose or an intention in mind, the act is likely to be performed more energetically and thus more successfully than when purpose is lacking. Wilson advocates purpose as an essential ingredient of human development. It is one thing to contemplate the stars as a mute observer: it is an entirely different thing to contemplate them with a highly developed intention. In examining the world of magic, Wilson has a very particular purpose; he wants to facilitate its becoming the science of the future. When this is achieved, who then will define humanity or even the individual in the limiting formulae of today's philosophy?

Wilson's movement from the Outsider to the Magician led him to an important insight into the individual. Each of us possesses what he calls 'a Ladder of Selves' – a multiplicity of personalities of ascending sophistication and maturity. The level of self – or rather the self at which level – we choose to be is largely a matter of the extent to which we have developed Faculty X.

In recent years, Wilson's work on the bicameral mind has gone a long way towards making the 'irrational' a little more respectable. On the surface of it a man who holds an orange in his hand and says that he is holding an apple is more or less absurd. (We assume that he is not deliberately pretending and really believes what he says.) But Wilson is aware that physiological facts not only explain the apparent absurdity but transform it into a threshold of exciting possibilities.

Within the human brain, there are two personalities: one residing in the left hemisphere, the other in the right. The self we know as self lives in the left side of the brain and is logical, rational, given to law and order. The other self, living in the right brain, is intuitive, spontaneous, irrascible. The left self dismisses magic as 'not happening': the right self is itself a magician, sometimes mischievous but at other times excitingly creative.

Wilson has pointed to the antithetical nature of the mind and has challenged us to find a synthesis that will bring immeasurable richness to our experience and a wealth of detail to our self-understanding. The alternative to such a discovery is to live a life under the dictates of what Wilson calls 'the Robot', an automatic response to any given situation that may serve some particular purpose admirably but which, if allowed to dominate our lives, will enmesh us in an all-pervasive feeling of helplessness and boredom.

In addition to the Outsider and the occult, there is a third significant area of study to which Wilson has turned his attention. This is the phenomenon of murder. Again, the interest is not peripheral: it finds its centre in Wilson's basic philosophy – the philosophy of a New Existentialism.

In the six books he has devoted to murder, Wilson posits the central thesis that modern murder is a typical reaction to boredom which in turn springs from a misunderstanding of the nature of freedom. Although the facts of murder have not varied much over the centuries, its motives have undergone considerable change. Where once men murdered for money or for other material gains, today they murder out of a sense of alienation from the world and a sense of meaninglessness within their own lives. This accounts for the increase of mass murder in the twentieth century.

The psychologist, Karen Horney, has argued that neurosis is a creative struggle on the part of the neurotic to come to terms with the pain he experiences. In much the same way, perhaps we must admit murder as an attempt at a creative act. Obviously it is not creative in terms of its victim, but from the point of view of the perpetrator, murder may be an act of self-assertion against a world that condemns him to insignificance. The act is a direct statement that the murderer 'is'; that he 'exists'. It is a passionate plea for the world to take notice of him.

My own conviction, in this context, is that love and hate is the same passion, or energy, directed at opposing ends.

To the extent that Wilson is correct about murder, the solution to crime is in view. If we can relieve boredom, that is, extend human beings in the direction of a realization of their own potential, we will have done much by way of reducing the crime rate.

There is further hope held out by Wilson. With the development of extrasensory perceptions such as those available through psychometry, telepathy and precognition, we are standing on the brink of a psychic technology which augers well not only in terms of our capacity to solve and even prevent crime but much more in terms of our development as civilised human beings. That we yet remain in need of civilising can be of no doubt in the minds of those who have read Wilson's *A Criminal History of Mankind*.

The mention of psychometry and telepathy will send many rationally-minded readers searching for cover. That is a great pity and we must acknowledge a great debt to Wilson that he has so consistently challenged established Science to come to grips with some of the abundant facts that it has chosen to ignore simply because they do not fit within its frame of reference. At the point where Science closes its mind to the inexplicable it becomes nothing more – and nothing less – than an arrogance.

In wedding his study of crime to his study of the occult, Wilson has been particularly cautious. He points out, for example, that he cannot find a single case where psychometry has led directly to the apprehension of a murderer. Yet he provides so many examples where psychics have assisted police in corroborating critical evidence that it is impossible to regard their involvement as an impertinence.

The philosophy of Colin Wilson is thus seen to have more than an individual reference. It constitutes an attempt to have society examine some of its most profound problems and resolve some of its deepest needs.

In examining the life and work of a number of twentieth century individuals, including Maslow, Reich, Shaw, Hesse, Borges, Gurdjieff, Lindsay and Ken Russell, Wilson has sought to identify their relevance to a world which needs a widened, deepened consciousness and a clearer pattern for individual fulfilment. In the application of his New Existentialism to their activities and insights he has drawn attention to the often tortuous struggle that becoming a full human being entails. Usually, he can be relied upon to find some new dimension to their work that makes them more accessible and more relevant to the man in the street. By contrast, the pedantic, logic-bound criticisms to which these studies have been subjected often read as descriptions of a witchhunt on the part of the reviewer.

To date, Wilson has produced thirteen novels and one novella. As this essay was being written he had a novel on Rasputin, *The Magician from Siberia* and another called *The Janus Murder Case* awaiting publication. His novels are all successful ventures into the craft of fiction in their own right but when they are regarded within the context of his total philosophy they become even more important. In each story we are confronted with the human struggle towards self-realization, set against a hostile environment. To be sure some of his characters are decidedly unpleasant but even these have their counterpart in life and they are all vehicles for Wilson's further development of a creative philsophy.

Wilson has always been very clear on the purpose of his fiction. In *The Craft of the Novel*, he points out that a novel derives its power from the novelist's struggle with a problem. Wilson's problem is the extension of consciousness, in freedom, towards an enrichment of personal identity. In *The Craft of the Novel* he recounts the following anecdote from Romain Gary's *The Roots of Heaven*:

In a German prison camp, the Germans are trying to demoralize their French prisoners by keeping them inactive. A prisoner called Robert suggests that they should play a game: to imagine that there is a girl in the hut. If someone gets undressed he has to hold up a blanket so that the girl cannot see him. If someone swears he must bow towards the corner and apologize. In a short time the 'girl' has raised the morale of the prisoners so much that the Germans become suspicious. The Commandant makes enquiries and finds out about their game. He decides to use psychological subtlety. He enters the hut with an escort of soldiers and tells the men that he knows they have a girl there and that they must hand her over. He will return the following day, he says, and his soldiers will escort her to the nearest brothel for German officers. Then he leaves. The men are in a state of consternation. They know that if they symbolically hand over the girl she will be gone for good. Their imaginations have given her life; she cannot be recreated at will. The next day the Commandant returns and demands the girl. It is Robert, as spokesman for the others, who tells him,

'We're not going to hand her over'. And the Commandant knows he is defeated; nothing he can do can rob the men of what they have created. Robert is arrested and everyone assumes they have seen the last of him. But he returns, thin and exhausted, but undefeated. He has learned the lesson of the imaginary girl. In solitary confinement he has imagined vast herds of elephants trampling over endless plains – a symbol of freedom – and this has preserved his sanity.

On this anecdote, Wilson comments:

This is one of the great parables of our age. Gary has grasped the secret of the power that lies at the heart of the human mind. Realism is not what happens to be most real to us at the moment. It is what we perceive in our greatest intensity. And the peculiar power of the imagination allows us to cling onto this vision after the intensity has vanished. The French soldiers have not merely conjured up an imaginary sexual partner; they have succeeded in recreating something of the mystery of the 'eternal womanly' and of their deepest motives for living. The girl is no phantom: she is a reminder of a deeper reality than the prison camp.

Gary's imaginary girl is an apt symbol for the very novels of Colin Wilson. They stretch us in the direction of a better, fuller self: they help us cope with the misery of our situation by reminding us that we are never without hope.

For me, one of the most important images in Wilson's fiction occurs in *The Mind Parasites*. Having freed themselves of the influence of the debilitating virus that has lived parasitically in their minds, severely limiting their capacity to function as real men, a group of scientists voyage into space and, as a result of their concentration, are able to move the moon in its orbit. It is a telling image, particularly when we note the persistent myth of a relationship between the moon and insanity. There is a profound sense, at least in the mind of Outsiders, in which the world in which we live is lunatic. To have the capacity to alter the orbit of the moon is to have the power to repair that lunacy and move towards a meaningful realism and a more personal existence.

In an interview with Daniel Grotta, published in *Oui* magazine,

Wilson expressed the view that future historians would regard him as a watershed between pessimism and optimism. It is not yet time for that claim to be written because we continue to languish in a painful malaise. It is a malaise that cuts us off from the integrity we seek. If we are to develop, it will be through the discovery of a new optimism and should we ever make such a discovery it will be, more likely than not, within the argument of Colin Wilson.

In a personal correspondence, Wilson told me of a discussion he had with a journalist in London when he visited that city for the launching of *A Criminal History of Mankind*. The journalist had sought from the publisher of a major London daily newspaper permission to do a piece on Wilson in relation to the launching. The request was denied with, according to the journalist, the suggestion that the very request was 'filthy'. Such treatment seems hardly appropriate for a man who has spent the past thirty years of his life struggling to point the way forward to a humanity desperate for direction. No one, including Wilson himself, is asking the world for unbridled adulation. What can be expected, and with every right, is that he will be treated with respect, integrity and not a little of the intuition that makes our everyday life more tolerable. Given that, Colin Wilson may yet lead us forward into a life rich beyond our wildest dreams.

Howard F. Dossor
Melbourne
1984

ONE

Civilisation and individual fulfilment

The last piece of work I finished, before beginning this essay, was a book about Abraham Maslow – a biography and study of his ideas. Towards the end of his life, Maslow came to feel increasingly strongly that 'human nature has been sold short' and that the cultural pessimism of the past century has closed man's eyes to his real potentialities for development. (It was my own expression of this conviction – in a book called *The Stature of Man* (1958) – that led us into correspondence.) According to Maslow, man possesses *creative cravings*, which are as important as – if less painfully urgent than – his need for food, security and sex. His revolutionary Theory Z – a theory of industrial management – suggests that industry could be made more efficient by taking this into account. A man's enthusiasm needs to be drawn out of him by a feeling of freedom and responsibility. Allow him the maximum of these moral vitamins within the industrial framework, and you get the best out of him. Treat him as a mere robot within a framework of rigid discipline – McGregor's Theory X – and you will get a certain degree of efficiency, but lose the bonus of sheer loving care, concern, the element that distinguishes the craftsman from the mere labourer.

Maslow believed that the same principle could be applied to society as a whole, and that the result would be what Ruth Benedict called a 'high synergy society', a society with a high level of co-operation and creative sympathy between its members. I agree with his general conclusion, though not entirely with his analysis. That is why I am glad of the opportunity to write this essay, which I regard as a kind of postscript of the Maslow book,[1]* an opportunity to explore problems I could only touch on there; and also, perhaps, as a kind of clearing-of-the-ground for a book about the significance of criminal violence in our society, to be called *Order of Assassins*.

* A superior figure in the text indicates a note or reference. These begin on page 270.

Let me begin by sketching a rough history of our modern ideas on civilisation. For the mere word arouses dozens, perhaps hundreds, of associations, and we may as well be clear what these are.

In the 1860s, Buckle's *History of Civilisation in England* produced almost as much controversy as Darwin; it was brilliant, aggressive and rationalistic. Buckle started from his loathing of Scottish evangelism, and a long analysis of the Spanish intellect is designed to show that religious bigotry prevents development. He was an enthusiastic advocate of science, and he saw this as the beacon for man's future. This was the gospel of progress in its simplest Victorian form – which is not to say that it lacks subtlety and penetration. Matthew Arnold's *Culture and Anarchy* (1869), has the same breezy feeling of optimism, although he places his faith in art – 'culture' – rather than science. He introduced the term 'Philistine' to describe the non-appreciative bourgeois, defended 'sweetness and light', and took a distinctly sniffy view of politics and politicians. The pendulum was already swinging in the direction of Pater and aestheticism.

It is not quite clear when the reaction began to set in, although aestheticism certainly had something to do with it – Blake had complained about the 'dark Satanic mills', a century earlier. In *The Outsider* (1956), I took Henri Barbusse's *L'Enfer* (1908) as a starting point; the hero is the detached, alienated man, who spends his evenings peering through a hole in the wall at the life that goes on in the next room. But Knut Hamsun's *Hunger* had treated a similar theme nearly twenty years earlier. And, as far as England is concerned, I am inclined to see in Saki's *Unbearable Bassington* (1912) the starting point of the new, jaundiced view of civilisation. This is a disturbing book, and deserves to be better known. The central character, Comus Bassington, belongs to the Wilde tradition of the irritating hero; the London 'society' portrayed is the society of Lady Windermere. But something had happened; there is a feeling of exhaustion and bitterness. The author is obviously rather sick of his own characters; *yet he has no alternative to suggest*. One interesting chapter pictures a different type of man, an adventurer who has retired to a small farm, who describes this kind of life as being 'like the old chronicles of mediaeval Europe in the days when there was a sort of ordered anarchy . . .'; but even he is not particularly happy in his self-chosen seclusion. And Comus, with his Wildean gospel of perverse frivolity, destroys his own potentialities. In the end, he is sent to Africa, and he dies of malaria and boredom. There is a curious sentence describing his feelings watching the native villagers: 'It was so utterly trivial to his eyes, so devoid of interest, and yet it was so real, so serious, so implacable in its continuity.' For years after I had read the book – at about 14 – this scene stuck in my head: Comus sitting there on a brown hillside, watching the muddy river and the ant-like activity of the people, and *feeling nothing whatever*. There is something symbolic about it, and I must come back to it later.

In the 1914 war, the 'civilization has failed us' theme became the refrain of every poet, novelist and critic. *The Waste Land* captured the mood definitively, with its comparison of the London crowds to the crowds in Dante's hell. And Freud, in *Civilisation and Its Discontents* (1930), developed a view that had occurred to him half a century earlier: that man pays for the conveniences of civilisation with severe self-deprivation, by placing himself in a strait-jacket that represses half his natural emotions and desires. Hemingway seemed to have unconsciously hit upon a symbol for his theme in *The Sun Also Rises*, with his hero who has lost his sexual organs during the war.

Perhaps the most interesting thing is that this mood comes through even in the fairly trivial fiction of the period between wars. Michael Arlen was brainless enough, scarcely more of a thinker than P.G. Wodehouse, but *The Green Hat* (1924) leaves the same bitter taste as Saki's Bassington. And I recall reading a novelist called Donald Henderson Clark in my early teens; his books were of the Scott Fitzgerald generation and, as far as I can recall, devoid of moral purpose; yet they produced in me the same feeling of barrenness, meaninglessness.

I suspect that an intelligent sociologist of the Edwardian period – say 1900 to 1910 – would have framed the indictment this way: 'Civilization has refined our emotions, refined our intellects, and at the same time, weakened the springs of vitality. We have taken Arnold's words to heart; we have become "cultured"; our sensibilities have been cultivated on Phidias and Euripides and Chartres and Michelangelo and Chopin. But you can't spend all your time absorbing the great works of the past. You have to keep coming back to this world of factories and taxicabs and the yellow press. And this is where the shock comes in. "Culture" has completely unfitted us for this awful world; we can't cope with it. Civilization is creating two basic classes: the intelligent, who loathe it, and the coarse go-getters who are thick-skinned enough to stand it. And, according to Darwin, the intelligent are bound to die out sooner or later, and the cretins shall inherit the earth.'

This explains, in a way, why Comus Bassington sat on his bare hillside and gazed blankly at the river; for all his frivolity, he was a kind of rarefied product. But it doesn't explain why the novels of Donald Henderson Clark have the same atmosphere and bitterness. His 'Millie' isn't an aesthete; she's a sex-loving little trollop. And Hemingway's novels are about vigorous heroes who enjoy sex and bullfighting, and Fitzgerald's novels are about a class of people who fascinated him, the glamorous rich. Why should they be subject to the same disease of life-failure?

Eliot, even in his pre-religious period, would have answered: Because modern life lacks a certain spiritual vitamin, some sense of values. But even that doesn't really convince when you think about Millie.

Perhaps the nearest thing to an answer occurs in that almost forgotten play of the twenties, *The Secret Life* (1922) by Harley Granville Barker. The play is mainly about people who are a little too intelligent for the modern world, who find its crudities and over-simplifications boring. Barker, I suspect was much influenced by Henry James, and the characters in his later plays remind one of the James of *The American Scene*. (But perhaps the classic statement of the 'over-intelligent' attitude is to be found in Hugo Von Hofmannsthal – particularly *The Difficult Man*.) One of the most interesting conversations in that cryptic play occurs towards the end, between Oliver – an over-intelligent, rather world-weary young man – and Lord Clumbermere, a sententious old industrialist who always wanted to be a Baptist minister. Clumbermere offers Oliver a job, running one of his pen factories.

OLIVER: If I ran your pen factory, I'd be for the pen, the whole pen, and nothing but the pen.

LORD CLUMBERMERE: Then you'd be little use to me. If we want

to make a good gold nib, it's religion we must make it
with . . .

OLIVER: But are you a devil, then, my lord, that you want to
beat the souls of men into pen nibs?

LORD CLUMBERMERE: I hope not. But if I am, Mr. Gauntlett,
please show me the way out of the pit. For I've tried to uplift
my fellows . . . gratis; that was a failure . . . at five per cent; that
wasn't quite such a failure . . . but it was all a failure
really.[2]

Oliver is saying that he could not put any real enthusiasm into
making pen nibs, but that he would do it conscientiously and
efficiently. Clumbermere says that if you want a good nib, you
need something more: that touch of *vital interest*, of enthusiasm.
('Enthusiasm' was, after all, a religious word a few centuries ago.)
Oliver replies, in effect: But nibs aren't *worth* vital enthusiasm,
and Clumbermere must be a devil (or perhaps only a demoniac
capitalist – Oliver has once been 'pink') to want to force men to
waste vitality on pen nibs. Poor, honest Clumbermere sees his
point all right; but he doesn't know how to answer. Of course it
isn't the *nib* you want men to put their soul into. The nib is just a
symbol; it could be anything, so long as it roused that spark of real
concern, of deep absorption, that starts the life-spring flowing. And
Clumbermere goes on, in his bewildered way, to state the
paradox. You try offering it at a price, and you immediately have
more success. Not a lot more, but a bit. . . . Clumbermere is, of
course, stating the old paradox of Tom Sawyer painting the fence;
Tom doesn't want to do it; but by whistling as if he's thoroughly
enjoying it, he has a queue of friends offering to pay him to let
them have a try. But as far as Clumbermere is concerned, it would
be no answer to try to increase the demand for his brand of
religion by raising the price. The product itself is at fault – it
would certainly never do for Oliver.

And there is the paradox. Oliver can reject Clumbermere's
Baptist religion because it is too crude for his subtle intellect. But
he has no answer of his own. Hence the frustration, the sense that
life is an absurd joke. It is the paradox of Edgar Lee Masters'
Professor Newcomer:

Everyone laughed at Col. Pritchard
For buying an engine so powerful
That it wrecked itself and wrecked the grinder
He ran it with.
But here is a joke of cosmic size:
The urge of nature that made a man
Evolve from his brain a spiritual life –
Oh miracle of the world! –
The very same brain with which the ape and wolf
Get food and shelter and procreate themselves.
Nature has made man do this,
In a world where she gives him nothing to do
After all – (though the strength of the soul goes round
In a futile waste of power.
To gear itself to the mills of the gods) –
But get food and shelter and procreate himself!

There is a summary of the problem of *The Secret Life*: what is the good of possessing these subtle powers of mind when you have no purpose to go with them?

If that problem was really as insoluble as it looked, then there is really a reason for pessimism as deep as Freud's. For the awful, simple truth seemed to be this: civilisation destroys man's vitality *at the root*. It destroys the *appetite to live* that made him create it in the first place. This was something those Victorian reformers and prophets of progress never foresaw that the 'good life' could lead to such boredom, such irritable, vague dissatisfaction. It made the social problems of the thirties seem horribly ironical. Very well, you loathed the braggadocio of the Italian fascists, the brutality of the Nazis, the State totalitarianism of the Soviets. But what had the decadent West to offer in their place? Nostalgic backward looks at the church in the Middle Ages, a Catholicism with an emphasis on Original Sin?

After the Second World War, the writers and literary critics went on expressing their various forms of pessimism. Beckett grew more resigned to life's meaninglessness; Céline grew more phantasmagoric; Durrell looked backwards to the 'religion of beauty' of the 1890s; Faulkner boozed himself to death; Hemingway shot himself. Only Eliot confounded everybody by getting happily married and thoroughly enjoying his last years. But then, he stopped writing. If he'd written poetry, it would probably have been in the vein of *Practical Cats*.

There had been certain clues, of course. . . . Clumbermere had been halfway there. While Eliot and Greene talked about the Church and Faulkner looked back towards the Old South, Clumbermere was thinking about pen nibs. The pen nib, not as an actuality, but as a symbol. And Shaw came close to it too. In *Heartbreak House* – a play about the boredom and vacuity of rich people – he has a dialogue that raises new concepts. Ellie Dunne intends to marry for money; Captain Shotover advises her against it on the grounds that it will kill her soul. Ellie protests that poverty will kill her soul just as surely; her soul needs to eat, music and pictures and books and mountains and lakes and beautiful things to wear and nice people to be with. Shotover can see her point, but he replies: 'You are looking for a rich husband. At your age I looked for hardship, danger, horror and death, that I might feel the life in me more intensely.' (He was captain of a whaler.) To this, Ellie might well reply (she doesn't) that she doesn't have that alternative, being a woman. Shotover would have an answer to that too; he is seeking what he calls 'the seventh degree of concentration'. He has recognised that *there* is the core of the problem. Hesse says somewhere that 'a long time devoted to small details exalts us and increases our strength'. The concentration need not be the fierce kind that makes the eyes bulge. It means basically a *gathering together of energy*, deliberately and conscientiously. Everyday consciousness is like a bucket full of holes; it leaks away vital energy all the time.

Slowly, a kind of answer was emerging. The real problem of civilisation is its non-stop *distraction*. It was Pascal's indictment of the fashionable society of his own time. Eliot catches it in *The Waste Land* where the society woman asks 'What shall we do tomorrow . . . What shall we ever do?' Running around in circles. And this applies as much to Dostoievsky's metaphysical heroes as to Donald Henderson Clark's Millie. Millie would never make a great deal out of her life; all she wants is something constant to *focus on*, to give her some sense of purpose and worthwhileness. The life of the big city may be superficially more exciting, but it acts as a prism, diffracting her vital energy all over the place and leaving her with an odd sense that life has cheated her. As to Dostoievsky, the problem that obsesses him is of the potential hero 'in a world in which there's nothing to do', no heroic focus for his energies. When Raskolnikov swings the hatchet, his rage is not directed against the old pawnbrokeress, or even against 'society', but against a life that offers him *nothing worthwhile to focus on*, to absorb his creative energies. And Stavrogin in *The Possessed* (a character about whom I have always been tempted to write a book) commits a whole series of absurd, paradoxical, masochistic acts, and then hangs himself, leaving a suicide note in which he explains that *he can find nothing to do with his strength*. Strength needs a focus, the spiritual equivalent of a magnifying glass; our civilisation offers it the equivalent of a prism. (The Stavrogin mentality also throws interesting light on the increase in motiveless crimes of violence, particularly in America: the Manson case comes to mind.)

But all this seems to support the general indictment. Man was not made for civilisation. For two million years he has survived on his wits and his strength. A few hundred years ago – the equivalent of yesterday in the life of an ordinary man – brain-power began to pay enormous dividends in comparison to physical strength. It changed him overnight from a hairless ape into a modern city dweller, a tender of machines instead of a tender of cattle. But how can he forget the instincts of the day before yesterday? He was a fighter and a hunter; now he goes to war in a helicopter and needs a licence to hunt. Three thousand five hundred years ago, the ancient Britons spent years erecting the monument known as Stonehenge, conveying some of its immense stones from Wales by land and water. Stonehenge is still standing; but the descendants of its builders possess no purpose that extends beyond the end of next week. It is not that man lacks the strength; he lacks anything *to do with it*. There is nothing much to keep him up to the mark. 'The comfortable life causes spiritual decay just as soft, sweet food causes tooth decay,' I have written elsewhere.[3] If you keep a large, active dog in a city basement, it will get overweight and bad-tempered. Man may not be the largest animal on earth, but he is by far the most active. Civilisation is the basement in which he is trapped.

And that, in general, is the 'case against civilization', as it might be presented to the ghost of Matthew Arnold by a modern sociologist. He might mention Briussov's story *The Republic of the Southern Cross* as a remarkable anticipation of the problem (it was written in the early years of this century): in this ideal republic, beneath a vast dome at the South Pole, the workers are all comfortably-off; but they have to live in identical houses and dress in identical clothes, and behave exactly like everybody else. Then one day, they all start to go mad; the madness takes the form of a compulsion to do the opposite of what is expected of them, to behave as irrationally and illogically as possible. Finally, the city is destroyed by the madmen, who die in its flames. The parable of 1900 looks uncomfortably like a prediction of what could happen in the year 2000 when the whole earth is one vast overpopulated city. . . . Even now, the rate of insanity and mental illness in the great cities of the world makes the story seem an inspired clinical guess.

Twenty-five years ago – directly after the war – it would have been difficult to go much further than this. Arnold Toynbee, writing the last volume of his *Study of History*, could only advise the West to 'cling and wait'. (When I interviewed him a couple of years ago, he said he was glad he was about to depart this world rather than just coming into it.)

In fact, interesting things were beginning to happen, mostly in psychology. Although American readers will be familiar with many of these, I must outline them here for the benefit of those who aren't.

Revolts against Freud had been taking place since Adler and Jung broke away in the pre-1914 period. Otto Rank 'defected' in the late twenties, and died a decade later. During that period, his most interesting contribution was the idea of the 'will to health'. Perhaps in reaction against Freud's emphasis on the sick impulses of human nature, Rank took the stand that man is *naturally* healthy – that his mental forces make for stability, health and balance. Just as water finds its own level. He never had time to elaborate this idea – at least, in psychological terms; his analyses were cultural and artistic rather than strictly psychological.

Abraham Maslow (born 1908) began as a behaviourist, working with Harry Harlow at Wisconsin on the intelligence testing of monkeys. Freud and Adler began to excite him in the mid-thirties.

MASLOW

SURVIVAL
SEX
SELF-ESTEEM

Whenever he read Freud, the sexual theory seemed self-evidently right; when he read Adler, the will-to-power theory seemed more convincing. One day, studying the behaviour of apes in the Bronx zoo, it struck him that the two theories could be synthesised; ape sexual behaviour was a function of dominance – the will-to-power contest between individuals. In effect, this made Adler righter than Freud; but not absolutely. On the most basic level, the animal's most urgent need is food and security; after that comes sex; after that, dominance and self-esteem. Assuming that this also applies to human nature, you might say that at the most basic level, Marx is right; men need food and shelter before everything else. Go higher up the ladder, and Freud is right; higher still, and Adler is right. This notion of a ladder suggested that human beings have a need for 'self-actualization', the expression of creative drives. (This also, of course, suggests another ladder, for creative drives might find expression in many forms, from collecting postage stamps to founding a religious order.) Maslow added a further step to the hierarchy of values: self-actualization, which becomes a matter of urgency only after the various lower 'value needs' have been satisfied.

A man who has satisfied the needs for security, sex, love, self-esteem and dominance ought to be a fairly healthy individual: so Maslow reasoned. In order to test whether such people naturally passed on to the self-actualisation stage, he had to study as many of them as possible. He looked for the healthiest people he could find. In fact – as he slowly came to realise – such individuals do not *have* to become self-actualisers; many of them stay quite happily at the self-esteem level. (He was in the process of investigating this problem when he died in 1970.) But a large number of people do become self-actualisers. But he also made anoher interesting discovery, as a by-product of his researches. The extremely healthy individuals often had near-mystical experiences of sheer delight in being alive. I say 'near-mystical' to give an idea of what I mean; but in fact, these experiences were, more often than not, oddly commonplace, and without any element of the 'supernatural' or ineffable. The individual would suddenly feel that all the troubles of life are worth it – and more-than-worth-it – or as if both he and the world had suddenly become more *real*. Maslow called these moments 'peak experiences'. His finding seemed to confirm

Rank's theory that man has a natural will-to-health that only needs to be given a chance to work.

The peak experience is an experience of meaning, of value – the opposite of the 'meaninglessness experience' that has played such an important part in modern literature – for example, in Conrad's *Heart of Darkness*, Eliot's *Hollow Men*, or the Marabar caves episode of Forster's *Passage to India*. In all these works about life-failure, disillusion, moral emptiness, there is usually – no, always – an assumption that the sense of meaninglessness is *deeper and truer* than the meanings that sustain everyday living. 'After such knowledge, what foregiveness?' asks Eliot in *Gerontion*; and according to Yeats in *Meru*, civilisation is held together by 'manifold illusion', and man's obsessive will to truth can only bring him at last 'into the desolation of reality'. The significance of Maslow's theory of the peak experience extended beyond psychology. For Maslow was saying that the feeling of desolation, 'when life loses its savour', is simply a matter of a certain kind of sickness, and has no more metaphysical significance than losing your appetite for cream cake when you have a fever. If a gramophone record of a symphony is slowed down, it makes the music sound strange and unreal; but this is completely irrelevant to an evaluation of Beethoven's Ninth Symphony; it certainly doesn't prove that it presents only an illusion of music.

I think it would be fair to say that Maslow was not too deeply concerned with the philosophical implications of his discoveries, although he recognised that they have religious significance. His conclusions can be simply stated. *If* human beings have a 'higher' nature which is just as instinctoid as their 'lower' nature, and *if* human nature has been 'sold short', then it might not, after all, be a foregone conclusion that humankind will destroy itself in pointless violence. The implications of his theory were anarchistic – in the precise signification of the word: the exact opposite, for example, of the view advanced by Golding in his fashionable *Lord of the Flies*, where it is implied that man's 'niceness' only goes skin-deep. Maslow felt that if human beings are given the right kind of freedom, the right kind of incentive to creativity, they will develop into creative and vital individuals. In fact, intelligent human beings *need* self-actualising activity as urgently as they need food or sex. One of his most instructive – and early – cases was of a young girl who even ceased to menstruate when she was trapped in a boring dead-end job. Part-time study at night school and the feeling that she again possessed a *future* completely restored her health. Maslow's 'idealistic' view when applied to industrial enterprises, proved to work triumphantly (for example, at the Saga Food Corporation in California – who, in gratitude, offered Maslow a fellowship which he enjoyed for a year before his death). The same method – applied without the theory – seems to be the basis of the economic recovery of West Germany and Japan since the war. The workers are treated paternally, their security guaranteed, and they are allowed to buy shares in the business: the result, a tremendous surge of enthusiastic effort.

When he died, Maslow was working out the details of how his Theory Z could be applied to society at large. The first and most obvious application would be the widespread adoption of Theory Z in industry. (As an Englishman who has watched his country wrecked by endless futile strikes in the past five years, I can vouch for the urgent need to apply Theory Z over here; but, being conservative and phlegmatic, no doubt we shall manage to delay applying it until the turn of the century.) Next – and now this is my own guesswork – the development of some kind of 'social participation' centres designed to increase creative co-operation. The fundamental aim, clearly, is to try to give people a sense of the worthwhileness of their own activity instead of feeling that nothing they can do will make any difference to society. G.K. Chesterton and his 'distributists' declared that man can only have such a sense – of being an active, living force – if he is part of a small community – hence the 'two acres and a cow' theory. Maslow said this is not so; a giant corporation – or even a giant city – *could* be run along Theory Z lines. If the human race seems to have been pretty inadequate over the last couple of centuries, this is because it has been governed by Theory X – authoritarianism.

The most interesting work, then, is still to be done; Maslow had not even made a start when he died, although he showed the way.

Since my own interest is centred around existentialism and phenomenology, the most absorbing question for me is: what are the philosophical implications of Maslow's view of human nature?

Before exploring this question, I must speak briefly about Viktor Frankl, whose discoveries in psychology parallel Maslow's. In a prison camp during the war, Frankl observed how far the physical health of the prisoners depended on optimism. When half-starved prisoners had something to hope for, their resistance to illness increased. Deprived of hope, they died. Their 'attitude' seemed to make all the difference, and in one of his most significant anecdotes, Frankl describes how the prisoners were made to stand in line outside a new camp throughout a whole night and the following morning; yet all were wildly happy because the camp had no chimney, and therefore no incinerator. When they had a reason to feel fortunate, lucky, the cold and their hunger were *overruled* by the mind.

Frankl's second major discovery was the so-called 'law of reverse effort', typified in his anecdote of the school drama group who needed someone to play a stutterer in their play. They chose a boy who stuttered, but when he got on stage, he couldn't stutter. Frankl later used this method with great success on obsessive patients. For example, a woman whose fear of germs had finally made her suicidal was simply persuaded to do the dirtiest work in the ward – clean up the vomit and wash out the lavatories; in a week or so, she was cured.

It seems to me that, in a certain sense, Frankl's discoveries are even more important than Maslow's. By this I do not mean to say that Frankl should be regarded as the greater psychologist. Maslow's discoveries were based upon a lifetime of experiment and observation; Frankl's seem to have been sudden insights. But they are incomparably fruitful insights. For they suggest (a) that neurosis may be a build-up of inner-panic akin to stuttering, rather than a symptom of subconscious disturbances, and (b) that physical health is more intimately and immediately tied up with the will – and therefore sense of purpose – than was previously suspected. And this was, of course, very much Maslow's own conclusion.

In his context it is also worth mentioning the 'attitude therapy' of Dan MacDougald, an American lawyer, which is an interesting application of the Maslow–Frankl principles (although Mac-Dougald seems to have developed them independently). MacDougald was struck by our powers of selective observation.

A cat's aural nerve can be connected up to an oscilloscope in such a way that when a bell is rung in the cat's ear, the needle of the oscilloscope registers the impulse along the nerve. But if a cage of mice is placed in front of the cat and the bell rung, the oscilloscope doesn't budge. The cat's concentration on the mice somehow increases the resistance of the aural nerve – like hanging a 'Don't Disturb' sign on a door – so it doesn't *hear* the bell. MacDougald calls this faculty 'blocking', and he believes that criminals are men whose faculty 'blocking' has placed them in an unpleasant universe to which the natural response is violence. It is rather as if you walked around wearing ear plugs and an eye shade and wondered why the world seems so dark and silent. In most criminals this negative way of seeing the universe is something automatic, of which they are not consciously aware. The MacDougald method of rehabilitation is to explain to the criminals about their faculty blocking and try to persuade them to change their attitudes to the world and their fellow prisoners. The results have been spectacular. But MacDougald's method would not work unless Maslow was largely correct – that there *are* 'higher ceilings of human nature', and that violence and anti-social activity are as abnormal as colour blindness.

All this amounts to an extremely non-Freudian picture of human nature. The Freudian picture shows man as a helpless creature at the mercy of inner-forces that he does not understand, and *cannot* understand, since they are concealed in the depths of the subconscious mind. His culture is an attempt to pretend that he is the master of his fate, the chooser of his values. His religion is a throwback to childhood, when he felt secure and confident and invulnerable in his mother's arms. . . . The Maslow–Frankl picture, on the other hand, asserts the exact opposite: the man possesses far *more* will, far more power over his mind and body, than he himself normally realises. And what is quite plainly implied – although neither of them actually said this – is that if he could learn to understand and make use of these powers, he would become more godlike than he can at present imagine.

There are, of course, many other rebels against the old 'reductionism' and 'scientism' that is our legacy from the nineteenth century. Maslow's polemic, *The Psychology of Science* was anticipated by Michael Polanyi's more massive and detailed

Personal Knowledge. Arthur Koestler has for many years now been synthesising the conclusions of many anti-behaviourist psychologists and many anti-reductionist biologists, notably in *The Act of Creation* and *The Ghost in the Machine.*[4] Naon Chomsky's linguistic theories are also 'Maslovian' in spirit, since he argues that language is not learned automatically – like a series of circus tricks or Pavlovian reflexes –but is structured by a sense of meaning (Maslow would say values) that seems to be above and beyond language. But I think it would be fair to say that the full significance of these various anti-reductionist theories can only be grasped within the framework of Maslow's 'new map of human nature'. The Maslow–Frankl theory constitutes the most *comprehensive* challenge to the nineteenth-century view of man as a mere creature of his environment.

But the real work, I repeat, remains to be done. Maslow sketched in the outline; we have to fill in the details. And this brings me to 'my own part in the matter'.

In *The Outsider*, I had stated that the basic problem was that of 'original sin'. I suppose I am one of those writers whose whole life is built upon a single insight – I am what Isaiah Berlin calls a hedgehog rather than a fox. I have always had a strong and deep feeling that there is something fundamentally wrong with human nature. Now it might seem that such an idea is in direct conflict with Maslow; but I shall try to show why it is not.

The most remarkable thing about human beings is the sheer *wideness and variety* of the consciousness of which we are capable. It is true that we appear to have lost certain faculties that are possessed by most animals – and also, perhaps, by young children: a kind of oneness with nature, an immediacy of response. I suspect, although I am not dogmatic about this, that many animals also possess powers that we might regard as 'super-normal' – extra-sensory perception, 'second sight'. The homing instinct may not involve *extra*-sensory perception; apparently it has been proved that salmon find their way home over hundreds of miles by a sense of smell; but in that case, 'normal' perception has been raised to a degree of fineness that makes the distinction little more than a quibble. Civilised man has lost most of that extreme delicacy of perception. On the other hand, he is capable of states of consciousness that might be described as godlike. His imagination can be touched in such a way that he catches some glimpses of the complexity of the universe: actually *feels and perceives* this complexity, at the same time grasping it with his intelligence. The romantics of the nineteenth century felt there was something tragic about this: that man should be capable of such tastes of piercing sweetness like a prisoner's glimpses of freedom through his bars. Freedom – the most beautiful and alluring of all human words. It arouses something at once painful and godlike in us. For there seems no practical way to achieve the reality of this vision in the grinding business of everyday living. As we approach middle age, the names of the poets – Shelley, Novalis, Hugo, even Goethe – cease to exercise the same magic; we suspect them of a kind of exaggeration. But you only have to turn to Keats's letters, and contemplate the intensity of his absorption in Shakespeare, Milton, Spenser, Homer, to feel again that this is an authentic vision. Keats is unhappy in the everyday world because he *has* stood on mental mountain-tops and seen far horizons; after that, the reality of everyday life gives him a certain claustrophobic feeling. I once called this 'the Bombard effect', after the French adventurer who sailed across the Atlantic in a rubber dinghy, drinking seawater and eating squashed fish, in order to prove that shipwrecked mariners do not have to die of starvation. Halfway across, he was spotted by a ship, and he made the mistake of going on board and eating a normal meal. It almost killed him, for when he got back into his dinghy, the squashed fish made him vomit for days. . . . The romantics were in the same position. After their glimpses of far horizons, everyday life produced acute nausea. (Thomas Mann has described this movingly in the Hanno sections of *Buddenbrooks*.)

I have always considered this 'the central question of philosophy. But what interests me is not so much the question of the 'intensity experience', the visions of freedom, as the phenomenology of this dreary everyday consciousness. If my car performs very badly, I know there is something wrong with it – perhaps even something very simple; perhaps I've left the handbrake on. So what is wrong with our everyday consciousness that it remains so rigidly limited? Does it run on the mental equivalent of train lines? In a book about Job, I once came across the phrase 'the great mystery of human boredom', and it instantly struck me as a revelation. There is something insane about it, like a man starving to death in a house full of food and drink. Obviously, there is no one so unimaginative and stupid as to deny that we are in an endlessly fascinating universe. The American bootlegger and murderer, Charlie Berger, looked at the sky as he stood on the scaffold, and said with sudden conviction: 'It *is* a beautiful world'. But it was a bit late to notice it; the trap dropped a moment later. Opposite my eyes, as I write this, is the criminology section of my library. As I look at the volumes of the Notable British or American Trials series, I again confront the great mystery of human boredom. Why did they kill? When you have analysed all their motives, you realise that the most important one has been left out of account: a kind of *devaluation* of the world; boredom. The gap between Bruno Hauptmann and John Keats was just about as wide as the human mind can conceive. One saw a debased reality in which a child's life was less important than a few thousand dollars; the other saw a reality always trembling on the brink of exploding into visionary meaning. What *precisely* was the nature of the difference between them?

Maslow, Frankl and MacDougald have all come up with partial analyses of the problem – the great mystery of human boredom. Maslow says that intelligent human beings have a need for self-actualising activity; if this need is denied, it goes sour. Habitually constipated people may develop cancer of the bowel; the consequences of creative constipation can be as serious. Frankl recognises the extent to which your own conviction of worthlessness and defeat erodes the sense of values. Freud's theory of neurosis developed from the study of hysteria – women who believed themselves partially paralysed or blind or deaf when there was nothing physically wrong. Frankl would say that most people have a similarly hysterical view of their psychic limitations or disabilities – as if psychic limbs had gone dead from lack of blood supply – and that the problem is to cure the self-division that causes panic. MacDougald would point to unconscious 'blocking' activities as the root of the trouble. All three are obviously right. But equally clear, to me at least, all three explanations fail to get to the heart of the problem. Put it this way: If 'mystical perception' were the norm among human beings, then these explanations *would* be adequate; they would explain how criminals and neurotics manage to fall so far below the norm. But there is also something seriously wrong with the norm, so that the criminal is only an exaggerated version of the norm.

I see this as an essentially evolutionary problem. Man is an animal, whose basic needs are animal. And the chief thing we notice about animals is their limitedness. My dog eats his dinner then curls up near the fire and sleeps. Certain things stimulate him. If he hears a clinking noise from his food bowl, he rushes into the kitchen to see if someone has dropped the remains of a steak in there. If I put on my hat, he looks hopefully, wondering if I'll take him for a walk. If I pick up a ball, he positively quivers with interest. But apart from this, his range of interests is limited. Game wardens in Africa know that lions and gorillas are equally limited. If you read Conan Doyle, or various other writers of the turn of the century, you will find that snakes are regarded as deadly, malevolent creatures; but they were anthropomorphising them. Anyone who has kept snakes knows they are also sluggish, limited, innocent creatures.

Man is also a animal, and he possesses the animal's limitedness to a large degree. His basic interests are food, security, sex, then a certain amount of amusement; (I think of those soldiers in *The Naked and the Dead*, playing cards for hour after hour as they wait to go into battle). And for most of his two million years, these have been the limits of his interests. However, civilisation was created by a different type of man, a type who possessed a greater curiosity and enterprise. And man is now living in a civilisation created by these above-average men: by Genghis Khan and Alexander, by Archimedes and Newton, by Plato and Goethe and Leonardo. The average man has probably changed very little since the first cities of Mesopotamia and Asia Minor, but he is living in a civilisation created by 'intellectuals'. And all its extraordinary activity only emphasises his simple desire to have a home and a wife and a certain amount of amusement. . . . That is to say, civilisation increases his natural *passivity*. It bewilders him, and it also protects him. Because we have all been dragged into technical civilisation by the back hairs, we all share this attitude of passivity.

And this, it seems to me, goes a long way towards explaining the romantic paradox: that man can have such clear glimpses of freedom, distant horizons, godlike possibilities, and yet feel himself so miserably limited and inadequate, so helpless and 'contingent' (to borrow a favourite word of the existentialists). To some extent, all intelligent people share this new, super-animal consciousness that has created civilisation, that made our ancestors labour to build Stonehenge. But then, there is that great bedrock of animal passivity in all of us. We can be stirred by great music or art, but we cannot see how its 'message' can be applied to actual living. The genuine idealist, Shelley or Shaw, is the rarest of all living creatures.

And so we are all in the position of some *nouveau riche* manufacturer whose wife insists on dragging him to the opera and art exhibitions; we are definitely not quite up to it.

The starting point of my own thinking was the romantic paradox: is man a god or a worm? It seemed to me that this question can only be answered by a minute phenomenological analysis of the experience of 'positive consciousness' – to find out whether it is, in fact, no more than a surge of emotional euphoria, or whether, as it seemed, it was a *perception* of a new possibility for human consciousness. For that is the basic question. If a romantic poet, looking back on one of those moments of visionary intensity, had to say: 'It was an illusion; the truth is the weakness and limitedness of my everyday self . . .,' what alternative had he to dying of despair?

Now it should be clear why I feel that Maslow does not go far enough (or rather, didn't live to go far enough). He recognises the importance of the peak experience – its relation to psychological health – but it remains *merely* an 'experience', a feeling. (It's amazing how often I'm asked after lectures: 'What is the *point* of peak experiences?') It is true that he also relates peak experiences to his theory of 'higher ceilings for human nature' and recognises that it has a kind of religious significance – or at least, a 'value' significance. But then, he emphasises that anyone can be a 'peaker', and that a peak experience can be *about* anything. One of his examples is of a hostess who had a peak experience after giving a successful party, looking round at the room littered with empty glasses and cigarette butts. . . . Which once again seems to reduce their significance.

The question as I expressed it was: How do we judge the objective content of the peak experience?

The starting point of my analysis was not Maslow, but Husserl. For it was Husserl who had recognised that mental activity cannot be described by chemical or physical analogies. All mental activities are essentially *acts*, analogous to reaching out one's hand or shooting an arrow at a target. A chemical process – for example, the combination of moisture with iron to form rust – lacks this element of *directionality*. The same is true of the various forces at work in a hailstorm – which otherwise may give an impression of power and purpose – but hardly directionality.

It is important to grasp the essence of Husserl's phenomenology, the theory of intentionality. Husserl said: *All* mental activities are intentional, no matter how much they may appear to be non-intentional. In this way, the body differs from the mind. For although my body is designed for activity of various sorts, it is also capable of non-intentional acts – for example, when I stumble and fall. Such acts are purely physical, like the hailstorm. *But the mind has no equivalent of the non-intentional act* – even becoming unconscious under anaesthetic. For in so far as consciousness exists, it is intentional. It may not seem so. You may feel that when you stare absent-mindedly out of the window of a train, this is non-intentional consciousness. But then, a moment's reflection will show that in so far as you become un-focused and mentally blank, you didn't have consciousness; what consciousness you still *had* – idly noticing the passage of scenery, so that when the train slowed down, you 'woke up' – was intentional. This is a controversial point among phenomenologists, and Merleau-Ponty believes that the consciousness we experience on the edge of sleep is non-intentional. This could just be so; if so, it only emphasises that all other forms of consciousness we know *are* intentional. To be conscious is to *grasp* with the fingers of the mind.

Although all consciousness is intentional by nature, it can obviously be more or less so. The kind of consciousness Mozart must have experienced when writing his last three symphonies in six weeks is obviously more intentional than the kind required for sunbathing, just as climbing a mountain is a more intentional physical activity than smoking a cigarette.

The significance of this seems to have been lost on phenomenologists. A man who is too lazy to take physical exercise becomes flabby and short of breath; his digestion probably deteriorates, and he may experience a vaguely nauseated feeling when facing his dinner. Similarly, if I watch television for too long, I experience the mental equivalent of this sensation. I get a feeling that the spark plugs of my brain are getting oiled up, so to speak. I feel a kind of moral dyspepsia. The reason that sensible parents are disinclined to let the children watch too much television is not that they have Victorian ideas about health and strength, but that they can see that too much TV demoralises the kids; they grow fretful; things get too much for them. The passivity involved in too much television causes a kind of leakage of vitality. The same is true of all mental activities. If I have been wanting to read a book for a very long time, and I finally get hold of a copy, I hurl myself into it; I read with total absorption; I savour every sentence. And when I have finished reading, I feel no 'moral dyspepsia; in fact, I may still feel as fresh as ever. If I read a book merely for the sake of passing the time, occasionally skipping a boring half-page or so, the moral indigestion builds up as I read. Highly intentional mental activity, like highly intentional physical activity – mountain climbing, bullfighting, shark fishing – produces a feeling of power and strength, of self-control, of vitality. The healthy person seeks out such highly intentional activity, because he knows it produces this feeling of strength. This explains why Hemingway spent his life risking his neck, big game hunting, etc. It also explains why Casanova or the author of *My Secret Life* spent his life chasing sex. It is an experience of *control* and power in which you feel more alive. As Nietzsche says, happiness is the feeling that obstacles are being overcome, that you are conquering.

The significance of this for phenomenology is considerable. For example, Sartre's novel *Nausea* argues that man's basic experience of the world is contingency, the feeling of his disconnection from it – what Camus calls absurdity. But the 'nausea' described is simply the opposite of the high-level intentionality described above, and is akin to the physical nausea experienced by people who take no exercise. In other parts of the novel, Sartre describes the peak experience with some accuracy: the sense of feeling hard, brilliant, shiny, like a 'precision machine'; that is to say the feeling of *control*, strength. But he is so committed to his view that 'consciousness is an emptiness' that he fails to grasp the significance of the experience. Similarly, Heidegger's work contrasts the feeling of inauthenticity with the feeling of authenticity experienced in aesthetic experience – reading poetry, for example –but fails to see that the difference between such inauthentic activities as 'gossip' and authentic activities like reading Hölderlin is a difference in the *degree of intentionality* involved.

The peak experience is a high-intentionality experience. Nausea and all other forms of mental sickness are low-intentionality experiences.

It must be firmly borne in mind that man takes it for granted that his mental processes are non-intentional, analogous to chemical processes. He finds that he gets bored in a dentist's waiting room. Why? Because there is a lack of 'reactive chemicals', so to speak. He sets out on holiday, and begins to feel altogether more alive. Why? Because, he thinks, new experiences keep dropping into his mind, like Alka Seltzer tablets into a glass of water, and producing a pleasing effervescence. . . . Ever since childhood, we have assumed this attitude: the mind is a glass of water; consciousness is passive. Husserl's view is not merely an interesting philosophical statement; it is one of the most revolutionary observations about human nature ever made. To understand it is difficult, because we are so completely accustomed to the 'natural standpoint'. This is why, when we suddenly grasp its significance in moments of great intensity, it seems to be somehow ungraspable, inexpressible in ordinary language. Yeats says that when a man is fighting mad, 'something drops from eyes long blind/He completes his partial mind. . . .' Because 'when a man is fighting mad', the passive fallacy is suddenly discovered to be an absurdity.

This also explains, of course, why Frankl's prisoners remained healthy so long as they were hopeful and died when they lost hope. The all important difference between high vitality and neurosis – and between life and death in a concentration camp – is the difference between high-level intentionality and low-level intentionality. The everyday consciousness of the average man could be compared to a half-deflated balloon or a tyre with a bad leak. In moments of intensity, he glimpses what life would be like with the balloon – or tyre – properly inflated. After all, tyre manufacturers advise the motorist to keep them inflated hard; if you drive on them when they are low, they wear out more quickly; and if you drive on a completely deflated tyre, you ruin it within minutes.

The 'law of reverse effort' can also be understood in these Husserlian terms. Because of the 'passive fallacy' of the natural standpoint, we shrink from effort, as a crippled man would shrink if you asked him to tap-dance. When a man is actually launched into excited effort – when, for example, he is fighting mad – the passive fallacy vanishes, and there is a curious instinctive 'rightness' about everything he does – an economy of energy, for example. But if he is not gripped by this curious confidence, he becomes self-divided. For example, a shy man, asked to make a speech, is aware of himself as a dual entity; he is aware of his voice – usually stammering – and of burning ears and cheeks. If some passion or anger carried him away, the self-division would vanish; he would feel himself a unity. While he is still shy and nervous, he is seeing himself simultaneously from two points of view, as active and passive. When he is carried away by excitement, he sees the 'passive self' to be an illusion, an error; in effect, he is glimpsing the truth of Husserl's assertion that consciousness *must* be intentional. Hypnotism depends upon taking advantage of human self-division to induce a state of error, the passive fallacy. The hypnotist sets up a conflicting mass of intentions, lending his weight to the passive ones ('You are feeling tired . . .'). In an obsessive subject, the two masses of intentions have reached a kind of equilibrium, and it is like driving a car with the brakes on. Frankl's reverse effort therapy advises the obsessive to actually use his will to achieve the result he is afraid of. ('Try to stutter', 'try to worry'.) As the patient *tries* to stutter (i.e. has the *intention* of stuttering), 'something drops from eyes long blind', and the passive fallacy vanishes.

There is another important point that must be made here. Human beings have a remarkable capacity for cutting themselves off from the external world, and descending into the realm of subjectivity. They say that Edgar Wallace could write a novel in a long weekend, and that Simenon can do a Maigret in eleven days;

this is a remarkable example of our capacity for subjectivity. But few of us use this power positively. Under any kind of stress or misery, we tend to descend into a subjective world of petty worry. And the result can be dangerous. Anyone with small children knows how easy it is for them to flood the bathroom. They may not be splashing violently, but a small wave travelling down the bath meets another small wave bouncing off the end and forms a reinforcement wave. Highly emotional people tend to do the same thing with anxieties. But not only highly emotional people. Once this mechanism is understood, it is seen to be of fundamental importance in all day-to-day existence. We habitually exaggerate the importance of present difficulties. We seldom feel relaxed and healthy enough to take a clear, objective view of our own lives. The consequence is that we are always working below our maximum level of efficiency. And only fairly unusual people possess the power to call the bluff of their emotions and restore a state of objectivity. Wordsworth's *Immortality* Ode offers an example of the process. He begins by making an apparently objective – and thoroughly gloomy – statement, that there *was* a time when all nature produced a mild peak experience, and that now that touch of 'glory' has passed away. He goes on to ruminate about the sense of 'magic' in childhood, and the way a feeling of imprisonment begins to descend on the growing youth. ('We have heard the key turn in the door/And turn once only . . .') But the odd consequence of this analysis of the 'long littleness of life' is that the 'timely utterance' makes him feel *strong* again. He has meditated himself out of his state of depression and subjectivity, back into a feeling of objective reality. It is like opening a window.

And again, I must point out, the feeling of poetic delight is a feeling of *strength*. Wordsworth confirms Husserl.

In the second book of my 'outsider cycle', *Religion and the Rebel* (1957), I analysed the problem that has concerned religious thinkers since Pascal; that civilisation *needs* a religion as if it were some important vitamin. Bergson distinguishes between two types of religion, dynamic and static, dynamic religion being the religion of saints and mystics – those who hunger and thirst after spiritual intensity – and static religion being the popular religion of dogmas and 'thou shalt nots'. The healthiest human beings are those with a sense of long-distance purpose, of values beyond the immediate contingencies of everyday living. Saints or poets experience a direct craving for such values; most people only notice their absence as a vague, uncomfortable feeling of suffocation. But the rise of the Nazi movement reveals how far a society craves a sense of long-distance purpose and ideals.

This same conclusion has been stated, in various ways, by many writers and thinkers of the past century: Dostoievsky (notably in 'The Grand Inquisitor'), Newman, Carlyle, Shaw, T.E. Hulme, T.S. Eliot, Arnold Toynbee, to name only a few. 'Civilization needs a religion as a matter of life and death' said Shaw, and he suggested (as Toynbee did later) that the answer might be a kind of synthetic religion that took the best from all the world's religions. I argued that this was no solution; it is like suggesting you could create a super-patriotism by persuading people to be patriotic about every country in the world. A religion seems to need to be held together by a certain amount of dogmatism and a belief in its *unique* capacity to ensure salvation. I concluded that either some totally new *form* of religion must appear, or society somehow learn to do without. This would be no hardship for the small percentage of people who are capable of 'dynamic religion', since they create their own anyway, but it might have unpredictable results on society at large – perhaps as dangerous as those foreseen by Briussov in *The Republic of the Southern Cross*.

The 'new psychology' has taken the first enormous, decisive step in solving this problem. At least, it is no longer completely deadlocked. If Maslow is right about 'higher ceilings for human nature', then the vitamin supplied in the past by organised religion can be supplied by other forms of creative activity. Industries work better if the workers are somehow given a greater sense of freedom, creativity, responsibility. Society as a whole will work better when we have devised ways of applying Theory Z to all its activities.

The more we consider this idea, the more exciting and satisfying it seems. Consider the argument of the Grand Inquisitor. He tells Jesus: 'You offered men freedom, you told them to seek their salvation with diligence. But most men don't want freedom; they don't want to think for themselves. They want bread and security, and they're perfectly willing to leave their salvation in the hands of the priests. . . .'

The argument looked unassailable. Maslow's reply would be 'You are mistaken'. It is true that men want food and security; but satisfy those needs, and higher needs develop. In order to get the best out of them, *all* men need a degree of freedom, a feeling of meaningful creative activity. If you can give them this, you have given them the same basic vitamin supplied in the past by religion. But in at least one respect, it is superior. Static religion encourages a passive, unquestioning attitude, which hardly favours self-actualisation; in fact, organised religion is often downright repressive. This is undoubtedly why many religion-orientated social theorists – Sorel, T.E. Hulme, D.H. Lawrence – had more than a streak of fascism in their make-up. Maslow's social theory avoids that pitfall.

All this is, of course, no more than a sketch for the new approach. It needs to be developed in two directions. First of all, we must consider how the application of Theory Z can be extended. At the moment it has shown itself remarkably successful in various industrial situations. (Robert Ardrey mentions a couple more in *The Social Contract*.) If enough manufacturers can be persuaded to try the experiment, we would be in a better position to understand its detailed working. Clare Graves of Union College, Schenectady, has done some valuable work in this direction. In a brilliant and suggestive paper on Deterioration of Work Standards, she lists seven levels of maturity ranging from 'autistic' to 'pacifistic individualistic', and points out that, as far as the industrial organisation is concerned, each person needs to be treated according to his level; to treat a higher level individual in terms appropriate to a lower level produces boredom, discouragement or revolt; to treat lower level individuals in higher level terms produces bewilderment or cynicism. She describes how, when these principles were applied in one large manufacturing plant, the result was a 17 per cent increase in production and an 87 per cent drop in grievances. Clearly, this is a valuable development of Theory Z.

But as far as I am concerned, the most interesting ground for development lies in the area of the phenomenology of creative consciousness. Our inner processes depend upon such imponderables as the individual's image of himself and his general attitude to his life-situation. At this point, I might risk an over-simplification, and say that what is now needed is an analysis as detailed and complex as Heidegger's *Being and Time* or Sartre's *Being and Nothingless*, but based upon Maslovian instead of reductionist principles. There is something preposterous and self-contradictory about these pessimistic analyses. When a man engages upon a major intellectual effort, he does it in a certain spirit of optimism – of expectation of some interesting result. We cannot imagine Newton writing the *Principia* in a state of neurotic gloom. And when Sartre concludes seven hundred pages of subtle and intelligent analysis with the announcement that it is meaningless that we live and meaningless that we die, and man is a useless passion, one cannot help feeling that his calculations have gone wrong somewhere. If he really thought so, he wouldn't have written the book. What is wrong, as I have pointed out, is the phenomenology of Heidegger and Sartre, which tends to be self-contradictory. 'Consciousness is intentional, but nothing intends it'; (i.e. there is no 'transcendental ego', no self to actualise). Moreover, the peak experience plays no part in the psychology of Sartre, and very little in Heidegger's. Their work is important and suggestive, but it has been supplanted by the insights of the new psychology as Descartes' *Le Monde* was supplanted by Galileo and Newton.

And what of the extraordinary discovery by Amaya – that when patients are connected up to an electroencephalograph, so they can watch their own alpha waves on a screen, they soon learn to produce intense peak experiences by controlling the alpha waves? Thought is man's attempt to gain control over his subjective processes; but he has always found them more frustrating and elusive than organising the world outside himself. Amaya's experiment suggests that the subjective process may be objectified and subjected to a new degree of control. The kind of analysis I am suggesting is also a step in this direction.

Sir Herbert Read began his introduction to Camus' *L'Homme Revolté*: 'With the publication of this book, a cloud that has oppressed the European mind for more than a century begins to lift.' I suspect that was premature; but I think there can be no doubt that the cloud *is* now lifting.

TWO

Existental psychology:
a novelist's approach

It is slightly embarrassing to find myself in this company of scientists and psychologists. I am a novelist, and I consider myself an existentialist philosopher. I happen to believe that there are certain things you *cannot* say in a treatise on philosophy which you *can* say in a novel.

There is a certain danger in being nothing but a thinker. Consider: At the time I am beginning this chapter, I should be writing a novel. I have got well into this novel – a kind of psychological thriller concerned with the 'dark room' and sensory deprivation – and I don't like to leave it. Because I have got myself into a kind of *creative* flow: The people and events have got me so interested that this interest has become self-perpetuating. It increases without much conscious effort on my part. Now if I spend a couple of hours on this essay, I shall find that I have narrowed down my senses and cut myself off from this source of 'inspiration'. My mind puts on its thinking harness, and at the end of a couple of hours, it can't get it off; it is stuck. Let me be clear, I am not denying that this thinking is also a creative process. But it puts my Pegasus into a tighter harness and gives him a heavier cart to pull. My intellect is like an oil derrick that tries to drill down to subconscious regions of my mind to release the same secret flow of vitality and affirmation that I may experience on a spring morning or on seeing a pretty girl or while listening to music.

All this lands me in the heart of my subject. (The novel will have to wait until tomorrow.) I am a phenomenologist, and my philosophical work is closely related to that of Husserl and Merleau-Ponty. But I have never yet opened a book on phenomenology that stated clearly the nature of its central obsession. Let me try this.

The robot and I

I am writing this on an electric typewriter. When I learned to type, I had to do it painfully and with much nervous wear and tear. But at a certain stage a miracle occurred, and this complicated operation was 'learned' by a useful robot whom I conceal in my subconscious mind. Now I only have to think about what I want to say; my robot secretary does the typing. He is really very useful. He also drives the car for me, speaks French (not very well), and occasionally gives lectures at American universities.

He has one enormous disadvantage. If I discover a new symphony that moves me deeply, or a poem or a painting, this bloody robot promptly insists on getting in on the act. And when I listen to the symphony for the third time, *he* begins to anticipate every note. He listens to it automatically, and I lose all the pleasure. He is most annoying when I am tired, because then he tends to take over most of my functions without even asking me. I have even caught him making love to my wife.

My dog doesn't have this trouble. Admittedly, he can't learn languages or how to type, but if I take him for a walk on the cliffs, he obviously experiences every time just as if it is the first. I can tell this by the ecstatic way he bounds about. Descartes was all wrong about animals. It isn't the animals who are robots; it's us.

There are times when I wonder whether I can really afford my robot. He costs so much to run, far more than my car. Admittedly, it is all my fault. When I was in my teens, I had a strong scientific bent. And I so hated being a teenager, a churning mass of emotions and embarrassments. I was like a man learning to skate, wasting a vast amount of energy and getting covered with bruises. So I set out to develop the robot, just as a factory manager would call in an efficiency expert. Soon he had things under control. He learned how to turn my emotional problems into symbols and equations and how to avoid some of the really destructive emotions that sometimes used to consume my energies like a forest fire. I soon found that I could think usefully and continuously, for hours on end if necessary. I could concentrate my mind on a problem with the precision of a microscope. I began to write books, and the books were accepted, which made life much easier. The trouble was that he became *too* damned efficient. It was all very nice being able to think efficiently and sort out my emotional problems. But life became so much duller. His obsessive tidiness used up so much time and energy. I would sometimes go for a country walk, and I couldn't hear the birds because his machinery was chattering along like an old typewriter. In a sense, he became my jailer. In my childhood, I was alway having marvelous experiences of freedom. Sometimes just coming out of school in the afternoon would make me burst with sheer joy, the feeling, 'I'm *free* – how lovely everything is'. Now, with this efficient, interfering robot, I have such experiences only once a year. When I threaten to get rid of him, he always points out reasonably that he saves me all kinds of unpleasant experiences too. And I suppose, looking back on it, this is true. One tends to remember the nice moments of childhood, but there were so many nasty ones. He said to me only the other day, 'Wilson, you're a fool. When I took you over, you were a stupid adolescent. You didn't really enjoy life because you disliked yourself too much. Well, you must admit you like yourself much more now. Why, because of me, you're much more *godlike* – let's not be shy of the word.'

I got to thinking about this. It was obviously true. I wouldn't go back to my childhood for worlds. It was a nasty, beastly time, and I hated it. And although I envy the way my dog rushes around on the cliffs, I wouldn't really like to be a dog either. I thought, 'There must be *some* way out of this stupid situation I've got myself into. There must be some way of outwitting this robot. After all, he's only a machine.'

It's really an interesting problem. Man has reached his present position on the evolutionary ladder because he is a tool-making animal, a machine-making animal ... in fact, a robot-making animal. But his sheer cleverness is proving to be his downfall (although I wouldn't have you suppose I am pessimistic about the issue). It is the same with my library. I started off with half a dozen books, and it didn't really matter where I kept them; I could always put my hand on a book when I needed it. Then I got carried away and began buying them by the dozen. I put shelves up all over the house. But I found I had to devote more and more time to keeping them in order, and finally I had to devise a kind of cataloguing system. Even so, it often costs me an hour to find a book. It's the same principle as when you're having a complicated argument, and you keep losing the thread of the argument and have to ask, 'What was I saying?' This never happens when you're discussing baseball.

But when I was discussing this with my robot the other day, he made a good point. He said, 'You're blaming me for all this, but it's your own fault. It's a case of the bad workman blaming his tools. I'm only your tool. You made me. And the reason I'm so unsatisfactory is that I'm such a crude piece of work. The real trouble is that you're lazy and self-indulgent. You complain that I take over when you're listening to a symphony. All right, take me to pieces and introduce some more complicated circuits. As to your complaints about the energy I waste, I've never heard anything more dishonest. *You're* in control of the energy supply, not me. By using the proper channels, you can get as much as you like.' 'But what *are* the proper channels?' I asked him, but he just shrugged and said, 'Don't be so damned lazy. Think it out for yourself.'

The Saint Neots margin   Let me underline this last point with an autobiographical digression. I promise it won't be too irrelevant.

Some years ago, I was hitchhiking up the Great North Road out of London, on my way to Peterborough. I was in a state of utter boredom and discouragement. It was a hot, dusty, Saturday afternoon, and there was little traffic on the roads. What made it worse was that I didn't much want to go to Peterborough. It was a rather dreary 'duty' call. And I wasn't much looking forward to going back to London either, since I had a particularly boring job at the time. So I was bursting with ennui and resentment – a feeling of total life rejection. If I'd had a bottle of whisky, I'd have got drunk and slept under the hedge.

After half an hour or so, a lorry stopped for me. This didn't improve my temper at all; I just thought it was about damned time. But after he'd been going for about twenty minutes, there was a knocking noise from his gearbox. He explained that he would have to stop at the next garage and get it fixed. So when he stopped, I got out and walked on. I was in such a state of boredom I didn't even feel annoyed about the inconvenience.

I wandered on for another half hour, getting hotter and more disgusted with life. Finally, another lorry stopped for me. Again, I didn't feel grateful; I was too tired. But after the lorry had been chugging along for twenty minutes or so, an odd coincidence occurred: There was the same knocking noise from inside *his* gearbox. This seemed too much; I felt that fate was persecuting me. The driver told me he'd have to drop me off at the next garage. However, he found that if he dropped his speed to about 20 miles an hour, the knocking noise stopped. The moment he got above that speed, it started again. So he got his speed up to about 19 miles, and we found that this seemed OK. He was as anxious to get to Peterborough as I was and didn't want to stop. So we both sat there, straining our ears for any sign of the knocking noise and keeping our fingers crossed. Finally, the driver said, 'I think we'll make it if we stick at this speed. It can't be anything serious'.

As he said this, I felt a great burst of elation. And then I caught myself feeling it, and thought, 'This is absurd. Half an hour ago, you were in a state of total disgust with life. Well, nothing has happened. It isn't as if you've found a £5 note or something. All that has happened is that *a threat of inconvenience has arisen, and now the threat has been removed*. So you're back where you started, and yet you are suddenly aware of your freedom!'

I saw I'd hit on an idea of profound importance. Why hadn't it given me pleasure when a lorry had stopped for me? There is obviously an area of the human psyche that can be stimulated by pain (or inconvenience) and *yet not by pleasure*. I recognised there in the lorry, that without involvement, commitment, participation – call it what you will – but without any emotional stake in what is going on, boredom leads to apathy, which may soon mount to utter distaste for life. So forcibly did this recognition come home to me that I named it by our location at the time – in the town of Saint Neots in Huntingdonshire – the 'Saint Neots margin'. It is basically an extremely familiar idea. It refers to that state of mind – of boredom, resentment, life devaluation – that we fall into so easily. Auden caught it when he wrote:

Put the car away; when life fails
What's the good of going to Wales?

'When life fails. . . .' That's the problem. Give people peace and quiet, and they soon want to commit suicide. Let a threat of inconvenience arise, and suddenly they're enjoying life again. I remember the early days of the war in England, how happy everybody was. And yet there is something quite mad about this peculiarity of human nature. It is like buying a powerful car and discovering that it will do 90 miles an hour *in reverse* and only 20 miles an hour going forward.

Now what happened to me, passing through Saint Neots, is obviously the answer to the robot problem. I had let myself get into a state of boredom and resentment. The threat of inconvenience made me snap out of it. It is true: our energies are almost infinite. But when there is no challenge, no threat, present, we tend to fall into a state of *sleep*. And in sleep, the robot takes over. It is a kind of vicious circle.

Freedom: 'The orgasm experience'

But having considered this negative side of the problem – the robot – let us take a look at its other aspect. My sudden flashes of freedom have a revelatory nature. I am inclined to refer to these moments as the 'orgasm experience' – understanding, by this, not merely the sexual orgasm, but any kinds of similar experience, due to music, poetry, a spring morning, your first Martini of the evening. [Maslow (1962) calls these 'peak experiences', but for the moment, I will stick to my own terminology.] Consider the meaning-content of these orgasm experiences and what they have in common. It will reveal, I believe, some very important conclusions.

To begin with, let us merely try to describe what happens in the orgasm experience. There can be no doubt whatever that the first word that comes to mind is 'freedom'.

When my six-year-old daughter has finished her bath, she is inclined to leave the sponge where you can knock it on the floor. And unfortunately, it is usually sopping with water, so that it squelches and makes a nasty wet mess. So if I see the sponge on the side of the bath, I place my index finger on it and press it gently. If it is full of water, the water appears in the depression around my finger. I cannot tell whether the sponge is full of water just by looking at it.

This image describes something else about the orgasm experience. What happens is that my 'mechanical threshold', my robot levels, have been pushed lower for a moment, and the freedom comes bubbling out. *In my ordinary, everyday state of consciousness, I am not aware of my freedom*; I can't see it or feel it, any more than I can see the water in the sponge.

Another interesting observation arises from all this. In my ordinary state of consciousness, the word 'me' refers to me, the personality – me, Colin Wilson. In the orgasm experience, I suddenly realise that this 'me' isn't me at all; *he is a robot*. The me called 'Colin Wilson' is entirely mechanical. The 'real me' is not mechanical; it is pure freedom. Pure freedom and energy, power to change my life, to do what I like. This is why in the orgasm experience, visible objects become so intensely beautiful. It is not the robot seeing them anymore. It is the real 'you'.

This, incidentally, is what mysticism is all about. Blake called the robot the 'spectre', but it is all the same thing.

The Princeton 'black-room' experiments (Vernon, 1963) only underline these points. I am 99 per cent machine or robot. Most of my consciousness tends to be a mechanical affair. If a sudden emergency – or stimulus – arises, my 'free' levels quickly take over. But in the black room, the robot part of me says, 'No emergency present – may as well go to sleep'. Sleep is the opposite of the orgasm experience, of the experience of freedom. But even when the body has had its fill of sleep after twenty hours in the black room, the robot continues to repeat mechanically, 'No emergency present; may as well sleep'. So the black room artificially induces the opposite of the freedom experience. And the longer you stay in it, the heavier the burden of consciousness becomes. Your only salvation under the circumstances would be to use your brain – to think, to develop ideas, to feel, if possible. But the darkness has you hypnotised or, rather, has the robot hypnotised. (Hypnotism is the science of taking command of the robot.)

Consciousness and habit   At this point I'll be autobiographical again for just a moment.

In my teens I read a lot of poetry. But there were whole days when poetry left me cold, particularly after a really boring and frustrating week at the office (I left school at sixteen). Sometimes, on a Sunday, I'd spend the whole day trying to snap out of this dreary state of coldness, of indifference. Yet it would be like trying to start a car when you've flooded the carburettor. Keats, Shelley, Wordsworth, Rupert Brooke – all would fail to touch me. Then sometimes, towards evening, it would seem that my sheer mental exhaustion was doing the trick. A warm glow would begin to pervade my brain. And then suddenly it was expanding, way beyond 'everyday consciousness'. It was as if a thick fog was lifting and revealing distant views of immense beauty. Occasionally these poetic experiences would rise to the level of genuine mystical insight. I was all freedom; it was like a sexual orgasm that could burn steadily for hours instead of seconds. There was a sense that human notions of good and evil are absurdly stupid and limited, based upon our spoiltness, our laziness.

These experiences left me with one certainty. Consciousness may be 99 per cent mechanical. But it is that other 1 per cent that counts. That 1 per cent, by continuous effort, can gradually subdue the other 99 per cent. It is a long and painful job, like pushing a stalled car uphill. Yet a point comes where you get over the top, and away you go. Sartre (1936) insists that consciousness is entirely mechanical, that its changes are mechanical changes, like the movements of the tides, sucked by the moon – that the sea has no power to move itself. He is a liar. It is hard work, but it can be done. It could be done a lot more easily if we understood the mechanism of the robot.

This examination of the robot is called *phenomenology*, and its basic techniques were laid down by Edmund Husserl (1912). At this point I should try to express how I see phenomenology. Every phenomenologist has a different approach.

If I am watching a weight lifter, I am aware of his effort; I can see it in the straining muscles, in the sweat on his forehead. I am aware that he has every *intention* of raising the weight. There is nothing mechanical about it; he is intensely aware of every ounce of effort that it is costing him.

When I was learning to type, I had the same agonised awareness of my intentions. But after months of practice it became a habit. Now if anyone saw me using this typewriter, they might think *I* was a machine, I am doing it so quickly and efficiently. But I'm not a machine. In spite of appearance, I *intend* every word that I type (allowing for misprints). Luckily most of my 'intentions' have been passed on to my robot. They have become mechanical. They are still intentions, but they are mechanical intentions. I am no longer painfully aware of them, as the weight lifter is aware of his intentions.

Consciousness is composed largely of mechanical intentions, habits. But they must not be mistaken for mechanisms. A mechanical intention is not a mechanism; it is half-and-half. When the sun comes up in the morning, that is a mechanism; it doesn't intend to. When my consciousness returns in the morning, that is partly a mechanism, but it is very largely my conscious intention. (The confusion here arises over the word 'conscious-ness'. We tend to use it as a kind of antonym of the 'unconscious'. In the sense in which it is used in phenomenology, consciousness *is* the mind – 'conscious' and 'subconscious'.)

These habit mechanisms are 'labour-saving devices'. They are intended to leave the conscious mind free for more important problems. And it is here that the problem arises. There is a whole number of reasons why we don't use consciousness to attack more important problems. To begin with, we get lazy. This is one of the more usual consequences of having labour-saving devices. Secondly, the habit mechanisms work so swiftly and efficiently that, before we know where we are, a 'problem' is being solved by habit, before new problems come along. So we get bored. Third, and most important, we tend to forget that a mechanical intention is not a mechanism. We start to take consciousness for granted. So the mind starts to get compartmentalised – just as a big business tends to get 'departmentalised', with each department working in relative isolation, only dimly aware of the others. What is here most important is that I don't allow this to happen. The boss should keep coming out of his office at the top of the building and taking a stroll around the works.

To put this in another way, consciousness is made up of intentions. Most of them are mechanical; a small number are conscious. And one gets a 'balance of power' situation in consequence. If too many of the intentions get 'mechanised', consciousness becomes robotic, automatic; you even *see* auto-matically; you stop *feeling*. In this situation – as I discovered in my teens – a real mental effort will change the balance of power and restore the necessary level of freedom to consciousness. It can be done purely instinctively, by what Blake calls 'mental fight'. Or it can be done far more consciously, by the various disciplines of phenomenology which consist in isolating intentions.

External stimulation and internal intentionality   It takes only a little thought to see that this matter of freedom is one of our most basic values. When you call a man a 'moron', you mean that he strikes you as largely mechanical, a robot – the vacant gaze, the automatic movements, and so on. (The word 'zombi' catches this even more distinctly – the robotic movements.) On the other hand, when you look at a highly intelligent and sympathetic person, you feel his freedom; you see it in his eyes.

The life of every animal is a continuous interaction with its environment. When I take my dog on the beach and throw a ball, he becomes twice as alive. If he is lying on the rug and I am reading, he promptly falls asleep because there is nothing to keep him interested. He *needs* the outside world to keep him alive and interested. The life in him simply wilts and collapses when the world doesn't present him with something to do.

The same kind of thing happens when a man of sixty retires to the country cottage he has always dreamed about – and is dead within a year of sheer boredom and inactivity. He has no inner resources to fall back on.

At first sight, the black-room experiments seem to justify the worst kind of pessimism about human nature. What Sartre said about his café proprietor in *Nausea* (1938), 'When his café empties, his head empties too', seems to be true of everybody. In the last analysis, there is not so much difference between Einstein and my dog. We are all dependent on external stimuli.

But then, consider a very simple and obvious matter: the sexual stimulus. Most animals need the smell of the female in heat to excite them sexually. Men have gone one stage further. They don't need the smell of estrus; the sight of a naked woman serves the same purpose.

But unlike any other animal in the world, man can also become sexually stimulated without the actual physical presence of the sexual object. That is, he can use his imagination to produce the sexual stimulus, even to the point of orgasm. We regard masturbation as a slightly shameful subject; but, viewed phenomenologically, it is one of man's greatest glories. He has such remarkable control over his *sexual intentions* that the presence of the physical object is unnecessary.

The Saint Neots margin problem can now be stated with more precision. If you peer into the darkness to distinguish some vague object, you are increasing the intentionality of your act of seeing. If you concentrate on some interesting problem, you are increasing the intentionality of your intellectual perception. And if you simply happen to be feeling healthy and optimistic on a spring morning, you can increase the general intensity of your consciousness by simply opening your senses; in this case, *all* the intentions are affected.

The one thing that human beings want above all others is the moment of freedom, of orgasm, of intense and ecstatic happiness – in short, a change in the quality of consciousness. Yet we leave this important function to our robot levels. Under circumstances of comfort the robot tends to take over. A man might spend years in prison dreaming of freedom. Yet within twenty-four hours of leaving the jail, he has lost his freedom. The intention he had directed toward freedom has vanished because he is outside the jail. The robot quickly takes over; consciousness yawns and goes to sleep. Freedom vanishes. In a paradoxical sense, he was freer in jail.

All this sounds pessimistic, but that is to miss the point entirely. For if you think about it for a moment, you will see that man is superior to the animal – in freedom – precisely because of the robot. Although an animal is never at the mercy of the robot, it has no freedom because it is stuck in the present. The whole purpose of the robot is to give man a certain *continuity of existence*, to save him from the meaninglessness of living in a perpetual 'present'.

Faculty X

This brings me to my final point, and the one with which I shall undoubtedly arouse most dissension.

When I was a child I was always fascinated by sheets of water. If

I went out on a long bus trip, I used to keep my nose glued to the windowpane in case we went over a bridge. Water always produced in me a strange and ecstatic excitement. But if the bus ever stopped near the water, I was always disappointed because there was nothing you could *do* about that strange desire. If I stared fascinated in a sweetshop window, I knew exactly what I wanted to do with the sweets. But what can you do with a sheet of water?

At about the age of thirteen, I came across a passage in Dr. Johnson's *Rasselas* (1759) that struck me as important. The prince remarks: 'Man has surely some latent sense for which this place affords no gratification, or he has some desires distinct from sense that must be satisfied before he can be happy'. That last part sounded like a description of my problem with the sheets of water. Yeats (1939) had made the same remark, speaking in a poem about a waterfall that he loved, yet knowing that if he touched it, it would be only 'cold stone and water'.

At a later period I christened this 'latent sense' or desire distinct from sense 'faculty X'. It seemed to me that all poetry and mysticism prove that man indeed possesses some faculty that he hardly ever makes use of. It woke up when Proust tasted the biscuit dipped in tea. It is the freedom experience. It accounts for that feeling of, 'Of *course*, how obvious!' in the orgasm experience.

I was also particularly fascinated by a couple of experiences described by Strindberg that seemed to reveal yet a new dimension of faculty X. On one occasion he was sitting in a café with a friend and trying to describe to the friend a conversation that had taken place some weeks previously in another café. He started to describe the other café in detail and suddenly found himself sitting there. Or rather, he was sitting in both cafés at once, with an odd effect of double exposure. The odd thing was that a door had appeared in a place where previously there was only a wall, and people were walking in and out of it – total strangers. With an effort Strindberg dismissed the hallucination and brought himself back to 'reality', that is, the first café. Yet it is a pity that he didn't take special note of the strangers and check up on whether they were really coming into the other café at that moment.

On another occasion Strindberg was ill and was longing to be with his family. He imagined the room with such intensity that he suddenly found himself standing in it (although it was many hundreds of miles away). His mother-in-law was playing the piano and looked up and saw him. When a moment later he disappeared, the old lady quickly wrote him a letter describing the 'apparition' and asking him whether he was well; she was afraid it was a precursor of death.

This appears to be the case of the Proustian experience taken a stage further, and it may well explain the many well-authenticated cases of apparitions of the living. However, I do not insist on it. It merely seemed to me, on reading these experiences of Strindberg (who was half insane when he had them), that his abnormal mental state had stimulated the normally latent faculty X.

But in view of what has been said above, it can be seen that there is no need to posit some faculty X. The moment man began to develop symbol memory, language, and so on, he had begun to create a new faculty. His very continuity is a new faculty, a new dimension of his being.

The spirit–body duality   In a brilliant passage in his autobiography, Wells (1934) compared men to the earliest amphibians, prehistoric creatures who wanted to become land animals but who possessed only flippers for moving around on land. After a short time on land, they had to get back to the sustaining medium of the sea. This, it seems to me, describes man's present position. His natural sphere is freedom, the world of the mind (which Teilhard de Chardin calls the *noosphere*). The problem is that he has insufficient control of the robot. And yet Shaw (1921) once remarked about evolutionary change, 'The brain will not fail when the will is in earnest'. The concept of faculty X has a certain importance in that it gives us a sense of something to strive for. A philosopher like Gilbert Ryle (1949), who insists that the old mind–body dichotomy is due to a confusion of language, may be right in many ways; but in the ultimate sense he is wrong. For there *is* a dichotomy, between our robot levels and our freedom.

If I happen to be reading a book like Wells's *Outline of History* (1920), I experience an odd sensation. To begin with, I become aware that I am not all that unique. There have been millions of species before man. I am merely a member of a species. One day, man may be as extinct as the dinosaur. I become aware of myself as a grain of sand on a universal beach.

At the same time, this humility is checked by an interesting reflection. I may be a mere grain of sand, but I am quite unlike all other animals in one important respect. My body may be doomed to die, but here is my mind, hovering over the page, contemplating eons of history with total objectivity. Physically speaking, I am a limited human being. Mentally speaking, I am as timeless and impersonal as the stars. I am a mind grasping the universe objectively, and it doesn't matter whether I am a duke or a dustman, a human being or a Martian, a man or a woman. For the time being I have transcended my everyday, 'human' aspects and have become a kind of immortal. Or, to use Husserl's language, I have placed the 'world' in brackets and become aware of myself as a transcendental ego.

It has been Husserl's achievement to give a new meaning to the spirit–body duality and to bring a new unifying principle into philosophy. Its full implications are so enormous that there are very few phenomenologists who have even started to grasp them. But let me try to outline them.

We develop 'intentions' as we develop a taste for foreign cooking. (In fact, such a taste *is* an intention.) If I pick up a difficult philosophical article, I have to force myself to read it. Six weeks later I may have grasped so many of its implications that next time I see the name of the philosopher on an article, I seize it with interest and devour it. My 'interest' was an *intention* which I developed, as I might develop a taste for olives. In a year's time my interest in this philosopher may be so deep as to seem a natural appetite.

According to Husserl all our appetites, all our intentions, are developed in this way; none are 'natural'. But they are passed on to our preconscious regions as habits, until we are no longer aware of them as intentions. Husserl's disciplines enable us to re-excavate these habits and to realise them as living intentions. This, in turn, takes away our boredom, our tendency to let familiarity breed contempt.

But it can be seen that what phenomenology has done is to

restore primacy to the will, as in the philosophy of Nietzsche or
Shaw. In revealing mechanisms to be buried intentions, it suggests
the possibility that the answers to all the fundamental problems of
the human psyche may be disclosed in terms of *willed intentions*
instead of mechanisms. This should bring a certain simplicity into
some of the classical psychological problems – for example, in the
psychology of sex, where no one has ever been able to suggest
how to draw a line between 'normal sexuality' and 'perversions',
i.e., between instincts and intentions. According to the Husserlian
view, 'instinct' is a misnomer; sex is simply a series of intentions,
buried at different levels, and therefore more or less accessible to
limited everyday consciousness. Again, Saint Augustine remarked, 'What is time? When I do not ask the question, I know
the answer' (Wittgenstein, 1953). Naturally; for the level of
everyday consciousness that asks the question has no contact with
the level of human intentionality concerned with time consciousness.

Beyond the robot   In short, the word 'robot' is also a misnomer in
this connection. He is actually composed of compacted layer upon
layer of willed intentions.

   A metaphysician might leap to the question of whether our
birth and death may not be interpreted as willed intentions. This
hardly concerns us here. We are concerned solely with the new
picture of psychology that emerges from Husserl. In a sense, it
could be likened to a kind of archaeology. When I speak of
'myself' in the everyday sense, I am speaking of the uppermost
layer of willed intentions. One layer below these lies the realm of
my acquired habits: typing, speaking French, reading, etc.
Another two or three layers down lie my sexual intentions, which
can actually be studied *as* willed intentions if I develop a certain
skill in descriptive analysis. The archaeological equivalent of these
layers would be Troy or Babylon. And below these lie the mental
equivalents of the Miocene, the Jurassic, the Carboniferous. Up to a
few hundred years ago, man's historical knowledge was limited;
now he can look back over a hundred million years of life. But his
psychological knowledge is still in its crude, prehistoric state. The
mind's archaeology must be made accessible to present consciousness: In this direction lies man's development.

Conclusion

It can be seen that I consider the basic problem to be that of the dead weight of consciousness. (I am here using the word in the phenomenological sense of the whole mind.) Man is in his paradoxical, neurotic, highly dangerous position because he has given too much of the control to the robot. If he is to have any real freedom, if freedom is to be more than a word that is mocked by the realities of politics and human weakness, then man must gain control over consciousness in a real sense. He has some slight control at the moment, but the muscle is undeveloped through lack of use. It will remain undeveloped while he is half asleep and unaware of its existence. His tendency to laziness – and mechanicalness – is the great obstacle. He must set out to develop this 'muscle' (which we might call faculty X) as consciously as a marksman sets out to develop a good aim. Man has to strive consciously to change the balance of power between his robot levels and his conscious intentions. His most valuable weapon is Husserlian phenomenology.

The hypotheses I've been describing, I might add parenthetically, should have some interesting repercussions on existential philosophising. For example, philosophers have traditionally treated the problems of man's contingency – his proneness to illness, accident, and death – as an absolute. But we know that a man in a state of 'freedom', in the 'peak experience', can stay awake as long as he likes. Sleep seems to be largely a mechanism of the robot. Everyone has noticed how difficult it is to stay awake when he is bored and how difficult it is to fall asleep when he is stimulated, intellectually or physically. Research on cancer indicates that it is partly a psychosomatic illness: that it tends to be a concomitant of psychological defeat, of surrendering to the robot. It is even conceivable that men who have managed an ultimate change of the psychological balance of power might discover that death, like sleep, is to a large extent a mechanism of the robot.

All this is speculation. What matters is that phenomenology has, so to speak, endowed human evolution with a conscious intention. It has revealed that man's incorrigible craving for optimism and purpose can be justified on basic epistemological grounds.

Moreover, there is a practical point of application. There is an amusing story abour Sartre, that after the war he would arouse audiences to fever pitch of enthusiasm by telling them, 'You are free; go out and claim your freedom'. But the enthusiasm never lasted for more than a few hours because the audiences never knew what to *do* – where to make a start.

Phenomenology *is* the start. It is also a direction. We face the absurd possibility that the creature we have called 'man' does not yet exist.

1967

THREE

Love as an adventure in mutual freedom

I write this as a phenomenologist. But since there are apparently as many kinds of phenomenology as there are phenomenologists, I had better begin by explaining what I understand by the word. I must also explain the way in which my phenomenology is a radical departure from that of Sartre, Heidegger, and Merleau Ponty – even, to some extent, from that of Husserl.

Most European psychology in the nineteenth century sprang from David Hume, who noted that when he looked inside himself to find the essential 'me', he only stumbled upon thoughts and impressions. For Hume, free will is an illusion, and our apparent freedom to think what we like, a misunderstanding. Man's mind, he maintains, gives an impression of free, purposive movement, just as the leaves on a windy autumn day seem to be in a hurry to get somewhere. But the leaves move because hot air rises, and our thoughts move because physical stimuli blow them around.

But Husserl objected that there is one important respect in which the mind differs from a windy day. When I think or feel or see, I think *about* something, I look *at* something; I fire my attention at its object like an arrow. A leaf doesn't care where it goes, but when I think, the thought cannot get started unless it knows its objective in advance. When I look at something, I must know what I am looking at before I can really grasp it. If I wake from a drunken sleep underneath a cane chair, I cannot grasp my situation until I have answered the question: 'What is this curious, angular-looking object over my face?' Until my mind has, so to speak, pinned it down by making an act of 'chair-ness', it hovers nervously over the chair, staring blankly. What is more, that act of chair-ness is exactly the same act you make if you close your eyes and imagine a chair. In other words, in order to see anything, we must imagine it. To look at a thing without this act of imagining would be not to see it, rather like reading these words with your mind on something else, and not taking them in. If your attention is an arrow fired at an object, this presupposes an archer. So Husserl denied Hume's assertion that there is no 'essential me'. He called this essential 'me' the transcendental ego.

Although Sartre claimed to be a disciple of Husserl, he reverted to the old Humeian position. He agreed that consciousness is intentional, but not because it is *fired* at its object by the essential me. It is, in fact, *sucked* towards its object, as air is sucked into a vacuum if you remove the cork, or as the tides are sucked by the moon. There cannot be an essential me behind consciousness, according to Sartre, because consciousness has no 'behind', any more than there is really a room behind the mirror.

It is hard to see how man can be free if Sartre is correct; however, according to Sartre, he is free, in some Pickwickian sense. The contradiction here should be easy to see. If consciousness has no 'inside', it has no 'works'. A parallel situation would be this: Someone hears about the earth moving around the sun, and says 'Ah, it must have clockwork inside it.' Someone else replies, 'No, it is quite solid inside. Its movement is due entirely to the sun.' The same goes for Sartrian consciousness – there is no clockwork, or anything else, inside.

My disagreement with Sartre is easily expressed. For Sartre, consciousness is a simple unity, like a plane mirror. But this leaves out of account one of the mind's most important parts: the robot. When I learn some new skill – a foreign language, typing, driving a car – I quickly pass it from my conscious mind to a subconscious robot, who does it far more efficiently than I can do it by conscious effort. So the mind is neither a unity nor a mirror. Its most important level is hidden in darkness. The full significance of this observation will appear in a moment.

There is an even more important matter that both Sartre and Husserl leave out of account. This is a quality of consciousness which I call 'relationality'.

This first came to my attention some years ago, and in order to make it clear, it would perhaps be simplest to explain the circumstances. I was driving through the Lake District, in a state of great mental clarity and intensity. I know the area well, and I observed that I was very clearly aware of what lay on the other side of the hills around me. I could say 'Over there lies

Derwentwater, and over there Helvellyn', and experience these places as *realities*, almost as if I could see them. Chesterton pointed out that we say thank you when someone passes us the salt, but we don't *mean* it. In the same way, I could now close my eyes and conjure up a picture of Derwentwater; but I wouldn't mean it. Yet, if some smell blown on the wind suddenly reminded me of Derwentwater, my mental image would take on reality; I would mean it.

In trying to define this state of mind, I found myself calling it 'weblike consciousness'. I had in mind the image of a spider in the middle of its web. It cannot see certain parts of its web which are hidden behind leaves. Yet it knows what is going on in every part of its web, since it can feel the vibration of every breeze, every slight movement of a leaf brushing a strand of web. In moments of intensity, consciousness seems to put out filaments of web to other times and other places.

Two years or so later, it suddenly struck me that *all* consciousness is weblike, by its very nature. If, for example, I am reading a book late at night when my brain is tired, I can understand each individual word or sentence, but it means nothing to me. Reading is a two-handed activity. One hand picks up the meanings of individual words or phrases, and passes these to the other hand, which holds all the meanings accumulated so far – rather in the manner of someone who picks up scattered sticks, picking up each stick with the right hand and passing them to the left hand, or tucking them in the crook of the left arm. A one-handed man could not pick up scattered sticks; and when consciousness is one-handed, it cannot pick up *meaning*, only individual meanings. The act of grasping meaning is an act of relating the new meanings to the totality of old meanings.

Sartre has said that consciousness *is* intentionality; i.e., that a consciousness that was not intentional would not be consciousness. I am inclined to doubt this; but it would seem to me more to the point to say that consciousness *is* relationality. I find it hard to conceive of a consciousness that is not consciousness of a pattern. Or, to put this more clearly, I find it hard to conceive of a perceived object that is not perceived essentially as a part of a pattern.

To take a crude example, I read *War and Peace*, and when I have finished it, consider that my knowledge of this period of European history is now reasonably adequate. Some time later, I become absorbed in the relations of the French and Russian courts in the eighteenth century, and read every book I can find that sheds any light on this. This, then, leads me to study the history of France and Russia since the fall of Napoleon. Then one day I reread *War and Peace*, and discover, to my astonishment, that it seems to be a different novel, full of meanings that I had failed to recognise before. My perception of *War and Peace* as a part of a vast historical landscape has deepened the meaning of the novel itself.

An obvious kind of assertion, perhaps, but consider its central point. If your older self could say to your younger self, 'There are things about *War and Peace* that you have simply failed to grasp', your younger self could read *War and Peace* with a microscope and still fail to grasp the deeper meanings. For these are not to be grasped within the novel itself, but through its relation to a larger canvas. The total meaning of the novel does not lie *in* the novel.

But then, surely there is such a thing as a meaning in isolation? Can I, for example, stare at my left index finger, and see in it isolation from the rest of my hand?

A moment's thought shows me that this is impossible. I know it as a finger; I know what fingers are for; and I know they are part of a hand. The reason I appear to see my finger in isolation is that the robot does the work of relating for me.

Or again, I glance at my watch while thinking of something else. A moment later, I have to look at it again to check on the time. I did not see the time, although I certainly saw the watch and the position of its hands. But 'seeing the time' involves a lot more than saying 'Half past two'. It involves a more complex thought: 'Half past two in the afternoon – an hour since lunch, two hours before tea time.' To see the time is to place it in relation to the rest of the day.

But now, here, for me, is the decisive leap in the argument. I am reading Eliot's *The Wasteland*, and I read the quotation from the beginning of *Tristan and Isolde*, '*Frisch weht der wind. . . .*' I experience the tingling sensation that A.E. Housman declares to be the test of poetry. Why? What has happened?

Only this: I have been reminded of a work with which I am familiar, and which has often moved me deeply. It is rather like a place in which I have been happy; it has established its own separate reality in my mind. Now this whole reality has been evoked by a single quotation. It is like the biscuit dipped in tea that reminds Proust of his childhood, in *Swann's Way*. The sensation of poetry is, in fact, merely an expansion of the ordinary relationality of consciousness. (It might further be remarked that the whole of *The Wasteland* is a series of such juxtapositions and evocations.)

One might, then, summarise this phase of the argument by saying that to see a thing truly is to see it in the widest possible field of relations. The 'nausea' that Sartre describes in the novel of that name is the sensation of seeing objects almost completely divested of meaning – i.e., of relations. Yet this is not to say *completely* divested of relations. An object completely divested of relations would not be seen at all, for consciousness would need to be totally passive to 'see' a thing in this way. (Even within the framework of Sartre's philosophy, there is a contradiction in his idea of nausea, for he implies that this nausea is pure perception, without prejudice or preconception – i.e., without *intentionality*; then, in the next breath, Sartre asserts that consciousness *is* intentionality.)

But we might symbolise an object perceived in nausea as a kind of tic-tac-toe square, like this:

where the X represents the object. There is a minimum of relationality around it. In normal everyday consciousness, the object is surrounded by far more relations (see p. 60):

But the larger the graph, the more alive and meaningful the consciousness. My 'weblike consciousness' must be thought of as a very large sheet of graph paper (see p. 60).

There is one more complication here that must be clarified.

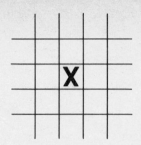

Even in limited, everyday consciousness, the graph is actually immense – but most of it is invisible. One must, as it were, imagine the lines of the graph continued with dotted lines to symbolise relations vanishing into shadowy realms beyond our 'immediacy consciousness'.

In experiences of weblike consciousness – poetic intensity – the dotted lines suddenly become solid.

This explains one of the basic problems of mysticism and poetry: the 'ineffability' of their insights. Anyone who has experienced weblike consciousness can grasp the reason for this. What is seen in these intenser states of consciousness is, in fact, what is *already known* to ordinary consciousness, but only known conceptually. William James has spoken of the sudden vision of 'horizons of distant fact' in states of mystical intensity, and this is very much to the point. The reason that the meaning content of weblike consciousness baffles expression is that it is already known to the limited everyday consciousness – but known conceptually, not perceptually. There is as much difference as between knowing a country from having studied a map, and knowing it from having lived there.

Now it can be seen why this notion of the relationality of consciousness throws a completely new light on phenomenology – in fact, virtually opens up new countries in phenomenology and existentialism. The existentialism of Sartre, Heidegger, and Merleau Ponty has a rather arid and sober nature; it seems to be largely an exhortation to man to face the unpleasant facts about himself. And all this arises from its theory of consciousness as a kind of helpless jellyfish, doing its best to deal with the world. The change of emphasis from intentionality to relationality suddenly reveals consciousness as possessing enormous and mysterious potentialities. In Sartre, states of poetic or mystical intensity are of merely 'chemical' interest; they do not affect his basic view of the nature of consciousness. For Sartre, consciousness is a jellyfish with blunt pseudopodia that appear to reach out, but which are really dragged out of it by the gravity of objects. There would be no point in examining the jellyfish through a microscope; it has no inside and no cause. The only interesting thing about consciousness lies in the nature of the intention that connects the jellyfish with the objective world.

I have tried to show that this view oversimplifies. The intentional act is, admittedly, interesting in itself; but far more interesting is what takes place within consciousness in any intentional act. As the intention reaches out to the object, inner intentions stretch out into the realm of the robot, striving to send spurts of power into the invisible areas of the web. Sometimes, for no understandable reason, the resistance of these inner circuits drops; the power flows into the hidden areas and we have a sensation that can only be described as being like the exclamation 'Of course!' These are the states in which all great poetry is written, and they are obviously a *perfectly ordinary potentiality* of human consciousness.

One further point. Hume divided sensations into two types: physical impressions and feelings, which are clear and definite, and mental impressions (memories, imaginings, thoughts), which are merely a *dim carbon copy* of physical sensations. On the whole, psychology has accepted this distinction.

Weblike consciousness denies it. What happens here is that our mental world, which normally seems so dim and feeble in comparison to physical actuality – a mere candle compared to the sun – suddenly takes on a glowing intensity. A kind of chain reaction starts, as in nuclear fission, and the result is a state of mind that is anything but a carbon copy of physical sensation. It exists in its own right, and may burn with such intensity that it is the physical world which becomes the candle against the sun.

It should be clear why it was necessary to say all this before entering upon the main subject of this chapter – the question of love and freedom. As is well known, Sartre's *Being and Nothingness* devotes a great deal of space to both subjects, and produces singularly discouraging conclusions. Love, according to Sartre, is a hopeless attempt by consciousness to escape its own loneliness; it could be summarised in Rupert Brooke's lines about lovers taking 'Their own poor dreams within their arms and lying/Each in his lonely night, each with a ghost'.

Sadism and masochism are also vain attempts to escape this 'lonely night', according to Sartre.

This view is a natural outcome of the Sartre view of consciousness as a passive emptiness, longing to feel itself filled. This can be seen with singular clarity in the following quotation from Simone de Beauvoir's *Pyrrhus and Cinéas*:

> I look at myself in vain in a mirror, tell myself my own story, I can never grasp myself as an entire object. I experience in myself the emptiness that is myself. I feel that I am not.

This is what one would expect from Sartre's psychology. Behind her eyes sits consciousness, like a shallow pool. It is basically a reflection of her environment – and at the moment, the main item in her environment is her own face in the mirror, with which she is completely, boringly familiar. Naturally, she feels nothing, and it seems to her that this state is an honest perception of what consciousness is really like. Feelings would only stir up the mud in consciousness and prevent her from seeing how shallow it is.

One might contrast this with the passage in Hesse's *Steppenwolf* in which the hero experiences a moment of weblike consciousness, about which he writes:

> For moments together my heart stood still between delight and sorrow to find how rich was the gallery of my life, and how thronged the soul of the wretched Steppenwolf with high eternal stars and constellations. . . .

This, in fact, is the experience whose possibility Simone de Beauvoir is denying. If Steppenwolf were to look into a mirror at this moment, he would not feel that 'I can never grasp myself as an entire object', for that is precisely what he is doing – or, at least, he is well on the way to it.

When the relational nature of consciousness is grasped, we see that Simone de Beauvoir was merely describing an extreme of low-pressure consciousness, close to nausea, and assuming it to be an accurate picture of all consciousness.

It is hard to see how one could convince Mlle. de Beauvoir of her error. One might try saying to her, 'You are starting to itch – first your left knee, then your right ear . . .' And then, as she reaches out to scratch herself, asking 'Where did it come from? Not your "consciousness" – you were watching it closely. Yet you undoubtedly made yourself itch. It follows that there is a part of your mind, not open to your observation, which produces the itch.' Or, even more simply, one might ask her to try to recall a tune, or the name of a character in a certain famous novel. After a moment's hesitation, she recalls the tune or the name. You then ask: 'But where did the tune come from? It walked into your consciousness, drawn forth by an act of intentionality. From where?'

I have tried to establish – and, I think, have established successfully – that the subject of love and freedom *can* be dealt with by phenomenological psychology, and, what is more, dealt with positively and creatively, not negatively and destructively, as does Sartre. Let us now undertake a more detailed analysis of love, attempting to remain within the phenomenological framework.

The aim of phenomenology is to brush aside preconceptions or assumptions that are not recognised as such. It once seemed self-evident that the sun revolved around the earth; it was necessary for Copernicus to perform a Husserlian epoché, a suspension of belief, before he could examine the truth of this assumption.

What, then, are the human assumptions about love that need to be suspended? They are so taken for granted that it is difficult even to state them clearly. In the romantic fiction of the nineteenth century, as well as in today's women's magazines, love is some immense, irresistible force that picks up human beings by the scruff of the neck and involves them in emotions that are the deepest they will ever experience – *Wuthering Heights* and so on. People 'fall in love'; they establish what Goethe called 'elective affinities', which somehow dissolve their separateness, creating a sort of unity.

I apologise for this vagueness; it lies in the matter under discussion.

Consider the alternative view. According to Blake, 'What men in women do require' (and vice versa) is 'the lineaments of satisfied desire'. That is to say, male–female relations are a transaction, like buying a cabbage from the grocer. What lovers are after is personal satisfaction, exactly as in a commercial transaction. They may be so mutually satisfactory that they are finally willing to give one another unlimited credit, offering satisfaction without the demand for immediate return. But it is 'established credit', just as in business; not pure generosity.

There is also the matter of 'falling in love'. But this will hardly bear scrutiny. Young people are very prone to fall in love – but then, they are emotionally hungry, and liable to fix on the most unsuitable objects, which would seem to suggest that they are projecting their desires rather than trying to enter into a two-sided relationship. We are inclined to label this emotion 'puppy love' or 'infatuation', indicating that we recognise its highly subjective nature.

Unfortunately, this recognition usually leads to a landslide of scepticism about the whole subject. The poet W.J. Turner writes:

Can the lover share his soul
Or the mistress show her mind?
Can the body beauty share
Or lust satisfaction find?

Marriage is but keeping house
Sharing food and company,
What has this to do with love
Or with the body's beauty?

If love means affection, I
Love old trees, hats, coats and things,
Anything that's been with me
In my daily sufferings.

And it is only one step from this to Rupert Brooke's 'each in his lonely night, each with a ghost', and Sartre's total nihilism on the subject.

Here is the analysis of love that I would propose as conforming to a fairly stringent reduction. Let me first of all state it flatly, without elaboration.

I would suggest that the normal use of the word love is inaccurate, that it contains several false assumptions. I have never heard of a case of falling in love that could not be analysed along the lines of the grocer and the cabbage. When the statue in *Man and Superman* protests that he has often been sincerely in love, Don Juan retorts: 'Sincerity . . .! To be so greedy for a woman that you deceive yourself in your eagerness to deceive her!' This kind of 'love' – greed for a desirable person – is surely a matter of possessiveness combined with self-deception.

On the other hand, the kind of love I feel for my children –
particularly when they are babies – is an instinctive protectiveness. I have included them within my personal radius, so that the
protectiveness I normally feel for myself extends to them too.
Protectiveness, in some respects, goes deeper than love. Is it self-
love that makes me fling up my hands when I stumble? Obviously
not; it is something much more primitive. My feeling toward my
children is an equally primitive protectiveness.

I can think of no example, either known to me personally or
through literature, of any case of love that could not be broken
down into the two elements of sexual desire (lust) and
protectiveness. There may or may not also be involved an element
of intellectual or personal sympathy of the kind that exists
between ordinary friends. (I can think of a great many marriages
in which it is lacking.)

I have to admit that, so far, I have said nothing with which
Sartre would not agree. But it is at this point that I would part
company with his analysis.

The last stanza of Turner's poem *Epithalamium* runs:

> I have stared upon a dawn
> And trembled like a man in love,
> A man in love I was, and I
> Could not speak and could not move.

In the same way, Shaw's argument in the third act of *Man and
Superman* is that love is given its peculiarly obsessive quality by the
fact that the lovers are in the grip of an evolutionary force that
transcends their personal involvements.

This, of course, is an argument that Sartre would condemn as
completely unphenomenological. Phenomenology is an extension
of Humeian scepticism. It deals in observables. To speak of an
evolutionary force is not only bad psychology; it is bad biology
and bad philosophy. The 'evolutionary force' is wishful thinking.
Julian Huxley commented that to attribute evolution to an *élan
vital* is like attributing the motion of a train to an *élan
locomotif*.

But it is always easier to demolish an argument by swinging a
sledgehammer of scepticism than to demonstrate it by detailed
and careful analysis. In this case, there are a number of reasons

why I cannot accept the sledgehammer approach. To begin with, Merleau Ponty has used phenomenological analysis to show that pure behaviourism cannot account for all mental activities. Arthur Koestler's attack on behaviourism in his important trilogy *The Sleepwalkers*, *The Act of Creation*, and *The Ghost in the Machine* follows similar lines, although for some reason, Mr. Koestler shows no awareness of what Merleau Ponty has already done. There is also a powerful movement, led by Sir Karl Popper and Michael Polanyi, to try to place the philosophy of science on a less positivistic basis. Some of Popper's arguments in *The Logic of Scientific Discovery*, particularly in the appendices added to the latest edition, strike me as quite conclusive.

Most important, for my purposes, is Maslow's contribution to psychology. Let me try to summarise this as I understand it.

Men differ from animals chiefly in that they may be driven by 'values' that cannot be reduced to such lower terms as the Freudian libido, the need for territory, food, security, etc. 'Man has a higher nature that is just as "instinctoid" as his lower nature. . . . This higher nature includes the needs for meaningful work, for responsibility, for being fair and just, for doing what is worthwhile,' he writes in the preface to *Eupsychian Management* (1965). Aldous Huxley once made a similar suggestion when he remarked that if man possesses a subconscious basement containing all his darker desires and instincts, why should he not possess an attic, equally inaccessible to conscious reflection?

It may be a relatively small proportion of human beings who urgently experience this need to live in terms of higher values, but it is also the most important section of the human race.

Man is an evolutionary animal. Of all animals, he is the one who most hates inactivity. A bored man will tap his foot or tap his finger against a chair arm. A bored animal will merely go to sleep. Man wants to move, to go. He is a big engine that needs to be geared to worthwhile labour if he is to operate at maximum efficiency. Or he could be compared to a river that must flow forward. If the river gets dammed up for some reason, it tends to run back up the valley and form a lake, which now becomes an amplifier of every minor frustration or neurosis.

Maslow's basic assertion is obviously that man's impulses toward higher values exist in their own right; they are not a sublimation of some lower impulse, a *faute de mieux*. In fact, Maslow's experiments with monkeys in the early nineteen-thirties seemed to demonstrate that monkeys will solve intellectual problems for the fun of it, and there therefore even a monkey cannot be wholly summarised in terms of its lower impulses.

What happens when the river gets dammed up is also the central theme of Frankl's psychology. There is Frankl's story of the schoolboy who stuttered badly – until asked to play the part of a stutterer in the school play, after which he was unable to stutter. Man was not intended for static self-contemplation and lack of purpose. He is only at his best when driven by purpose – the higher the better. This is the theme of Shaw's *Man and Superman*, and, more recently, of the Spanish existential philosopher Zubiri, for whom man is only truly himself in action.

I am here summarising a large body of evidence in a hasty and unsatisfactory manner; lack of space demands this. The evidence has not in any way contributed to my own conviction that the evolutionary drive cannot be dismissed as wishful thinking; this was already the central theme of my book *The Outsider* (1956), written before I was aware of any of this evidence. I refer interested readers to the six volumes of my 'outsider cycle' (1956–65), and to my *Introduction to the New Existentialism* (1966).

All this should make it clear why, although I accept Blake's 'lineaments of gratified desire' view of love, I have no sympathy with the Sartre vacuum.

Maslow, then, has answered Nietzsche's question 'Freedom for what?' with an evolutionary affirmation. 'Freedom for the expression and development of man's higher instinctoid nature.' Love in itself is not necessarily a part of this higher nature; it may be a fairly low-level expression of lust, protectiveness, and the need for emotional security. But it may become a vital part of this higher instinctoid expression, blending it with it so as to become an indistinguishable part. The love story of the Curies offers a convincing example of this. But the higher expression need not necessarily be connected with love. There is no evidence that Bernard Shaw's marriage made the slighest difference to him as a creative thinker, except to provide him with three meals a day. H.G. Wells' sexual relations were frankly promiscuous and physical, but there is no evidence (in his work) that his 'higher nature' was in any way starved. Clearly, he was in some ways an immature person, which explains the obsessive need for seduction; to judge by his later work, however, his creativity was unaffected.

But the really interesting problem is the question of the nature of freedom for modern man. And here I must admit that I do not see how this word can be defined except in evolutionary terms. Man is probably about two million years old. For about three quarters of that time, he showed no advance at all. Then the rate of evolution slowly accelerated. One of his greatest advances was his collaboration with the dog, and his realisation that certain animals would obey him instead of fleeing from him, if he treated them right. Then came husbandry, with the discovery that he could survive by growing things instead of hunting, as the next greatest advance in human history. And it was probably this slower, more contemplative pace of life that caused the development of religion and then of art.

Art, as Julian Huxley never tires of pointing out, is perhaps the greatest advance of all. For it is basically the discovery that man is not permanently 'stuck in the present', like a needle tracing its inevitable course over a gramophone record. He possesses a mental being, 'those thoughts that wander through eternity', as Milton says. According to Robert Ardrey, this was the beginning of his downfall, for he now had to see himself as something more than a part of nature; he had to believe that he was somehow the centre of the universe. Whether one agrees with Ardrey or not (and I don't), it has to be admitted that all real evolution – truly human evolution – has sprung from this belief in his central significance. It endowed him with a new, altogether more aggressive attitude toward nature. One has only to read any popular book on Stonehenge to grasp clearly what this means; read of the enormous effort entailed in quarrying stones in Wales, then dragging them overland on rollers, then floating them on rafts up the Bristol Channel, then more rafts, then more rollers – until they are finally dragged to the middle of Salisbury Plain, to take their place in a monument that probably took a hundred years to build.[1] To imagine that state of mind of the priests when they looked at the finally completed temple is to realise that the human will to achieve is a force that makes glaciers and volcanoes and earthquakes seem modest and feeble. It is this force that has continued to operate, from Archimedes' pulleys to the discoveries of Pasteur and Fleming, and that has made man the most incredible phenomenon that this planet has ever seen.

But the changes of the past two hundred years have been too abrupt. We cannot adjust to them. And as a result of this feeling of confusion and bewilderment, we have Samuel Beckett's tramps looking blankly at the universe and muttering 'Nothing to be done', and Sartre's assertion that 'man is a useless passion'. We are at our best when responding to challenges; and compared to human life five hundred years ago, our civilisation is a huge feather bed.

The problem of freedom now arises. We have plenty of freedom in the physical sense; we are surrounded by it. And now the Frankl syndrome begins to operate. Left to itself, with no purpose, consciousness begins to feed upon itself. Frankl's story of the stutterer makes this clear enough. When told to use his conscious control to go ahead and stutter, the will goes into gear; energies flow into their proper circuits; the being is unified by purpose. And the neurotic symptoms vanish. Man becomes what he *should* be – what evolution intends him to be. (It is worth commenting here that the sexual orgasm offers man one of the clearest insights into what consciousness *could* be like if he could learn to unify his being through purpose with the same intensity that his sexual instinct can unify it.)

Man is not himself without purpose. And it has been the great achievement of humanistic psychology to recognise this from purely experimental premises, without wishful thinking or idealising.

It may seem that this paper has failed to come to grips with its subject: love as an expression of mutual freedom. But, in fact, it has been necessary to argue in this somewhat roundabout way in order to reach this subject.

The kind of unity of being provided by a strong sexual stimulus is largely nonreflective; it rises from the realm of the robot. But most of our purposive activities are less powerfully instinctive, so that they require a conscious self-image to hold them together.

Here is an anecdote that illustrates my point. When the BBC

built the first soundproof studios for broadcasting music, they discovered that orchestras played badly in the 'dead' studio. An orchestra likes to *hear itself*, to hear its sounds bounced back off the walls of the concert hall. A friend of mine was given the amusing job of connecting up a circuit that would pick up the sound of the orchestra, and relay it back to them a fraction of a second later through loudspeakers situated around the studio, thus producing an artificial echo. As soon as they could hear themselves, the orchestra played twice as well.

We all need 'mirrors' to reflect our activity if we are to function at our best. And this is surely the deep significance of the male–female relation. There is, of course, the simple fact that in merely stimulating one another sexually, they are providing one another with an experience of deep instinctive unity. But the sexual side of marriage is bound to be affected by habit, so this aspect is hardly important over a long period. But the way in which each of the partners operates as a mirror for the other remains of permanent importance. Freedom cannot operate on a long-term basis without a clear self-image, and the purpose of the marriage partner is to provide this self-image.

There are, of course, many other ways of providing a self-image. To mention only one: a writer produces his book because it is his mirror, which confirms the direction of his evolution. While Alexander's slave was told to whisper 'Remember you are mortal', a writer's book is there to whisper 'Remember you may be immortal'.

Ideally, a love relationship serves the same purpose. Each of the partners is provided with a new self-image, one that differs radically from the reflection thrown back by parents and schoolteachers and work colleagues. Each serves as a magic mirror in which the other sees himself reflected *in terms of potentiality*. (It also follows, of course, that sexual relations can be the most destructive thing in the world if either of the partners lacks belief in the other's potentiality.)

Let me finish on a warning note. It is true that a love relation is, ideally, an illumination of one another's freedom: that is to say, potentialities for evolving. But real evolution – of the kind we see in the case of great artists, musicians, philosophers, scientists – is not dependent upon this kind of encouragement. Would

Beethoven have been a greater composer with an admiring wife? Would Goethe have been a greater poet if he had married an intellectual equal instead of the stolid and peasant-like Christine Vulpus? Almost certainly not. On the other hand, a downright unsuitable marriage – such as H.G. Wells's first marriage, or Einstein's – may actively hinder creativity.

While love undoubtedly presents the possibility of an immensely important adventure in mutual freedom, I have to admit frankly that I cannot call to mind a single case of a great man – or woman – whose evolution has been heavily dependent upon the freedom mirrored by the love relation. And the reason may be the one given by Socrates in the *Symposium*: that in highly evolved human beings, the love of another person tends to serve as the stepping-off point for more universal enthusiasms. And at this point in the discussion, it may be that psychology gets uncomfortably close to theology.

1972

FOUR

Spinoza – the outsider

Spinoza has the curious distinction of being the least influential of the great philosophers.

To someone approaching Spinoza for the first time, this is the most obvious and puzzling thing about him. Every history of philosophy devotes a chapter to Spinoza, and no one seems to doubt his right to so much space. But why is he so important? What other great philosophers did he influence? Where can we find any trace of his ideas – no matter how diluted – in the modern world? There are still plenty of traces of Platonism and Aristotelianism and Cartesianism – even Hegelianism. By comparison, Spinozism seems to have been a kind of dead end – his ideas influenced a few eighteenth-century Deists, and a few nineteenth-century atheists, then seemed to fade away. History has played the same trick on a number of other philosophers who seemed highly significant in their own time – Reid, Lotze and Eucken, to name a few at random. So by what right does Spinoza continue to occupy his position in the histories of philosophy?

Of course, the *Ethics* is obviously a philosophical masterpiece. But even this only underlines the problem. For it is essentially a closed system. And in philosophy, closed systems are at a disadvantage. Nietzsche continues to exercise more influence than Schopenhauer, not because he is a better writer – he is not – but because he left most of his questions unanswered. The same goes for Kierkegaard and Husserl and Wittgenstein. The great systematisers – Hegel, Lotze, Whitehead – are somehow too impressive; they kill all desire to take up where they left off. Spinoza's *Ethics* is considerably shorter than Lotze's *Macrocosmos* or Whitehead's *Process and Reality*, but its geometrical propositions make it look even more impregnable. Goethe used to read it in Latin, but I can think of few modern poets who would attempt it even in English.

Nietzsche made the same point about Spinoza in *Beyond Good and Evil*, in a scornfully hostile passage. And, oddly enough, came close to putting his finger on the reason for Spinoza's fascination for other thinkers. He attacks the 'tartuffery' of Kant, then turns his fire on Spinoza,

> the hocus pocus in mathematical form, by means of which Spinoza has clad his philosophy in armour and visor – in fact, the 'love of *his* wisdom', to translate the term fairly and squarely – in order to strike terror into the heart of the assailant who would dare to cast a glance on that invincible maiden, that Pallas Athene; how much personal timidity and vulnerability does this masquerade of a sickly recluse betray.

And then he goes on to make one of his most celebrated statements:

> It has gradually become clear to me what every great philosophy up till now has consisted of – namely, the confession of its inventor, and a sort of involuntary and subconscious autobiography.

Now Nietzsche is not entirely wrong to look askance at Spinoza's 'armour'; his own polemical and dramatic methods are certainly more striking. But when he suggests, in effect, that we forget the philosophy and look at the philosopher, he immediately provides the answer to his own attack. Anyone who knows the slightest amount about the life of Spinoza knows that it is nonsense to speak of his personal timidity and vulnerability. Like Nietzsche – another sickly recluse – he revealed remarkable courage and inner strength. His greatness lay, to a large extent, in his capacity for 'outsiderism', in standing alone, apart from society, in renouncing the pleasures that make life tolerable for most of us, and transcending personal needs in pure creativity. Once we have come to admire this courage and inner strength, we can also see how it is reflected in the 'impersonal' form of the *Ethics*. Like Plotinus, Spinoza believed that a philosopher should leave the personal behind. He began a semi-autobiographical treatise – *On the Improvement of the Understanding* – but seems to have left it unfinished. But his major work was an assertion, both in form and content, of the transcendental nature of philosophy. Nietzsche is defiantly polemical. Spinoza is defiantly scientific.

Now those of us who know something of the history of philosophical logic since Leibniz will be inclined to shake our heads. Russell and Whitehead pursued a related dream; so did Hilbert; Frege and Gödel brought their edifices crashing. I am inclined to believe that Spinoza's work is vulnerable to the same sort of criticism. But before I consider this possibility, I would like to follow Nietzsche's prescription, and examine the philosophy as part of the personal development of the philosopher.

For a contemporary Englishman, the background to Spinoza's philosophy is almost impossible to grasp. This is partly because the battles Spinoza fought were won two centuries ago. There is still plenty of religious – and racial – intolerance in the world; but now no intelligent person accepts it as norm. We find it almost impossible to imagine a time, for example, when the majority of people approved of the Inquisition – or a least, took it for granted. (As an imaginative exercise, we might try it in reverse, and envisage a completely vegetarian society that regards our meat-eating as a horrible, grisly remnant of the Dark Ages.)

So to even begin to understand Spinoza, we have to make an effort to understand the long-standing persecution of the Jews in Spain and Portugal – an effort that is aided by our proximity in time to the Nazis. In 1492, three hundred thousand Jews were expelled from Spain, and thousands died of starvation or in shipwrecks. Some took refuge in Portugal; they were made to pay a high price in exchange for a limited period of time there; those who were unable to leave when their time was up were enslaved. The others moved on to further sufferings.

The Spanish atrocities against the Protestants in the Netherlands are an equally brutal and horrifying story. So when the Dutch revolted and threw off the Spanish yoke, Jews and Protestants felt they were united by a certain common cause. This is why Spinoza's grandfather – a Portuguese Jew who had been forcibly 'converted' to Christianity – came to Amsterdam. The Jewish community found religious freedom in Holland.

All of this may enable us to understand – even if we fail to sympathise with – the religious bigotry of Spinoza's co-religionists. From Voltaire to H.G. Wells, rationalists have shaken their heads over Jewish religious fanaticism, and suggested that it is an unfortunate reaction to centuries of persecution. (This argument is hardly convincing; intense devotion to their religion has been a Jewish characteristic since long before the Diaspora.) Whatever the reason, it seems clear that Jews – like Christians and Mohammedans – have been capable of a pretty high degree of bigotry and intolerance in matters of religion. Spinoza wrote:

> The love of the Hebrews for their country was not only patriotism, but also piety, and was cherished and nurtured by daily rites till, like the hatred of other nations, it must have passed into their nature. Their daily worship was not only different from that of other nations (as it might well be, considering that they were a peculiar people, and entirely apart from the rest), it was absolutely contrary. Such daily reprobation naturally gave rise to a lasting hatred deeply implanted in the heart: for of all hatreds, none is more deep and tenacious than that which springs from devoutness or piety, and is itself cherished as pious (*Tractatus Theologico-Politicus*, 17).

From which we may infer that Spinoza would have thoroughly approved the 'forecast' made by H.G. Wells in *The Shape of Things to Come*:

> And yet . . . in little more than a century, this antiquated obdurate [Jewish] culture disappeared. It and its Zionist state, its kosher food, its Law and the rest of its paraphernalia, were completely merged in the human community. The Jews were not suppressed; there was no extermination . . . yet they were educated out of the oddity and racial egotism in little more than three generations.

In his early teens, Spinoza had a chance to observe this 'antiquated and obdurate' bigotry at first hand. Uriel Acosta was a Portuguese Jew of considerable eminence; in Lisbon, he had permitted himself to be forcibly converted, and risen to an important position in the service of the State. Preferring freedom, he moved to Amsterdam and reverted to the religion of his fathers. Acosta had a passionate belief in reason, which he carried to aggressive extremes. A treatise pointing out that the traditions of the Pharisees were at variance with written Law was taken as an unfriendly act by the Jewish community, while another work questioning the immortality of the soul provoked bitter fury. He was twice excommunicated from the religious community, and the sentence was lifted only when he grovelled in the dust on the threshold of the synagogue, allowing the congregation to walk over him. Being a man of spirit and intelligence, he was soon excommunicated a second time, and the 'retraction' was repeated. When he rebelled a third time, the community united to force him into submission; he wrote a violent denunciation of the elders, and shot himself. The story aroused enough controversy to be turned into a popular drama by Gutzkov. Spinoza was fifteen when Acosta killed himself in 1647. By that time, he was already aware that his own temperament was basically rational and scientific, and must have anticipated a similar fate.

Spinoza lacked Acosta's hot-headedness; his motto was *Caute* (caution). There were many pressures on him to conform; his father and grandfather were prosperous merchants; in the small, closed Jewish community of Amsterdam, the highly intelligent youth was inevitably a person of some prominence. He showed considerable distinction as a student of the Talmud; from this he passed on to Jewish philosophy and Cabbalistic mysticism. Unlike the empirical Anglo-Saxons, Jewish communities are inclined to take a certain pride in their more brilliant sons. Spinoza's father probably had every reason to assume that he would, in due course, become the religious and intellectual leader of the community.

It would be fascinating to know at which point Spinoza himself realised that this was out of the question – that his commitment to reason would inevitably sunder him from the society of his co-religionists. Possibly it happened as a consequence of the suicide of Acosta. It must certainly have taken many years to develop into a powerful and settled conviction, sufficiently strong to enable him to bear the shock of total rejection when it came. Dates are unfortunately lacking in the biographical materials, so it is not clear when he first began to abandon his attendance at the synagogue. Nor do we know how soon thereafter he abandoned caution and allowed himself to express his increasing scepticism to other young men. But common sense suggests that it was fairly close to his twenty-fourth year – when he was excommunicated.

As Nietzsche's Zarathustra points out, separating oneself from the herd is a painful and exhausting process. Nietzsche was the son of a Protestant clergyman, and went through the same experience. His letters and autobiographical fragments make clear the spiritual agonies he suffered; yet nineteenth-century Germany was an entirely different matter from seventeenth-century Amsterdam; to begin with, there were educators like Schopenhauer to turn to. Spinoza's equivalent of Schopenhauer was Giordano Bruno, and Bruno was burnt alive for his freethinking. Spinoza's agony must have been even greater than Nietzsche's. Logic suggests that he kept his rebellion to himself for as long as possible.

Neither do we know how much pain the break finally cost him. We are told only that he was summoned before the Rabbins and elders of the synagogue in 1656 and accused of 'rationalistic' views, such as that angels do not exist, that the soul might simply be another name for life, and that the Old Testament says nothing of immortality (the opinion that had caused Acosta's downfall). We are told that Spinoza stood his ground, declined an offer of an annuity if he would continue to conform to the external practices of his religion, and that when he still refused, there were violent threats of excommunication. The struggle may have continued for days or weeks. Finally, on 27 July 1656, there was a solemn ceremony of excommunication, which was, in effect, a spiritual execution. G.H. Lewes describes it:

> High above, the chanter rose and chanted forth, in loud lugubrious tones, the words of execration; while from the opposite side another mingled with these curses the thrilling sounds of the trumpet; and now black candles were reversed, and were made to melt drop by drop into a huge tub filled with blood. This made the whole assembly shudder; and when the final *Anathema Maranatha!* were uttered, and the lights all suddenly immersed in the blood, a cry of religious horror and execration burst from all; and in that solemn darkness, and to those solemn curses, they shouted Amen, Amen!

How far this description is accurate is open to question; but the actual formula of excommunication, published by van Vloten, makes it clear that it comes fairly close to the actual spirit of the

ceremony. The aim was to break Spinoza and throw him into the
outer darkness, to make him feel that his wickedness had led to his
total rejection by every decent man and woman.

Shortly thereafter, to emphasise that he was now some kind of
human offal, a fanatic attempted to stab him to death in the street.
The blow missed and tore his coat. Lewes says he 'walked home
thoughtful' – a statement that reveals his inability to imagine
himself into the situation. Spinoza must have walked home
shattered and traumatised, realising that there was now no point in
trying to salvage a little security and normality from the situation.
He had to turn his back on the world of his childhood and accept
solitude and exile. When he left to live outside Amsterdam, he
must have felt like some wounded creature dragging itself away to
die. All of which sounds melodramatic; but then, Spinoza's
situation *was* a subject for melodrama.

It is interesting, and by no means entirely futile, to ask: What sort
of philosopher might Spinoza have become if he had been born
into a non-Jewish community – perhaps in England or France?
We know that his philosophy was deeply influenced by his studies
of the Talmud, and by the peculiarly intense nature of Jewish
Theism. But then, he had also read certain mystics – like Ibn
Gebirol, Moses of Cordova and Bruno himself. As an Englishman
or Frenchman, he might have been equally influenced by Plato
and Plotinus.

I am willing to be corrected, but it seems to me that Spinoza's
temperament was scientific and logical rather than religious.
Under different circumstances, he might have been another
Descartes, or Newton, or even Shelley, a 'beautiful and
ineffectual angel'. By temperament he was a Platonist and
something of a Stoic. (Significantly, Goethe used to travel with
the *Ethics* and the *Meditations of Marcus Aurelius*.) That is to say, he
was an idealist in the Platonic sense, one who agrees that our
human purpose is to lift the mind beyond desires and trivialities,
beyond merely incidental beauties, to contemplate the truth and
beauty of the universe itself – as Socrates explains in the
Symposium. In a sense, it is quite inevitable that a great philosopher
should be a Platonist, since the basic aim of philosophy is to rise
beyond the 'triviality of everydayness' to a bird's-eye vision of

broad generalities. Einstein compared the scientist to a town dweller who enjoys getting into the country, to contemplate mountains and lakes instead of endless bustle and chatter. Individual scientists and philosophers may differ in a thousand ways; but all share this common impulse to achieve a 'bird's-eye view'.

The evidence of his book on Descartes suggests that Spinoza was basically a rationalist who, under different circumstances, might have learned to accept some modified form of Judaism (as Descartes and Leibniz accepted Catholicism), while his main interests were directed towards a kind of critical philosophy. In which case, we might only know his name as an obscure commentator on other philosophers, a minor disciple of Descartes, like Geulincx (Spinoza's fellow countryman).

Whatever else the effect of the excommunication, it must have driven all tendency to amateurism and dilettantism out of his system. It faced him squarely with the question of what he really believed, and whether his belief was worth the discomfort and loneliness he had to endure. At least the bigotry of his fellow Jews accomplished one important result: it prevented him from ever taking intellectual freedom for granted as some basic human right, like the air we breathe. Having paid such a price for it, freedom of thought became a positive ideal, a kind of religious conviction.

But then, reason itself seems a feeble battle cry. On its most familiar human level, it is little more than the ability to add up a column of figures correctly. Descartes's radical doubt only led to a self-contradictory Dualism. (If the world is mind and matter, how do they interact?) If Spinoza was to justify his sacrifice, his freedom had to lead to something a little more inspiring than that.

It led, of course, to that gigantic philosophical counterpart to *Paradise Lost*, Spinoza's own Promethean effort to justify the ways of God to man, the *Ethics*. In the meantime, as an intermediate step, there came the *Theologico-Political Treatise*, a seminal work of rationalist criticism of the Bible. Issued anonymously in 1670, it caused widespread controversy and ran through many editions. When his identity became known the book was denounced as an instrument 'forged in Hell by a renegade Jew and the devil'. It is, of course, a remarkable work; but if Spinoza's reputation rested on this alone, he would be classified with Voltaire and Tom Paine as a moral rebel rather than a philosopher. It was the *Ethics* for which Spinoza spent his life preparing, the great Hegelian synthesis, the Ultimate System. (In fact, Spinoza never wrote the projected work: the book was have is no more than an outline.) The *Ethics* was his answer to his old master Morteira and the other elders who had expelled him.

In his two-volume work on the philosophy of Spinoza, Harry Austryn Wolfson has pointed out the dozens of influences that went to make up the *Ethics*, from Plato and St Anselm to Bruno and Descartes. Yet it was Whitehead who remarked that Western philosophy could be regarded as a series of footnotes to Plato, and it would not be inaccurate to regard the *Ethics* as an enormous commentary on the *Symposium*, with its view that man's highest aim is contemplation of universal truth. From the modern point of view, the *Ethics* has been written back to front. The final Part (V) deals with man's aims and purposes, Parts III and IV with the emotions, Part II with the mind, Part I with God and the universe. The last three Parts are an attempt at a phenomenological psychology of man, the first two at a metaphysics.

I shall not attempt a summary of the *Ethics* – which would take far more space than I have available – but confine myself to some general comments. This is basically an immense and static System, based on the mystical notion that God *is* the universe, and vice versa. One commentator remarks that Spinoza does not assert the existence of God; he asserts that existence *is* God.

That sounds the kind of meaningless and irritating proposition that makes logical positivists reach for their revolvers. But, in fact, Spinoza is prepared to argue his way towards it step by step, starting from man and his problems. The first and most basic question is obviously: why, if God is the universe, is there such a thing as evil? To which Spinoza replies that there isn't. All creatures have their own trivial, personal view of evil and good, based on their desires and needs. A cold wind seems bad to a man who has just fallen in the canal; itself, the wind is neither good nor bad – just air in motion, according to natural laws.

Man himself is merely a fragment of the whole – a leaf on a tree, a blade of grass in a field. His basic aim is self-preservation, and this governs his notions of good and evil. His powers are obviously very limited indeed. He is not body *and* soul, as Descartes taught; the mind is the mirror of the body. Here we seem to be fairly close to the psychology of Hume and the empiricists – and possibly of Gilbert Ryle – in which mind is a product of the body as smoke is a product of fire. But it is also worth bearing in mind the view of Whitman and D.H. Lawrence that man is a living unity, and that 'mind' and 'body' are two sides of the same coin, so to speak. Spinoza's basic feeling seems to come closer to this attitude.

The emotions cause man to be a slave to nature and its forces; understanding and self-control can free him from this slavery. Maugham borrowed the title of Part IV – *Of Human Bondage* – for his novel about an intelligent man's irrational slavery to a worthless woman, and the book is a fairly accurate reflection of Spinoza's view of the emotions. 'Evil' is basically ignorance. Man achieves freedom by using his understanding to dispel it. Selflessness is not a virtue; all of us are self-seeking, but the wise man seeks things of permanent value; the stupid man is misled by his emotions to strive for unworthy aims and objects.

All this sounds drearily deterministic; it is certainly thoroughly naturalistic, only one step away from the naturalism of Hume or the total materialism of nineteenth-century thinkers like Büchner. Religious people will object that it denies human freedom; idealists that it denies transcendental values; evolutionists that it offers a static universe. Aware of these objections, Spinoza takes a bold leap into theology, and leaves all his opponents startled and bewildered. The world consists of shadow and substance – Plato's 'form' and 'idea', Schopenhauer's 'Will' and 'illusion'. Spinoza calls them 'mode' and 'substance'. 'Modes' are the temporary forms of the basic underlying reality. This reality is God. God is infinite and incomprehensible; in our worm-like state (at one point, Spinoza compares man to a worm living in the bloodstream of the universe), we can only see two of God's attributes – thought and extension. There are millions more which are beyond our comprehension.

All the same, because we are fragments of God, we possess the ability to rise above our mere humanity and glimpse the essential nature of the universe and of God. So the aim of life is clear: to increase the understanding.

It becomes possible to see why Spinoza ceased to exercise any profound influence in philosophy after the seventeenth century. His 'improvement' of the Cartesian dualism is not really acceptable on any practical level. To accept it as satisfactory, you have to rise to Spinoza's idea of God as one with nature, then transfer this mystical idea to the human realm. It is very hard – in fact, it requires a kind of mental sleight of hand – to see mind and body as somehow inseparable – at least, without slipping into the materialist viewpoint that mind is merely a product of body. The trouble is that human experience keeps making us aware of ourselves as mind *and* body. We say 'The spirit is willing but the flesh is weak'. Every day of our lives we become aware of ourselves as two conflicting forces. So monist solutions, no matter how logically satisfying, fail to appeal to our common sense.

But all this is far from the whole story of Spinoza's declining influence. Altogether more serious is the kind of criticism implied in Nietzsche's comments about 'unconscious autobiography'. Apart from the accusation of 'timidity and vulnerability' – which we have seen to be unfounded – Nietzsche is accusing Spinoza of being a kind of liar, or at least, a self-deceiver.

Admirers of Spinoza may shrug and ask why Nietzsche deserves to be taken so seriously. The answer is that Nietzsche's attitude has become, to a greater or lesser extent, the attitude of modern philosophy. And not merely 'existential philosophy' – the school with which Nietzsche's name is usually associated. Kierkegaard – the founder of existentialism – criticised metaphysical 'Systems' on the grounds that trying to shape your conduct according to one of these systems is like trying to find your way round Copenhagen using a map of the world on which Denmark is the size of a pinhead. In short, that a System is too much of a 'bird's-eye view' from whose dizzy altitude the real world becomes practically invisible. And this is a matter in which logical positivists find themselves in total agreement with existentialists. Both agree that philosophy ought to deal with reality as we actually know it, not with some idealistic abstraction. And so, for practical purposes, we may regard Nietzsche as the spokesman of the whole anti-metaphysical point of view. Let us, therefore, try to grasp the essence of Nietzsche's objection to Spinoza, and the existentialist viewpoint from which it sprang.

Interestingly enough, most of Nietzsche's references to Spinoza
– they can easily be tracked down through the index to his
Collected Works – indicate his sense of kinship; he speaks of him
as 'the most upright of sages', and praises his stoicism and self-
sufficiency. And Nietzsche was too self-analytical not to be aware
of the parallels between himself and the Jewish philosopher. Both
were 'sickly recluses'; both were 'outsiders', rejected by their own
community, living in rented rooms on a low income, devoting
themselves to the life of the mind. Neither were celibate by
choice; both had fallen in love and been rejected; both shrugged
off the disappointment and turned back to the serious business of
creating a 'revaluation of values'. Both were men who, in the
words of Husserl, had had 'the misfortune to fall in love with
philosophy'. Both were obsessed with truth. Clearly, then,
Nietzsche's rejection of Spinoza was no sudden flash of irritation.
There were two other major figures towards whom Nietzsche's
attitude was equally ambiguous and ambivalent: Socrates and
Wagner. It was where Nietzsche felt most attracted that he felt the
need to reject most violently.

The attraction is easy enough to explain. Spinoza *is* an
immensely attractive figure. Goethe regarded him as a kind of
saint. 'None had spoken so like the Saviour concerning God as
he,' he told Lavater. And Bertrand Russell, who is predictably
hostile to Spinoza's metaphysics, nevertheless describes him as
'the noblest and most lovable of the great philosophers'.

All of which makes us aware that the truth about Spinoza – as
we intimated at the beginning of this essay – is that any attempt to
judge him must start from Spinoza the human being. Judged *in
vacuo*, the *Ethics* may be 'noble', but it is rather repellent. And as
speculative philosophy – according to Moore the art of arousing
thought in other philosophers – it has been a great deal less fruitful
than Hume's *Essay*, Kant's *Critique* or Husserl's *Ideas*; in
appearance, at least, it is a little too inhumanly perfect. It is when
we have come to know Spinoza the man that we are in a position
to appreciate him as the author of the *Ethics*.

What we admire is the man of incredibly tough moral fibre who
stood up against the whole age, the 'prophet who contradicted the
Prophets', as Goethe called him. Apart from Nietzsche, the other
'outsider' he most resembles is the mystic William Blake, another

intransigent visionary who lived a life of neglect (although Blake at least had a wife to share it with him). Spinoza's enemies drew strength from bigotry and the opinion of 'the herd'. Spinoza not only stood alone; he refused to be embittered or prejudiced. Yet in spite of his mystical love of God – which he equated with knowledge – we feel that Spinoza saw the world through natural eyes. If he is a martyr, it is to reason, not religion.

And reason is simply the intellectual form of freedom. In the *Tractatus Theologico-Politicus* he is concerned with religious and political freedom. In the *Ethics*, he becomes concerned with the freedom of the spirit itself, man's longing to escape all the limitations of the earth and of his own weakness. He avoids the usual snare of religious pietism. He has little use for pity, and none for humility, which he regards as hypocrisy or weakness. He dismisses the usual notions of good and evil; for Spinoza, as for Nietzsche, virtue is based on power and ability. Neither does he have any use for the view of Socrates, that since the philosopher spends his life trying to escape his body, death is some kind of consummation. Altogether, he seems to have escaped most of the fallacies that Nietzsche most detested.

And yet it is at precisely this point that Nietzsche and Spinoza part company. Nietzsche was physically sickly, but he carried his gospel of power to its logical conclusion. When he conceived the idea of Zarathustra, the preacher of the Superman – he was above the lake of Silvaplana at the time – he wrote on a slip of paper: 'Six thousand feet above men and time'. The idea that came to him was that all religions and philosophies have so far been mistaken about the highest good. It does not lie in moral virtue, or in self-restraint, or even in self-knowledge, but in the idea of *great health and strength*. This, says Nietzsche, is the fundamental constituent of freedom. Once man has these the others will follow, for most of his evils – and his intellectual confusions – spring from weakness.

It follows that the philosopher should recognise man as inadequate – 'human, all too human' – and strive to bring about the advent of the superman. For Nietzsche, reason is a manifestation of strength. Man's chief duty is to nurture his strength and his optimism, and to teach men to strive to evolve.

Now Spinoza quite definitely sets his face against evolutionism – or teleology – in the appendix to Part I. Since God is perfect, he asks, how can he have mere purposes? Admittedly, he seems to risk self-contradiction at this point. For he admits that God is 'partly' personal, and that will and thought are among His attributes. Nevertheless, we would be mistaken to think of God as sharing such personal qualities as desire and purpose. For a moment, we seem to glimpse Spinoza's mental picture of God; some unthinkable gigantic creature, like nature itself, breathing quietly in its sleep, unconsciously producing all the activity we see around us as a mere by-product of its tremendous breathing.

For Spinoza, man's ultimate perfection is to achieve 'cosmic consciousness', to transcend all his mere emotions, and to rise on wings of reason to the contemplation of this vast indifferent godhead.

Now at a fairly early stage in his career, Nietzsche had admired Socrates above all other philosophers; it seemed to him that the ultimate good was Thought. Then, in *Human, All too Human*, he turned against his old masters and ideals; he comes to feel that thought is trivial and unimportant compared to life. He ceased to believe in thought or reason as the vehicle that would transport man to the infinite. The thinkers, from Socrates to Kant, are deniers of the body and of life. And Spinoza, he feels, is unrealistic; he scornfully dismisses 'the no-more-laughing and no-more-weeping of Spinoza, the destruction of the emotions by their analysis and vivisection, which he recommended so naively'.

And so his indictment of Spinoza amounts to this: that the philosopher, rejected by society, withdrew into solitude and sought consolation in thought. He 'transcended' his humanity by rejecting it, dismissing the emotions as trivial. Now Nietzsche, like Blake, believed that the right way to transcend the emotions is to outgrow them; *not* by starving them to death. Zarathustra loves life; he loves nature; he loves to see pretty girls laughing and dancing. Spinoza's solution smacked to him of sour grapes.

This is not to say that Nietzsche did not believe in thought, or in self-discipline. But he believed they were only part of the answer. If a man is hungry, he cannot satisfy his belly by thinking about food. But he can use his intelligence to find ways of obtaining food. And it is better to find food than to talk yourself into believing you are not hungry. It is better to have a wife – or mistress – that to find ascetic reasons for condemning sex. To over-indulge the emotions is disastrous for the philosopher; to starve them in the name of reason is just as bad.

Basically, then, Nietzsche is accusing Spinoza of producing a false solution to the problem of the philosopher. Nietzsche created a new concept of the philosopher; not merely Rodin's thinker, sitting with his chin in his hand, but a whole and complete human being – something like Plato's philosopher-king. In *Man and Superman*, Shaw has a thoroughly Nietzschean definition of the philosopher: 'he who seeks in contemplation to discover the inner will of the world, in invention to discover the means of fulfilling that will, and in action to do that will by the so discovered means.' Obviously, Spinoza fulfils the first clause triumphantly. But he erected this activity of contemplation into the whole duty of the philosopher, his ultimate aim and purpose. His only 'action' was to write and think, and he attempted to give his ideas an air of icy self-sufficiency by casting them in the form of Euclidean propositions. It could be argued that his book justifies inaction, withdrawal from the world.

Since Nietzsche, this notion of the philosopher as the complete human being has become an integral part of the twentieth-century philosophical tradition – and not only for existentialists. A.N. Whitehead expressed it forcefully in his last book *Modes of Thought*:

Nothing can be omitted, experience drunk and experience sober, experience sleeping and experience waking, experience drowsy and experience wide-awake, experience self-conscious and experience self-forgetful, experience intellectual and experience physical, experience religious and experience sceptical, experience anxious and experience carefree, experience anticipatory and experience retrospective, experience happy and experience grieving, experience dominated by emotion and experience under self-restraint, experience in the light and experience in the dark, experience normal and experience abnormal.

It is true that few philosophers measure up to this standard; but most existentialists nevertheless take care to bear it in mind.

At which point I must 'declare my interest', and explain the nature of my own approach to the problem. My first book, *The Outsider*, was concerned with such men as Spinoza and Nietzsche – men whose inner development demanded a rejection of society – and often their own rejection *by* society. Whitehead defined religion as 'what a man does with his solitude': and since such inner-development usually demands a withdrawal into solitude, it would probably be true to say that most 'outsiders' are concerned with religion – although often of a highly personal and mystical kind.

In the great ages of religion, such men could usually find refuge in the Church. They might still be 'outsiders' – like Eckhart and Savonarola and St Francis and St John of the Cross – but they could nevertheless find in the Church a creative outlet for their energies. Outsiderism – the sense of not belonging to a society – could be justified as a need to belong to a still higher society – of saints and god-seekers. So, in a paradoxical sense, there *was* a place for 'outsiders' in society.

Then, for better or for worse, the Church ceased to be the dominant intellectual force in society, even if it could still bully Descartes into suppressing his major work on the universe. Modes of thought were 'secularized'. The man with a powerful urge to inner development now had to find his own way to self-realisation. Spinoza was one of the first of these 'outsider' figures. Two centuries after his death, 'outsiderism' had become the intellectual disease of the West. My own interest in the subject arose from the fact that so many of the great Romantics of the nineteenth century died tragically – either through insanity or disease or suicide.

But because the sickness had become so widespread, it was easier to reach a diagnosis. Many of the Romantics, from Shelley and Kleist to Van Gogh and Stefan George, were inclined to believe that life is fundamentally tragic. Man has brief glimpses of god-like intensity, but they vanish and leave him trapped in 'this dim vast vale of tears'. Yet other 'outsiders' took a less pessimistic view. William Blake insisted that man consists of three components: body, emotions and intellect. When intellect – which he called Urizen – is allowed to dominate, it becomes a force for evil, and the Fall occurs. In a healthy human being it must combine with emotion and body; these then give birth to a fourth component, imagination (Los). Half a century later, Dostoievsky – another seminal existentialist thinker – expressed the same view symbolically in the three brothers Karamazov. Ivan, the intellectual, comes close to insanity by suppressing emotions and body in the name of intellect.

Nietzsche, we have seen, reached the same position; but only after he had purged his system of the pessimism of Schopenhauer, which had totally dominated his early thinking. And having achieved optimism at the price of ruthless self-vivisection, he became violently intolerant of thinkers like Socrates and Spinoza, whom he regarded as 'life-deniers', glorifiers of 'Urizen'.

We may feel that, in the case of Socrates, this is hardly fair. Socrates was a soldier as well as a thinker; he could apparently out-drink and out-march his friends as well as out-think them. He held love to be as important as reason, and seems to have regarded the health of the body as equally important (as did Spinoza). Nevertheless, Nietzsche condemns him as an arid rationalist who allowed reason to dominate his life. The citizens of Athens who condemned Socrates to death seemed to believe that he was primarily a sceptic – a sneerer. Nietzsche seems to feel they were not entirely wrong.

And what of Spinoza? I would suggest that, while Nietzsche's 'existential criticisms' were, to a large extent, justified, there are nevertheless elements in Spinoza's temperament that Nietzsche left out of account because he was unable to understand them. His criticisms apply to the naturalistic part of Spinoza – Spinoza the sceptic – not to Spinoza the mystic.

Now to a modern reader, Spinoza's psychology seems as inadequate as John Stuart Mill's. Here we feel most strongly that Spinoza's insight was limited by the strength of his reaction against contemporary 'unreason'. He begins Part III by stating aggressively that most writers on the emotions have treated them as if they belonged to the realm of the 'soul'; he, Spinoza, proposes to treat them as if they obeyed the usual laws of nature – which he proceeds to do in a manner worthy of Somerset Maugham. No doubt his method was a salutary shock to most of his readers. But after three centuries, it has ceased to be shocking. Freud went much further in 'reducing' man to a bundle of uncontrolled impulses. And there are modern behavioural psychologists who have gone even further. Now the reaction is setting in. Many of us feel that the naturalistic view of man leaves out more than it puts in. The philosopher St Martin pointed out that the kind of 'humility' that insists that man is a mere grain of sand on some universal beach leads to laziness and cowardice. It is easy enough to demonstrate that every man suffers from the delusion that he is the most important being in the universe (what Robert Ardrey calls 'the fallacy of central position'), but it is too easy to slip into the opposite assumption – that he is the least important being in the universe. Even Freud's naturalistic psychology opened up all kinds of strange possibilities – for once we have admitted the existence of the subconscious, we have taken a long step away from naturalism. (This is why some behaviourists have refused to acknowledge its existence.) We find ourselves having to decide on the possibility of a 'collective unconscious', which in turn may lead to questions about telepathy and psychokinesis, and whether the subconscious mind may be responsible for poltergeist phenomena. Spinoza would have dismissed all these as superstitions.

Probably the closest modern equivalent to Spinoza's psychology is the 'existential psychology' of Sartre. Sartre's first book, *A Theory of the Emotions*, stated the thoroughly Spinozist doctrine that an emotion is simply another name for frustration; when we want something and we act, we feel no emotion; it is when we want something and are frustrated that we feel emotion. The more elaborate psychology of *Being and Nothingness* is constructed on this foundation. Emotion is basically an attempt to deceive ourselves. But for Sartre, there is no God, so the trivial drama of human stupidity and self-deception is played out against a background of universal emptiness.

On the other hand, comparison of Spinoza with Sartre makes us realise that Sartre is in one respect immensely more sophisticated; he had grasped Husserl's insight that all consciousness is *intentional* – that each perception is fired towards its object like a grappling hook. This in turn led Husserl (though not Sartre) to the notion of a 'transcendental ego' presiding over consciousness and ultimately responsible for intentionality; he came to see philosophy as the task of uncovering the secrets and mysteries of the transcendental ego. We might say that Husserl counterbalanced the Freudian Unconscious with the notion of a Superconscious mind.

Again, many non-naturalistic psychologists have felt that the most basic and interesting fact about human consciousness is that *there seems to be something wrong with it*. Pascal and Newman chose to call it 'original sin'. But it was also recognised by Gurdjieff, who said that our problem is that 'ordinary consciousness' is a form of sleep. While we are asleep, says Gurdjieff, we are little more than machines. He would have said that Spinoza's psychology is simply the psychology of the machine. What interested Gurdjieff was the possibility of awakening from sleep and utilising some of the hidden potentialities of consciousness. Again, we are close to Husserl and the 'secrets of the transcendental ego'.

So Spinoza's psychology, while brilliant and full of insights, will strike most modern readers as simplistic, not to say mechanistic. It is perhaps significant that he called his Part IV 'Of Human Bondage', while Pascal wanted to call the equivalent book of his own psychology 'The Greatness and Misery of Man'. One feels sometimes that Shaw's remark about Shakespeare applies equally to Spinoza: that he understands human weakness, but not human strength.

But then, the essence of Spinoza lies not in his vision of man, but in his vision of God. And here we see why Nietzsche found it impossible to come to grips with this aspect of his thought. In this respect, Nietzsche was a thoroughgoing nineteenth-century rationalist, like Tennyson and Emerson and Carlyle; he might have an idealistic hankering after the transcendental or the absolute, but in his heart of hearts he believed God to be a crude superstition, a hangover from the ages of unreason. Spinoza, on the other hand, felt himself at home in a great mystical tradition that can be traced back in ancient India, China and the Middle East. In all natural things – practical things – he felt himself to be a reasonable, natural human being. But he felt that a point came where human knowledge had to recognise its own inadequacy.

G.K. Chesterton once pointed out that mystics should not be considered less rational and practical than other people; on the contrary, they are often more rational and practical because they know precisely where their knowledge begins and ends. One of the oddest things about mystics is that they often seem to have very precise insights into the nature of God. As they struggle to express these insights, with immense clumsiness, you feel that this is not romantic verbalising; they are struggling for precision, but language defeats them.

I do not know whether Spinoza knew anything about the mystics of China or India, or even about the Sufis; what is quite certain is that he would have felt perfectly at home in their tradition, as he did in the tradition of Cabbalism. For these mystics, God was not an idea, but a reality. They experienced God in moments of deep insight or of sudden intense ecstasy. A hungry man is not more certain of the existence of hot soup than the mystic is of God.

In this sense, God is an insight, a 'bird's-eye view' of the universe. I should say, perhaps, that God is *experienced* as an insight. Man is confined in the narrowness of personal existence, and all his habits seem determined to keep him trapped, like some prisoner chained to the floor of his cell by an iron collar. The philosopher observes with pity and irony the triviality that wastes the lives of most men. He feels that they are stuck in the present like flies on flypaper. His aim is freedom, and he knows that the first step is to avoid the flypaper. So the two parts of the *Ethics* on human bondage should not be regarded as a comprehensive psychology so much as a series of moralistic observations on human nature, of the kind that can be found so abundantly in the writings of the religious philosophers, from Boethius to Loyola.

What is perhaps most difficult to understand from the 'natural standpoint' is that once a man has clearly grasped the nature 'of human bondage', he may quite suddenly experience a deep intuition of the nature of freedom. The Hindu saint Ramakrishna was about to kill himself with a sword when the 'Divine Mother' revealed herself, overwhelming him with a tremendous vision of *meaning* – of some vast torrent of universal energy that drives nature like a giant dynamo. Nietzsche himself experienced this vision on at least two occasions, and felt that it transcended all human ideas of good and evil. And Bertrand Russell – another 'sceptic' – once identified the source of his own scientific inspiration as 'the very breath of life, fierce and coming from far away, bringing into human life the vastness and fearful passionless force of non-human things'.

This is the mystic's basic realisation, and to some extent, it is accessible to all of us, at least by analogy. I may *say* that I know what a rose smells like, yet when I first smell a rose bush in spring, I realise how much I had forgotten. The reality is somehow so much more real and rich than anything I could conjure up mentally in midwinter. And the same goes for all the meaning of the universe. We are cut off from meaning as a prisoner in the deepest and dampest dungeon in the Bastille is cut off from the sunlight. The prisoner may imagine the sunlight; he may even dream he is outside; but when he actually feels the sun and breaths in the air, he realises that the mind is absurdly inexpert in conjuring up absent realities. The mystic 'knows' a little of the nature of God by pursuing this analogy – by imagining a reality a thousand times as great, and a thousand times as real and startling, as a spring morning. Of course, the imagination is totally inadequate; yet it *can* catch a glimpse of this vision of meaning. And this is enough to make him aware that all our human 'knowledge' is crude and absurd and totally inadequate. The reality is so infinitely rich that it is absurd to speak about 'evolution'. In believing that the universe could 'evolve', we are merely projecting our human inadequacy on the ultimate reality. . . .

And now, perhaps, we can begin to see the paradox of Nietzsche's criticism of Spinoza. In effect, he read the last four parts of the *Ethics* and accused Spinoza of mistaking his intellectual concepts for reality. If Spinoza had been alive, he would have pointed to the first part of the *Ethics*, and accused Nietzsche of using the word 'reality' without the faintest insight into its meaning. Yet this, too, would have been unfair. Nietzsche also had his glimpses of that 'breath of life', fierce and blowing from far away. The two great philosophers approached the same basic concepts from opposite points of view. Both had glimpsed the reality, but they called it by different names.

And ultimately, Spinoza had the last word. For ultimately, Nietzsche became a Spinozist. That may sound absurd; yet how otherwise can we interpret the idea of Eternal Recurrence? It makes no sense in the context of Nietzsche's evolutionary philosophy. Yet it makes sense to a mystic. Nietzsche began his life as a disciple of Socrates and the stoic philosophers. He swallowed Schopenhauer's Buddhistic pessimism. Then came the 'visions', the glimpses of 'bliss rising from the depths of nature' (as he expressed it in *The Birth of Tragedy*). Nietzsche transcended good and evil – and Socratic 'reason'. He came to feel that man owes allegiance only to that 'fearful passionless force of non-human things'. He preached the superman. And then, as his imagination grasped for a moment the concept of the super-human, he saw that ultimate force as something too vast to be contained in such a mere human concept as evolution. In the angels' chorus at the beginning of *Faust*, Goethe had written:

Es schaümt das Meer in breiten Flüssen
Am tiefen Grund der Felsen auf,
Und Fels und Meer wird fortgerissen
In ewig schnellen Sphärenlauf.

(Against the cliffs with roaring song
In mighty torrents foams the ocean
And cliffs and sea are whirled along
With circling orbs in ceaseless motion.)

Imagine this vision multiplied a thousandfold and you have an approximation to Spinoza's vision of God – and Nietsche's vision of that mighty ultimate force behind the universe. 'Circling orbs in ceaseless motion' – eternal recurrence. It became Zarathustra's ultimate affirmation, beyond the superman. And so, in the end, the vision of Spinoza and the vision of Nietzsche blend into a kind of unity.

From our point of view, it is fortunate it happened so late in the day. Philosophers are never so entertaining – or so instructive – as when they are beating one another over the head.

1977

FIVE

'Dual value response' . . .
A new key to Nietzsche?

'I must, I *must*, before I die, find *some* way to say the essential thing that is in me, that I have never said yet – a thing that is not love or hate or pity or scorn, but the very breath of life, fierce, and coming from far away, bringing into human life the vastness and the fearful passionless force of non-human things.' The quotation, oddly enough, is by Bertrand Russell, from a letter written to Lady Constance Malleson in 1918; he was having a love affair with her at the time, which may explain the uncharacteristically romantic tone.[1] It has always struck me as one of the most Nietzschean sentences written in the twentieth century. It also helps to answer a basic question about Nietzsche: why his work has shown such extraordinary vitality since his death in 1900. All philosophers who are worth anything keep trying to say that 'essential thing': that feeling of the infinite world of *objective meanings* that surrounds us, waiting to be gathered like apples in an endless orchard. But philosophy attempts to say it by circumscribing a subject, plodding around it like that greedy peasant in Tolstoy's 'How Much Land Does a Man Need?' And when he has finished, he is breathless and exhausted, and the 'thing' remains unsaid.

This is the challenge of Nietzsche. There is something about him that cannot be pinned down. Eminent interpreters have been trying for years: George Brandes, A.R. Orage, Karl Jaspers, Walter Kaufmann, Martin Heidegger. Heidegger probably comes closest to the essence of Nietzsche; not in that monstrously prolix book, which loses the essence in comparison with Plato and Descartes, but in some of the shorter pronouncements, such as the essay 'Nietzsches Wort "Gott ist tot" ' in *Holzwege*. For Heidegger allows us to see that what fascinates him about Nietzsche is also what fascinates him about Hölderlin – something elusive, but oddly real – something like a smell or taste, or that madeleine dipped in tea that reminded Proust of his childhood. 'Knowledge is in essence the schematisation of chaos' says Heidegger in his book on Nietzsche. But in that case, is the aim of philosophy really knowledge? We can agree that the aim of physics or chemistry is 'to know', for when I know something about nature, it gives me power over nature, or rather, an aid to power, just as a railway timetable gives me an aid to travel. But I am a living being, in continual direct contact with the world, with 'life', and philosophy is basically my attempt to *adjust* to the world, to my own life. A baby's problem is not simply to know his mother, but to *suck her milk*. The philosopher's problem is not simply to know 'life', but to get to grips with it. And by that, I do not mean 'commitment' to some merely human problem. I mean in the sense that Russell meant; somehow *contacting* the 'breath of life, fierce and coming from far away', and the 'fearful passionless force of non-human things'. For it is this actual contact that gives the philosopher what he needs most – his vision, his feeling of direction and meaning. Philosophy cannot operate *in vacuo*, because, unlike science, it does not have a clear and well-defined object. Its 'object' is illuminated by flashes of vision, by a sense of wonder.

Nothing is harder to grasp than this. For after all, when a philosopher has written a book, it *looks* like a book on physics; it seems to be full of 'propositions' that relate to the 'real world', and so on. It is only when you examine it more closely that you realise that its 'content' is much closer to the content of a poem or a symphony, that it suggests a *way* of seeing, of feeling, and not 'knowledge' at all. What is a symphony *for*? It is designed to put you in a certain mood, to mould your feelings; but not in the same straightforward way as a cigarette or a glass of whisky. It aims to cause you to 'open up', so as to change your normal relation to the world around you, to see things you hadn't noticed before, to experience a sense of mystery and excitement. And ideally, to an intelligent reader, a volume of philosophy does *exactly* that. Philosophy is *very* closely related to music; and hardly at all to physics.

Jaspers remarked in an essay ('On My Philosophy') that Nietzsche became important to him 'as the magnificent revelation of nihilism and the task of going beyond nihilism' – a strange-sounding remark if one thinks of Nietzsche as the philosopher of the 'breath of life', of the Dionysian upsurge of vitality. And Heidegger also lays emphasis on Nietzsche's nihilism, his anti-metaphysical trend, in the essay 'Nietzsches Wort "Gott ist tot" '. How is it possible for two 'existential' philosophers to regard Nietzsche as primarily a nihilist? What is nihilism anyway? The Russian revolutionary Pisarev stated its credo: 'What can be smashed should be smashed,' which sounds like Nietzsche and his hammer; but Pisarev was talking about the political institutions of Tsarist Russia, and Nietzsche was not remotely interested in this kind of nihilism. The nihilism of Turgeniev's Bazarov consists largely in atheism and materialism à la Büchner, and Nietzsche's atheism (if that is what it was) has nothing in common with Büchner's. The 'God' who was dead was closer to Blake's Old Nobodaddy. So what precisely does it mean to call Nietzsche a nihilist? What Nietzsche wanted to 'smash' is stated clearly and repeatedly in his work, in *The Antichrist* for example: 'All these great enthusiasts and prodigies behave like our little females: they consider "beautiful sentiments" adequate arguments, regard a heaving bosom as the bellows of the deity, and conviction a criterion of truth'. What is being attacked here is German romanticism – Schiller, Jean Paul, *et al.* – with its 'Kantian' moral tone and Rousseau-istic gush. If this makes Nietzsche a 'nihilist' then Jane Austen is a nihilist for satirising the same kind of thing in *Northanger Abbey*. Jane Austen's mockery sprang from a firm sense of reality; so did Nietzsche's philosophising with a hammer. People who dislike Nietzsche – Bertrand Russell, for example – dislike him because they do not share his sense of reality. When they attack him, they have the relatively easy task of pointing out the contradictions inherent in his 'irrationalism', and the potentially dangerous nature of his superman doctrine. People who admire Nietzsche – including Jaspers and Heidegger – share his basic intuition; they do not object to his 'contradictions' because they can see how each opinion was an expression of this basic intuition. In some cases, the expression was more careless or bad-tempered than in others; hence the 'contradictions'.

Now *if* that is true, then real understanding of Nietzsche can only come from a grasp of this basic intuition. And in order to define this, we must speak of a psychological phenomenon which, as far as I know, has never been described in standard textbooks. I have called this, for want of a better term, 'dual value response', and it has some relation to the religious conversions described by William James. A situation that has aroused a neutral or negative reaction quite suddenly arouses a very positive response; black becomes white, as it were. It is most typical of poets and mystics, but I think that everyone experiences it at some time. Yeats describes such an experience in the poem 'Vacillation'; it took place in a London teashop:

> While on the shop and street I gazed
> My body of a sudden blazed;
> And twenty minutes more or less
> It seemed, so great my happiness,
> That I was blessèd and could bless.

If we choose to take a reductionist viewpoint, we can, of course, dismiss this as a mere 'feeling'. I shall try to show that it is, in fact a *perception* of value, and can be analysed precisely in phenomeno-logical terms.

Nietzsche was unusually subject to 'dual value response', perhaps because of his invalidism. A man whose health never fluctuates seriously takes up a certain attitude towards the world – what he enjoys, what is a nuisance – and maintains it year in and year out, until it becomes a habit. The invalid swoops up and down like a swallow; in the morning, life seems a burden; by evening he feels magnificent, and life is self-evidently good.

The exact mechanism of this becomes clear if we consider how we make our moment-to-moment judgments on situations. Let us take a hypothetical situation. I am on holiday, and my car breaks down in a lonely place. My first response is gloom, for there is no 'positive side' to this situation, no 'bright side' to look on. This is 100 per cent nuisance. Another car comes along. My spirits rise. The motorist offers to take a look under the hood. He says that it could be a broken pump, which is fairly serious; my spirits sink. Then he notices that the lead is off one of the spark plugs; the trouble may be less bothersome than I thought; my spirits rise. Perhaps the absurdest thing is this: that if I succeed in effecting some kind of repair, and I drive on, I may find that I feel much happier than I felt before the breakdown – an absurdity because I had nothing to worry about then, and now I know that I may have to spend an hour hanging around at the next garage. *Obviously, our 'value response' to things that happen to us is, to some extent, quite arbitrary.* 'An adventure is only an inconvenience rightly considered,' says Chesterton, 'an inconvenience is only an adventure wrongly considered.'

Why is this? Because our 'responding mechanism' has the power to *change focus*. It is as if I possessed a sort of combination of telescope and microscope. I can either look at a situation 'from a distance', to get the over-all effect, or I can focus upon some minute particular. I change focus as I need to. For example, if I am in process of changing the spark plugs, and I drop the spanner in the deep grass, I switch instantly from my over-all view of the whole job to this smaller problem of finding the spanner. But in switching to the smaller task, I must not lose sight of the larger one. If I glance up from my search for the spanner, and see that the car is running away downhill because I forgot to leave it in gear, I realise that I have made a fundamental mistake – of forgetting the general in order to concentrate on the particular.

Nietzsche's life affords many examples of 'dual value response', two of which are particularly striking. The first is described in his letter to Carl von Gersdorff. It took place in the year 1866, when Nietzsche was 21, and often in a state of fatigue and depression. Climbing a hill called Leusch, he took refuge from the rain in a peasant's hut, where the peasant was slaughtering two kids, while his son looked on. Nietzsche was not fond of the sight of blood. But 'the storm broke with a tremendous crash, discharging thunder and hail, and I had an indescribable sense of wellbeing and zest'. He added: 'Lightning and tempest are different worlds, free powers, without morality. Pure will, without the confusions of intellect – how happy, how free.'

The second experience occurred in 1870, when he was serving in the ambulance corps during the Franco-Prussian war. He had been in the cavalry, but a fall from a horse had caused severe complications. One evening, after a hard day's work with the wounded, Nietzsche was walking along the Strasbourg road, alone. Cavalry came up behind him; he drew under a wall to allow them to pass. It was his old regiment; as he watched them pass, he experienced again the sense of tremendous exaltation. Later, he told his sister that this incident was the origin of his philosophy of the will of power: that as he watched these men riding to battle, perhaps to death, he realised suddenly that 'the strongest and highest will to life does not lie in the puny struggle to exist, but in the Will to war, the Will to power'.

Both are clear examples of sudden and total *change of focus*, from a state of fatigue and self-pity into a state of exaltation. What happens is, to some extent, explained in William James's important essay 'The Energies of Men':

> Every one is familiar with the phenomenon of feeling more or less alive on different days. Every one knows on any given day that there are energies slumbering in him which the incitements of that day do not call forth, but which he might display if these were greater. Most of us feel as if a sort of cloud weighed upon us, keeping us below our highest notch of clearness in discernment, sureness in reasoning, or firmness in deciding. Compared with what we ought to be, we are only half awake. Our fires are damped, our drafts are checked. We are making use of only a small part of our possible mental and physical resources. In some persons this sense of being cut off from their rightful resources is extreme, and we then get the formidable neurasthenic and psychasthenic conditions, with life grown into one tissue of impossibilities, that so many medical books describe.[2]

He goes on to point out that when mental patients sink into a condition of depression and exhaustion, 'bullying treatment' often works. 'First comes the very extremity of distress, then follows unexpected relief.'[3]

Now James is obviously right to emphasise that what we are dealing with here are underground energies, invisible reserves way below the surface of our conscious awareness. Being so far below the surface, they are not available for conscious inspection. When a crisis is forced upon us, our first response appears to verify the certainty of being close to exhaustion, 'the extremity of distress'. The gauge seems to register an empty fuel tank. And then, abruptly, the needle swings back to indicate 'full'. The gauge was telling lies. We had reserve energy tanks, and the emergency has caused them to connect up.

All this has obvious implications for morality. For what, on the whole, is our definition of evil? 'Evil is physical pain,' said Leonardo; we associate it with the cruelty, the oppression of the weak by the strong. If you saw an old lady with arthritis walking painfully upstairs, and you set your bulldog on her, that would be cruel. But suppose the emergency made her skip upstairs like a goat, and the arthritis vanished? . . . The whole business of the 'dual value response' introduces an ambiguity into matters of morality. Yeats's wise old Chinamen, in 'Lapis Lazuli', look down on the tragic confusion of history, but their 'ancient glittering eyes are gay'. Unlike Arnold Toynbee, they are not appalled by 'the cruel riddle of Mankind's crimes and follies'.

Bertrand Russell's response to this kind of Nietzschean philosophy is whole-hearted condemnation. Nietzsche was a sick weakling who had compensatory fantasies of power. . . . But it is all rubbish and double-talk. Good is good and bad is bad, and if Nietzsche cannot tell the difference, that is because his romanticism made him incapable of thinking clearly. . . .

Nietzsche's reply would be that it is Russell who is not thinking clearly, or rather, who misunderstands the nature of philosophical thinking. Thinking is not a linear process that could be carried out by an adding machine; it depends upon *insight*, and *insight* depends on an upsurge of vital energy. It is true that it *can* occur without; something may 'dawn on you' for no particular reason; but a problem is more likely to be solved in a flash of vitality than not. Current thinking on the nature of the insight process – in Polanyi's *Personal Knowledge*, in Bernard Lonergan's *Insight*, in Maslow's *Psychology of Science*, in Koestler's *The Act of Creation* – is wholly on Nietzsche's side. Husserl's phenomenology had established the same point in the first decade of this century, but is was not generally understood then. Perception is intentional, a *reaching out*, not a passive process. But philosophical thought is a process of perception, and therefore depends upon the drive, the energy behind it. It also follows that under-energised thought will actually falsify the objects of perception. To put it another way, thought requires a bird's eye view, and a bird requires the lifting power to hover in the air. A worm's eye view is not necessarily false, but it is a close-up, and its perspectives are distorted.

These insights are very gradually becoming familiar to

philosophers nearly a century after Nietzsche went insane. Nietzsche did not possess the *concepts* to undermine the currently accepted attitudes of his time. If he had bought and studied Franz Brentano's *Psychology from the Empirical Standpoint*, published in 1874, he might have realised the significance of the concept of intentionality; but that is doubtful, since Brentano himself did not grasp its full significance. (It was left for Husserl to develop it into a powerful philosophical tool.) Nietzsche was forced to attack the 'linear' philosophy of his time in the manner of a dive-bomber, swooping dangerously from above. This is the reason that Nietzsche's work is fragmentary. It is not that his thought is disconnected; only that, since his own basic insight remains constant, he is always being irritated into pointing out the fallacy of current attitudes. It is an unsatisfactory way of doing philosophy; to begin with, it encourages a continual state of irritation or excitement, which is wearing for the nerves. A philosopher should start from 'first principles' and work outward, as Kant and Hegel do – as even Schopenhauer does. Husserl was luckier. He was also irritated by the psychologism, the relativism, the nominalism, that had permeated philosophy since Locke. But he demolished them with irrefutable arguments in the *Logical Investigations*, and laid his own foundations. Nietzsche completely lacked foundations in this sense. His work is a series of brilliant guerilla raids on enemy positions; but a guerilla is at a psychological disadvantage, being a man without a home, without an established position. The two polemics against Wagner are superb; but one can sense Nietzsche's underlying envy of Wagner. Wagner had his Bayreuth, his Cosima, his disciples; he could get on with the business of creating, of building. And Nietzsche could only criticise, like a disgruntled reviewer. . . .

Nietzsche's fundamental insight was a feeling about human beings and their relation to the world, to 'life'. It was a vision, in the sense that we speak of the vision of a painter or a novelist. Expressed in words, it was something like this: human beings are permanently 'under the weather', permanently unhealthy – a disease for which the complexity of civilisation is partly to blame. Because they are so poor-spirited – human, all too human – their vision of the universe is also poor-spirited. Like one of James's neurasthenics, they stagger around in a state of self-pitying fatigue, permanently listless and miserable.

But the theory of meaning that I am propounding in this essay states that meaning is perceived correctly and objectively only when the mind can perceive it from a distance, from *above*, like a bird. And this in turn requires a certain energy – in fact, a tremendous energy and drive. Early space rocket engineers worked out that a space vehicle would have to travel at seven miles per second to escape the earth's gravity. And thought needs a comparable kind of speed and drive to escape its own limitations and to become objective. Or one might compare human thinking to an under-capitalised business that can never get clear of its debts. 'Close-upness deprives us of meaning', and human beings are permanently too close-up to their lives, to their trivial problems, to see things objectively. They need a touch of the frenzy of Dionysus to make them snap out of their neurasthenic state, to grasp their own possibilities and those of the world. . . . Nietzsche's philosophical books are a series of judgments on the nineteenth century from his own 'bird's eye view' – a view that struck most of his contemporaries as 'ruthless' and a little paranoid.

Nietzsche suffered under one tremendous disadvantage that has never been sufficiently emphasised by his biographers. Living in an age of Prussianism and prudery, he was unable to give sex the central place that it should occupy in his philosophy. D.H. Lawrence and Frank Wedekind were the first moderns to be able to do this.

We do not find much about sex in books on Nietzsche: a few paragraphs about Lou Salomé, speculations as to whether he reakly picked up a venereal disease from a prostitute. . . . It was natural for Brandes and Orage to think of Nietzsche as the solitary thinker, brooding idealistically on Kant and Socrates and Wagner, and only occasionally wishing that he had a wife. . . . But in this age of frankness, we know that sex occupies a central position in the lives of most human beings. In the mid-thirties, before the days of Kinsey, Abraham Maslow did a study on the relation between dominance feelings and sex in women. His conclusions, briefly, were that women fall roughly into three classes: high dominance, medium dominance and low dominance. Low dominance women actively dislike sex; it frightens them, and they regard the male sexual member as ugly. High dominance women, with rare exceptions (due to puritanical upbringing) love sex, tend to be promiscuous, masturbate, and regard the male sexual member as an interesting and delightful object. (Medium dominance women, predictably, share characteristics of both classes.) I am not sure whether anyone has done a comparable study on men, but I am fairly certain that it would turn up the same results: that there is an immediate, direct relation between male dominance and sexuality. And male sexual dominance differs slightly from its female counterpart in having an element of sadism. By this I do not mean a desire to cause pain; but the attitude of a cat towards a mouse, (i.e. the feeling that the mouse is both a plaything and a meal). Even the most highly dominant females, Maslow found, enjoyed having a more highly dominant lover; in fact, they could not give themselves completely to less dominant men. In one case, a woman would provoke her husband into a quarrel, in which he would treat her very roughly; after which, they made love. Female sexuality has a masochistic element; male sexuality has a sadistic element – the cat licking its lips as it watches the mice wandering innocently past. Even in the closest love relationship, this element remains.

Now Nietzsche was beyond all doubt highly dominant. He was physically courageous; he had fought duels (if only friendly ones) and been a fine horseman. He had the dominant man's attitude to women, 'don't forget your whip', etc. Unless one supposes that Nietzsche's puritan upbringing inhibited him for life, it would be logical to suppose that he spent a good deal of time in auto-erotic fantasies.

I make this point because we ought to bear in mind that the sexual orgasm is the commonest form of the 'dual value response', the moment when the world is seen as if from a higher plane, when the negative becomes positive. Again I must emphasise the *extreme* nature of 'dual value response'. Most moralists suggest that ordinary values are too materialistic, too much a compromise with the trivial values of everyday life. But in Ibsen or Tolstoy or Russell, there is a plain and evident *connection* between 'everyday values' and the higher values being suggested: people should be more honest, more compassionate, public-spirited, etc. In Nietzsche, as in D.H. Lawrence, there is a lack of this 'connection', a feeling of a *gulf* between the everyday standpoint and this vision of reality. The only other examples of a similar vision who come to mind are religious mystics. Pascal, for instance. But Pascal's vision differs as fundamentally from Nietzsche's – or Lawrence's – as Nietzsche's does from Tolstoy's; it is religious in the most essential meaning of the term, involving a sense of man's nothingness and God's greatness. Nietzsche, like Lawrence, has a fairly high opinion of himself; he feels this kind of abnegation to be a form of intellectual cowardice. He is not genuinely atheistic in spirit, being too much of a poet, but his sense of 'another standard of values' – *other* in the most profound sense – is quite unconnected with any notion of God. And this, I would argue – indeed, I would state dogmatically – indicates that the standard is derived from sexual experience. I regard Nietzsche as a sexual mystic, in the same sense as Wedekind or Lawrence. There is no other *type* of human experience, religious, moral, aesthetic, natural, that carries with it this insight of a standard of values that is alien, non-human, 'other'. (The quotation from Russell with which I began this essay is an exception, and I cited it there as an unusual example of the Nietzschean vision.) It could be argued that music is an exception, and there is some truth in this. It is just possible that Nietzsche's 'dual value response' came from music, particularly in view of Nietzsche's response to Wagner – until we recall the later revulsion from Wagner, the preference for the 'mediterranean' lightness of Bizet. A baffling change of loyalty; why Bizet, who is delightful, but no more profound that Chabrier? But then we must remember *which* Bizet – *Carmen*, that Wedekind-like study in sexual slavery, in the power of the eternal feminine.

The above comments should not be interpreted too simply. I am not suggesting that Nietzsche spent his days masturbating, and that his basic vision – of 'dual value response' – was derived from a kind of phenomenological analysis of the meaning-content of the orgasm (although I am not discounting this either). I am suggesting that Nietzsche was what we would now call highly sexed, *very* highly sexed, that women represented for him an alluring mystery, and that his 'dual value response', like D.H. Lawrence's, arose from the intensity of his consciousness of this mystery. (If I had space, I could elaborate an interesting parallel with David Lindsay, the author of that strange masterpiece *A Voyage to Arcturus*, a work in which 'dual value response', the feeling that all 'human' values are totally false and that 'true' values are totally *other*, is taken even further than in Nietzsche; for Lindsay, although a shy, puritanical man, was also obsessed by the sexual mystery.[4])

Sexual response *is* dual value response, by its basic nature. This is recognised in popular wisdom – for example, 'A standing prick has no conscience.' Sexual response is basically a kind of shock, as all pornography recognises. A man in a state of sexual excitement is aware that he is channeling forces that have no connection with his everyday 'social' personality. Sexual response is a spark leaping the gulf between our everyday standard of values and that 'other' standard, oddly non-human. All the attempts to domesticate it with religion, morality, even humour, fail because they ignore its non-human – its Dionysian – nature. Thomas Mann's Nietzschean composer remarks in *Doktor Faustus* that the words of the marriage ceremony – 'These two shall be one flesh' – are nonsense, because if they were 'one flesh' they wouldn't attract one another; it is the alienness that causes the attraction, and which continues to do so as long as the marriage has a sexual basis; it cannot be domesticated.

Nietzsche is important because of his uncompromising honesty, because he remains an honest votary of Dionysus. He suspects – as we all do – that it may be impossible to reconcile Dionysus with civilisation. The Greeks came to terms with Dionysus by worshipping him. Christian civilisation tried suppressing him in the name of morality, and has more recently tried turning him into a decent member of society in the name of 'sexual freedom'. The argument goes that if men and women can find a new uninhibited sexual relation, the old 'class war' between the sexes will vanish; the cat will lie down with the mouse, and will be quite cured of his desire to make a meal of her. Nietzsche would have smiled grimly and recommended a reading of *The Bacchae*.

Heidegger said that Nietzsche was important because he is the culmination of European metaphysics – in fact, its end. Such a view obviously makes Nietzsche extremely important *in himself*. I am suggesting the opposite: that what we call Nietzschean philosophy – meaning his critique of nineteenth-century values –

is not particularly important, while even his philosophy of evolution, of the superman – has been largely superseded by Shaw, Teilhard, Julian Huxley. I would suggest that Nietzsche is not particularly important for what he said, but rather for what he found it impossible to say. One might say that all his work is a commentary on the incident on Leusch, and that unfortunately, he did not possess the analytical tools for understanding it. For the incident on Leusch suggests a theory of meaning that Nietzsche was able to understand intuitively, but not logically. It suggests that 'meaning' is not available to our ordinary, everyday, two-dimensional consciousness, and that consequently nearly all our humanistic values and ideas are false. But meaning *is* available to a far more highly energised consciousness. The search for philosophical truth should aim for Shaw's 'seventh degree of concentration' rather than Russell's kind of analytic procedure in which philosophy is not basically different from mathematics.

If Nietzsche had been a contemporary of Husserl, the two might have formed an unexpected alliance. For the relationship between the two is closer than appears at first sight. To begin with, both regarded themselves as psychologists, in the basic, pre-Freudian sense. But the relationship goes deeper than that. I will try to elucidate briefly.

Brentano, Husserl's predecessor, recognised that all mental acts must be directed at an *object*. We love someone or something, we think *about* something, we imagine a situation, etc. Brentano was concerned to oppose Hume's view that thoughts are a kind of casual by-product of the brain, created *accidentally* by its processes of association; so Brentano emphasised the purposive nature of thought. Husserl went further. He stated, to begin with, that there *is* a reality 'out there', which is just as fascinating and complex as it seems. But, he added, this reality is quite invisible to us unless we make the necessary 'intentional effort' to apprehend it. An obvious example is glancing at your watch for the time; if you are engaged in conversation you can *see* the position of the hands, yet still fail to register what time it is. And so it is with all perception; you grasp the richness and complexity of reality only insofar as you make the requisite effort to do so. Opening your eyes is not enough.

If Nietzsche had lived long enough to read Husserl's *Ideas* (by which time he would have been 68), I suspect he would have instantly seen the connection with his experiences on Leusch and the Strasbourg road. In both cases, an exciting stimulus caused him to make an *effort of will* over and above what he had intended a few minutes earlier. The immediate result was an enormous sense of enrichment of 'reality'. Let us ignore the feelings of delight that accompanied the insight, which is irrelevant, and concentrate on *what* he saw. The world, which, five minutes before, had seemed a miserable and tragic place – and certainly pretty dull – was suddenly perceived as infinitely complex and interesting.

If Nietzsche had known about separating the intention from its object – the noema from the noetic act – he would have ignored the stimulus itself (the shepherd killing the goat, his old regiment riding past) and concentrated on the *way* that an act of will had 'boosted' his perception. So we might have been spared a great deal of misleading stuff about Cesare Borgia (that egotistic roughneck), and later assertions that Nietzsche was the forerunner of Hitler. But – far more important – Husserlian phenomenology would have taken an important stride forward. Husserl might have grasped clearly what is inherent in his philosophy of intentionality. If our 'gaze' is a spear thrown towards its object, then *meaning* depends on how hard you throw it. Perception is not merely 'reference to an object' (Brentano). It is not merely the intelligent effort of interpretation (Husserl). It is the process *of the will*. The will enters into it as directly as into lifting a heavy object; and it can be intensified by an effort of the will, of concentration. Perception is a process that can be brought to the same kind of perfection as playing the violin or doing acrobatics. All this is inherent in Nietzsche.

Perhaps the more immediate and useful application of the idea lies in psychiatry. Neurosis may now be seen as a kind of dialectical process, a 'downhill dialectic' so to speak. On Leusch, a violent stimulus and a violent effort (for in Husserl, a response *is* an effort) cause Nietzsche to burst through to a higher level of mental health and a deeper perception of value. Conversely, a tendency to slip downhill (into passivity), together with a belief that this is the *logical* response to a situation in which effort is 'not worth-while', leads to the de-energising of consciousness, a loss of meaning, and to a situation in which the meaninglessness seems to be the result of honest perception and logical response to it: in short, a vicious circle. Perhaps the most optimistic consequence to be drawn from Leusch and dual value response is that man is free to choose, *and that a choice of effort is automatically a choice of meaning.* Students of modern existentialism – particularly as Jaspers, Heidegger and Sartre present it – will see that this view flatly contradicts the currently accepted position on freedom and meaning. It is an interesting thought that, philosophically speaking, Nietzsche should be regarded as the successor of Sartre rather than as a predecessor.

1972

SIX

An integrity born of hope:
Notes on Christopher Isherwood

There is a passage in Stephen Spender's autobiography, *World Within World*, that has fascinated me since I first read it – in the early fifties. He is speaking of his first meeting with Isherwood:

> Auden had spoken of Isherwood in a way which made me think of him as The Novelist, who, applying himself with an iron will to the study of material of his work, was determined to live the life of the Ordinary Man, going to the office in a train, dancing in dance halls at seaside resorts, dressing with a studied avoidance of every kind of distinctiveness, and so on. Isherwood, according to Auden, held no opinions whatever about anything. He was wholly and simply interested in people. He did not like or dislike them, judge them favourably or unfavourably. He simply regarded them as material for his Work. At the same time, he was the Critic in whom Auden had absolute trust. If Isherwood disliked a poem, Auden destroyed it without demur. Should he select one line for praise and condemn the rest, then Auden skilfully inserted this one line into a new poem . . .

And he goes on to remark that, 'just as Auden seemed to us the highest peak within the range of our humble vision from the Oxford valleys, for Auden there was another peak, namely Isherwood, whilst for Isherwood there was a still further peak. Chalmers [Edward Upward].'

I suppose what is fascinating here is what looks like deliberate legend-building. All ambitious young people read the lives of great men, lingering over the early struggles, and wondering what the critics of the future will be saying about themselves. And wondering what they ought to be *doing*, at this moment, to provide

110

the critics with something interesting to say. Auden, Isherwood and co. seemed to have the right idea. They set themselves up as the Next Generation (after Joyce, Huxley and Eliot) and achieved literary eminence by a kind of *coup d'état*. I, for one, felt their methods were worth studying. . . .

Yet of the group, Isherwood seemed to be the odd man out. Auden and Spender were starting where Eliot left off, writing about the world of aeroplanes and pylons and guerilla warfare. Upward's prose in *Railway Accident* and *Journey to the Border* was as complex and allusive as you would expect from someone who knew his *Ulysses* by heart. By comparison, Isherwood seemed deliberately naive. There was no evidence that he'd ever read anybody – except possibly the early novels of Knut Hamsun, which have the same artless directness. How could he reconcile being The Novelist – one of the company of Balzac and Dickens and Tolstoy – with this deliberately low-key approach?

It must have been about five years later when I realised that I had been the victim of my own preconceptions. My own first book, *The Outsider*, had appeared in 1956. I had become friendly with Stephen Spender, who was then editing *Encounter*, and I met Isherwood at his house. We immediately plunged into a discussion about Gerald Hamilton, the original of Arthur Norris, the hero of *Mr. Norris Changes Trains*. A few weeks before, I'd been giving supper to Gerald and a couple of other friends when my girlfriend's parents arrived with a horsewhip – they had found out we were living together. Gerald vanished, and made for the nearest telephone box. Half an hour later, half the photographers in Fleet Street were on my doorstep, and details of the uproar were on most of the front pages the following morning. Anyone who has read Isherwood's novel will note that Mr. Norris had not changed in twenty-five years . . .

I found Isherwood a puzzling character: gentle, self-effacing, not at all awe-inspiring. Yet there was something about him that I couldn't put my finger on, as if he wasn't quite what he seemed. What he *seemed* to be was a fairly typical member of that thirties generation of writers and poets, many of whom were rather upper-class, English public school types. To my mind, it has always seemed that there is a definite disadvantage in belonging to this class, which has provided so many members of the Foreign

Office, the BBC and the publishing world. They seem to *belong* to
their world in a rather oppressive way, not merely as if they'd
been stamped with it, but as if the stamp went all the way through,
like the letters on a stick of Blackpool rock. D.H. Lawrence used
to grind his teeth about them, but that seems to me unfair. Upper
middle-class upbringing has rooted out any element of what might
appear to be self-assertion or egoism; good manners is to be like
everyone else. So the male of the species becomes accustomed to
suppress any stirring of impatience or originality. Shaw once said
you can't learn to skate without making a fool of yourself; the British
middle-class attitude seems to be that, in that case, you hadn't better
skate at all. The result seems to be considerably more oppressive than
being brought up in a Jewish ghetto or a west side slum.

Now on the surface, Isherwood seems to be a typical member
of his class – even to adopting a slight American accent because it
would be impolite to be oppressively British when he lives in Los
Angeles. Yet I immediately sensed that, in some off way, he had
slipped out of the strait jacket and was free. It struck me that this
might have been due to spending so many years in America, and
leaving his childhood thoroughly behind; but then, many
Englishmen of his class spend their lives abroad, and never leave it
behind, as his cousin Graham Greene never tires of observing.

When I got home, I found an old Penguin copy of *Mr. Norris
Changes Trains*, which I hadn't looked at in five years, and started
to re-read that delightful opening on the train:

My first impression was that the stranger's eyes were of an
unusually light blue. They met mine for several blank seconds,
vacant, unmistakably scared. Startled and innocently naughty,
they half-reminded me of an incident I couldn't quite place;
something which had happened a long time ago, to do with the
upper fourth form classroom. They were the eyes of a
schoolboy surprised in the act of breaking one of the rules. Not
that I had caught him, apparently, at anything except his own
thoughts: perhaps he imagined I could read them. At any rate,
he seemed not to have heard or seen me cross the compartment
from my corner to his own, for he started violently at the sound
of my voice; so violently, indeed, that his nervous recoil hit me
like repercussion. Instinctively, I took a pace backwards . . .

I found myself trying hard to remember what that reminded me of: that detached, observant first-person narrative. Then it came: Henry James; the James of *The Aspern Papers* and *The Sacred Fount*. Not that Isherwood's narrator 'Chris' is ever as complicated or analytical as James's mouthpiece. Yet, as I now suddenly realised, the basic spirit behind Isherwood's enterprise is Jamesian. Professor Sampson once compared James to a man who looks at life through a magic mirror, like the Lady of Shalott, always the observer, never the participant. What is the difference between James's mirror and Isherwood's camera?

The idea struck a deep chord of sympathy in me because of my own obsession with James and his methods. From the age of about seventeen to twenty-one, I had regarded James, quite simply, as the greatest of all English novelists. I envied him the good fortune that had allowed him to spend his life as an observer, watching the world from 'outside', as uninvolved as a Buddhist *arahat*. (These were the days, of course, before Professor Edel's biography had revealed that James was anything but uninvolved.) To see life from the point of view of pure intelligence, free of the stupid emotions that seem to possess and ultimately to destroy most people . . .

Joyce had glimpsed the same idea, but from a purely technical point of view. *Ulysses* begins as a 'phenomenological' novel, told as if it had been observed by some kind of machine, a combination of camera and tape recorder. Those opening descriptions of Mulligan and Stephen are even a little pedantic; the movie camera is unselective; it would pay the same attention to a man blowing his nose as to a man committing suicide in despair. This phenomenological technique reaches a kind of climax in the chapter in the newspaper office, where the complexity of the material finally defeats the camera-tape recorder. It must have struck Joyce at this point that he had been cheating. The phenomenological novel should be unselective, free of the author's prejudices, so to speak. But when newsboys are shouting, machines are pounding, and half a dozen people are speaking at the same time, the author has to be as frankly selective – or biased – as Dickens describing the death of Little Nell. Thereafter, Joyce abandoned the attempt at the 'camera' novel, and began to brood on the paradoxes of language as a 'mirror' of reality. The remainder of the book is a hall of distorting mirrors.

In James's novels, the attempt at 'purity' had also ended in a kind of contradiction. The premise of the James novel is life observed in a plane mirror of intelligence: again, a kind of phenomenological novel. The disadvantages began to show early, in *Daisy Miller*. The reader wants the narrator to marry Daisy; that would be the emotionally satisfying conclusion of the story; but in the interest of detachment and observation, they have to remain separated, and Daisy has to die. The trouble with this plane mirror method – excluding emotion, excluding everything but the novelist's curiosity, as he prowls around with his magnifying glass – is that it makes for rather flat endings. This is typified in *The Beast in the Jungle*, that story about a man who feels that his destiny is to be completely unique – and who finally discovers that its uniqueness consists in the fact that he is the one man in the world to whom nothing, absolutely nothing, will ever happen. But we can begin to see the disadvantages of pure detachment earlier than this, in *The Sacred Fount*, when the narrator exerts so much intelligence in an investigation that remains on a level of trivial gossip. (The vampirism implied in the novel *could* have been made interesting, but E.T.A. Hoffmann would have been the man to do it.) The later novels have their admirers – Graham Greene admits to re-reading *The Golden Bowl* regularly – but again, one feels that the method has got out of hand, and that the intelligence, which was supposed to provide a faithful reflection, is now distorting the world; the characters seem unreal.

In both Joyce and James, the problem seems to arise because the novelist is untrue to his original conception: of being a camera. For the moment he attempts to exclude himself from the scene, to photograph a group of people who exist only in his own mind, he is only pretending to be a camera. It would be more honest if, like Anthony Trollope, he turned to the reader and said: 'And now reader, shall we make Lucy marry the squire . . .?'

At which point, it may be worth asking: But why *should* the novelist want to be a camera? Is not the whole enterprise dishonest – or at least, muddled – from the beginning?

The answer to this question can be seen by referring to any of the early camera novels, from Knut Hamsun's *Hunger* or Rilke's *Malte* to *Ulysses* and Olyesha's *Envy*. I began *The Outsider* with an analysis of a typical 'camera' novel, Barbusse's *Hell*, in which the narrator simply relates what he sees through a hole in the wall of his room. The 'camera' novel is essentially the 'outsider' novel. It is about a man 'outside' everyday life – what Husserl called the communal life-world – looking in. There is a tremendous gain in intensity and subjectivity. And that word reminds us that one of the earliest 'camera novels' was Kierkegaard's *Either/Or* – not, perhaps, strictly a novel, but certainly achieving a kind of philosophical detachment, combined with subjective intensity, which is typically Jamesian.

So it becomes possible to understand how Isherwood could see himself as The Novelist – even, perhaps, as the Great Novelist – without abandoning his humanistic creed of truth, attention to detail, and refusal to get overblown. The philosophy – such as it is – may have come from Forster, but the essential idea came from Kierkegaard, via Rilke, James, Joyce and Aldous Huxley. (I am not suggesting that Isherwood was influenced by any of these – except possibly Huxley – but that this is where we should look for literary parallels.) The ideal is a peculiar kind of honesty – an honesty that becomes almost a monkish vocation. The aim is to tell the truth – about oneself and other people – with a precision and honesty and thoroughness that would have alarmed Rousseau. The aim could be compared, for example, to that of the Impressionists, who got tired of muddy academic paintings with gold-tinted skies and brown grass, and insisted on trying to give a more accurate idea of how a river really strikes you if you open your eyes and *look* at it, look with honesty and humility, and without preconceptions.

Readers of Isherwood's first novel *All the Conspirators* – started when he was twenty-one and published two years later – might be forgiven for feeling that the results of the method are hardly spectacular. But then, most first novels are at least partly autobiographical – designed to allow the writer to get some of his pet obsessions off his chest – and this is no exception. At the end of his remarkable tribute to his parents, *Kathleen and Frank* (his father, Frank Isherwood, was killed in the First World War) there is a kind of wry acknowledgement to his mother for the part she played in making him a writer by infuriating him into rebellion. It is a curious ending for this nostalgic and moving book. When he speaks of an episode of 1928, when his mother remarked 'I can't think why they want to bury that ridiculous Thomas Hardy in the Abbey' and he left the room in a rage, one feels that, even after forty years, his blood still boils as he thinks about it. *All the Conspirators* is written in this mood.

The main impression it makes on the unprepared reader is of triviality. The blurb of the recent British edition states that it is about the 'Evil Mother who destroys her son'. This seems to be pitching its claims a bit high. It describes how the hero decides to throw up his boring office job to become a writer, the rather muted conflict with his mother, and his decision to run away from home, which ends in his collapse from some undefined illness. But at the end of the novel, he is talking cheerfully with his rebellious friend Allen Chalmers, and one senses that his next attempt to escape his home will be more successful. His mother seems rather stuffy, but scarcely evil – this novel never reaches the intensity of Ivy Compton-Burnett. Its main interest is that it gives us a very clear picture of what Isherwood had to fight against, the suffocatingly dull and respectable middle class background. Edward Upward's novel *In the Thirties* (1962) throws an interesting side-light on *All the Conspirators*. Upward is, of course, Allen Chalmers, and both novels open with a description of the same seaside holiday, which Isherwood and Upward took together. In Isherwood's novel, Chalmers represents revolt and strength and freedom, as well as a sane, pipe-smoking normality. Yet *In the Thirties* has the same oppressive, suffocating atmosphere as *All the Conspirators*. It is about Upward's decision to join the Communist Party, and one feels that he is only jumping out of the frying pan into the fire. Middle class respectability has so eaten into his soul that you feel there's nowhere for him to escape *to*. Writing about it thirty years later, in this novel and its sequel *The Rotten Elements*, Upward still gives the impression of being trapped, of never having acquired the escape velocity to leave behind his respectable background.[1] The impressive thing about Isherwood is that he *did* escape.

Anyone who has been exasperated by *All the Conspirators* would hardly be reassured by the next novel *The Memorial* (1932). The technique is reminiscent of Aldous Huxley's *Point Counterpoint* of four years earlier; modern readers will be reminded of Angus

Wilson. It is about a group of middle-class, rather cultured people in the 1920s, and again we are aware of how oppressive Isherwood found the whole milieu. 'Eric turned away from the window, deeply sighed. He was weary – weary to the bone.' Yet the book is finally far less oppresive than *Point Counterpoint* or *In the Thirties*: the reason being that Isherwood so obviously *likes* people. He writes of them with the sae kind of keen observation and sympathy as E.M. Forster – Carolyn Heilbrun has commented on the 'roundness' of Isherwood's characters. This gives the novel an inner glow that saves it from negativeness.

From the first words of *Mr. Norris Changes Trains* (1935), you can see that Isherwood has achieved his freedom. He has still not quite achieved the confidence to speak of himself as Christopher Isherwood, but in all the essentials, William Bradshaw *is* 'Chris'. (Even the names are his own middle ones.) Isherwood's 'British' characteristics – his detachment, his good manners, even his shyness – have now ceased to be a disadvantage and have become his strength. For he is no longer trapped in a mood of self-disgust. He is thoroughly enjoying himself in contemplation of Arthur Norris, exporter, amateur communist and sexual pervert. The humour and piquancy arises from the contrast between the rather sordid goings-on and Isherwood's butter-wouldn't-melt-in-your-mouth prose.

> The first person I saw was Anni. She was standing in the middle of the room. Arthur cringed on the floor at her feet. He had removed several more of his garments, and was now dressed lightly but with perfect decency, in a suit of mauve silk underwear, a rubber abdominal belt and a pair of socks. In one hand he held a brush and in the other a yellow shoe-rag. Olga towered behind him, brandishing a heavy leather whip.
>
> 'You call it clean, you swine!' she cried in a terrible voice. 'Do them again this minute! And if I find a speck of dirt on them I'll thrash you till you can't sit down for a week.'
>
> As she spoke she gave Arthur a smart cut across the buttocks. He uttered a squeal of pain and pleasure, and began to brush and polish Anni's boots with feverish haste . . .

In *Kathleen and Frank*, Isherwood comments about his mother: 'She can't have cared much for *Mr. Norris* – its humour was too sour, it was too preoccupied with drinking and dirty rooms and lowlife types to suit her taste . . .'. In measuring the distance from the impotent rebel of *All the Conspirators*, one becomes aware of how far Isherwood has come in five years. And how far the impetus that has driven him towards freedom has been his mother. He has found a subject as remote as possible from Kensington – so remote that it has even freed him from the need to cock a snook at Kensington. So the negative element that made the first two novels rather oppressive has vanished. The surprising thing about *Mr. Norris*, in spite of the brothels catering for perverts and the brooding shadow of Nazism, is that it is such a sunny and open-hearted book. Berlin has given Isherwood his freedom just as certainly as Paris and Zurich gave Joyce his; but this Artist as a Young Man has no need for silence, exile and cunning, and apparently no resentment about the things he has fought so hard to escape.

I re-read the book after reading *Kathleen and Frank*, and was surprised to discover that one of its most remarkable qualities is its honesty. In the last pages of *Kathleen and Frank*, Isherwood speaks openly of his homosexuality, comments on how difficult it would have been to tell his father about his taste for 'boy-love', and describes swopping anecdotes with a homosexual uncle about the boy-bars of Berlin. None of this, of course, emerges in either of the Berlin novels, although in *Goodbye to Berlin* the narrator rather demurely admits that he is 'queer'. (In context, it sounds as if he is joking.) We hear nothing about the boy-bars –except that 'Chris' visits them as an observer – and Mr. Norris's masochism is oriented towards girls, not men. It *ought* to give the whole thing a slight air of *mauvais foi*, as in Proust, where you find yourself wishing that Marcel had had the courage to admit that Albertine was really Albert. Yet in Isherwood this is not so. It does not matter that 'Chris' allows us to assume that he is a perfectly heterosexual young man, and that in the dramatised version, he even gets Sally Bowles pregnant. The pruderies of the thirties were such that it was still not possible to admit openly to homosexuality, even if only for legal reasons. (Stephen Spender was able to write about it openly only after the war, in *World within World*, and Auden only spoke about it frankly – in a magazine interview – shortly before his death.) But what is absolutely clear is that this thoroughly irks Isherwood. Part of his hard-earned freedom was the right to be defiantly honest; so he steers as close as he possibly can to admitting it in the Berlin novels, and seems to try to make up for the suppression by an additional honesty about himself and his motivations. It is this feeling that Isherwood is a totally honest man that gives all his novels – but particularly the four 'Chris' novels – their durable quality. (It is worth bearing in mind that Forster, whom Isherwood admired so deeply, and whose generation was even more inclined to reticence on the subject, wrote his own homosexual novel *Maurice* in 1914, and although it was impossible to publish it, defiantly passed it around to all his friends, so that everyone knew of its existence.)

Of all Isherwood's books, *Goodbye to Berlin* is the most stunningly successful. The method, the subject and the style have all come together to produce one of those oddly 'perfect' books. I put 'perfect' in quotes because in the Jamesian sense, it is far from perfect; it is all over the place: three bits of diary and three long-short stories. In spite of which, it has that air of never putting a foot wrong. It is not necessarily the best of Isherwood's books; both *The World in the Evening* and *Down There On a Visit* are in many ways more substantial and impressive products of the novelist's craft. (Next to *Prater Violet*, the *Paul* section of *Down There On A Visit* is my favourite among all the things he's done.) Yet it has the curious perfection of a healthy child.

This is due to an interesting combination of ingredients. To begin with, as 'Chris' himself recognises, this is because he has cast himself in the role of a camera, the Jamesian observer. But he has gone one step further that James. The narrator of *The Turn of the Screw*, *The Aspern Papers* and *The Sacred Fount* is basically a lay figure, an excuse for getting the story told. Now Isherwood is too good mannered to take refuge in this kind of objectivity; like a well-bred Englishman, he is anxious to hide his superiority. So he enters the story as a real character, apparently revealing himself as well as Sally and Otto and Bernhard. 'Chris' is not, of course, Isherwood; he is also a lay figure; but Isherwood pulls the strings so convincingly that we hardly notice. And this lay figure of *Mr. Norris*, *Goodbye to Berlin* and *Prater Violet* is perhaps Isherwood's most skilful creation. (I exclude the Chris of *Down There On A*

Visit because he is visibly older and wiser.) He moves around, forms relationships, makes mistakes, yet succeeds in remaining the ideal camera. What Isherwood has suggested is that 'Chris' is a shy young Englishman, brought up in a pleasant, normal middle-class home, sexually rather restrained and backward, like all well brought-up young Englishmen, and motivated chiefly by a naive curiosity about people that is as scientific as Darwin's interest in butterflies. Now we know from *All the Conspirators* that Chris's home was no more pleasant and normal than one of Ivy Compton-Burnett's country houses, and we know from Isherwood's remarks at the end of *Kathleen and Frank* that his sex life in Berlin was fairly lively. But Isherwood's reasons for omitting these is not practical but artistic. To produce faithful reflection, one needs a plane mirror, and 'Chris' is carefully ground until he provides the necessary standard of fidelity.

The next thing one needs, of course, is something to reflect in it. *All the Conspirators* and *The Memorial* have the same feeling of fidelity as the Berlin novels; but *what* they are reflecting lacks urgency; you admire the precision of the writing without getting very involved with the characters. Hemingway had a similar problem: that flat, faithful, reflective prose was at its best when reflecting war or violence; it lost much of its virtue when the subject became more everyday, as in *Islands in the Stream*, *Across the River and into the Trees*, and many of the short stories. Like Hemingway at Caporetto, Isherwood happened to find his ideal subject in the Berlin of the early thirties. His own slightly ambiguous attitude towards his subject gives the whole thing an additional sharpness and clarity. He does not take up a violently moralistic attitude towards his pro-Nazi landladies, and his attitude towards Otto – who is what would nowadays be called a 'yob' – seems oddly compassionate. So the human values remain; the violence is understated – and therefore all the more shocking. The story of the Nowaks, with its poverty and muted tragedy, might have been written a generation earlier by one of the 'socially conscious' writers like Hauptmann or Sudermann; but that fact that it takes place in this brutal, disintegrating society gives it added force.

At which point, it is necessary to stand back and admit that some of the virtues of *Goodbye to Berlin* are accidental. A hostile critic would point out that he writes with such gusto of the Nowaks because he is seeing it all with startled, middle-class eyes. The result is that it is a little *too* cold and detached. A writer like D.H. Lawrence would have shown more sympathy for the miserable Frau Nowak, with her sordid, dreary life. Dickens would, of course, have cried tears all over the place; and I'm not sure that I wouldn't have preferred this to Isherwood's objectivity, which seems to me to have a faintly cruel flavour. (No doubt this is because my own home background was closer to the Nowaks than to Kathleen and Frank's Kensington – so my attitude is biased.) It was sound artistic judgment to keep Chris asexual – except for the brief and dreamlike episode with Frau Erna in the TB sanatorium – but also a practical necessity. Sally Bowles's promiscuity rather shocks him, as it would have shocked his mother. If he'd been less shockable, and if he'd absorbed his Zola and Colette and Joyce and Hemingway and Fitzgerald – not to mention *The Green Hat* – he might have decided that Sally, with her green fingernails and dead-white face, was all rather old-fashioned, and kept her in only as a minor character. Which would have been our loss. This same hostile critic would not have absolved Isherwood of the responsibility of wanting to shock his mother in the abortion scene.

All of which is probably true enough. Yet it seems rather trivial to hold it against a book that is as well integrated as *Goodbye to Berlin*. It is rather like saying that Blake painted in watercolours because he was no good with oils; it may be true, but it is irrelevant if you consider the miraculous use he made of the watercolours. Isherwood 'uses' his own accidental virtues with supreme artistic skill and cunning, and the result is anything but accidental.

By the time *Goodbye to Berlin* finally appeared in book form, in 1939, Isherwood was already on his way to America. Since leaving Berlin he had written two plays with W.H. Auden – and would write another – a volume of war reporting, and that excellent autobiography *Lions and Shadows*, which makes us aware that Auden was as responsible as Upward for making Isherwood kick his way to freedom. And then, from the creative point of view, there was a dry-up of ten years; *Prater Violet* and *The Condor and the Cows* were the next major works, and both appeared in 1949. And 'major' is here used in a relative sense; *The Condor and the Cows* is a travel book – hardly the most significant literary form – and *Prater Violet* is basically a long-short story like *Sally Bowles*. *Prater Violet* is, in my opinion, one of Isherwood's most successful works, and this is largely because he again makes use of the brooding, menacing atmosphere of the thirties and the rise of Nazism. The story is ostensibly about his involvement in a preposterous 'escapist' musical film; Bergmann, its German director, feels the full irony of the contrast between this cachou-scented nonsense and the Reichstag Fire Trial, which is at present taking place in Germany.

From the point of view of Isherwood's development, the most interesting thing about the book is the sense of 'Chris's' involvement with Bergmann and the tragedy of Germany. He is no longer cold and detached, and rather enjoying the superiority his detachment gives him. Many changes have taken place since the days of *Sally Bowles* and *The Nowaks* – the most significant being Isherwood's 'conversion' to Vedantism. This has not, of course, made any basic change in Isherwood's character – even conversion could scarcely do that. Even in *The Memorial* and *Goodbye to Berlin*, his great human warmth had been apparent. James Joyce's integrity had the effect of making him rather remote and formidable; Isherwood's has always been combined with a kindness and concern for other people that make him anything but formidable. He seems to share with Angus Wilson a desire to keep himself 'cut down to size', in case anybody should make the mistake of overrating him. (This may be the chief reason why, as Carolyn Heilbrun has pointed out, he has been so consistently undervalued as a novelist.) In the early novels, he kept this personal quality in the background as he kept so many of the qualities of the real Christopher Isherwood; his Englishness made him intensely averse to anything that looked like showing off. If the Vedantism is to be given any credit, it is simply that it seems to have made him lose his reticence about his human qualities.

At the same time, *Prater Violet* makes us more intensely aware than ever before of the limitations of this interesting method that Isherwood has chosen for himself – trying to be a 'pure' novelist in some super-Jamesian sense. By the rules he has laid down for himself, he is not allowed to keep voluminous notebooks of observations, which can then be elaborated into ideas for stories or novels, fleshed out with invention and technical know-how. I have already commented on the resemblance between the basic ideal of Isherwood and Hemingway – to *tell the truth* as it had never been told before. The trouble is basically that a novel is a pack of lies. If a novelist really wanted to tell the truth, he'd write history or autobiography. He doesn't; he wants to *create*, and to make his creation *seem* as truthful as possible. That is to say, to use a culinary analogy, the truthfulness is a method of cooking rather than an ingredient of the pudding. A good writer achieves the effect of truth even when lying, and a bad writer – you can finish the epigram for yourself. (Hoffmann's *Mme de Scudery* is as absurd a story as he ever invented, yet reads like a piece of factual journalism.) Isherwood and Hemingway could be compared to painters who have imported photographic techniques into their work; their problem thereafter is to find subjects that photograph well.

Prater Violet achieves an apparently unsurpassable level of clarity and simplicity; it is so straightforward that it looks naive. This is the beginning:

> 'Mr. Isherwood?'
> 'Speaking.'
> 'Mr. Christopher Isherwood?'
> 'That's me.'
> 'You know, we've been trying to contact you ever since yesterday afternoon.' The voice at the other end of the wire was a bit reproachful . . .

It ends in the same casual way: 'As for Bergmann, *Prater Violet* got him the offer of a job in Hollywood. He went out there with his family, early in 1935.'

It is only in re-reading some of its finest scenes – such as Bergmann's imitation of the Reichstag Fire Trial – that one becomes aware of Isherwood's marvellous craftsmanship.

Yet *Prater Violet* seems to be a dead end. Isherwood's 'mirror' had been so effective because the monstrous figure of Hitler dominated the background; his fundamental subject had been the contrast between public and private life. (It was a formula that Solzhenitsyn would later use so effectively.) Now he had moved to the country – of all countries – where there was no startling contrast between public and private life. And he had gone to the city of all cities where there was no clear line between illusion and reality – Hollywood. Nathanael West had almost stifled to death there. It was almost as if Isherwood had gone back to the Kensington of *The Mermaid*.

When his next novel, *The World in the Evening*, appeared in 1954, it was clear that he was making an extraordinary, almost heroic effort, to deal with these new circumstances. And this is also characteristic of the three novels that followed – his total output to date. Creatively speaking, each one of them has involved a far greater effort than any of the Berlin novels. None is a complete success, and one comes close to failure. Yet it seems to me that this is due to the nature of the problem rather than to Isherwood's response to it. I have found myself, on the whole, more absorbed in these later novels than in the earlier ones – but rather in the way that an audience pays more attention to a gladiator in a tight corner than to a gladiator who is winning. Perhaps a slightly less dramatic analogy would be a spectator of a chess tournament, wondering how a Master is going to get out of this one . . .

At which point, let me try to state the problem in its most general terms, so we can be clear about the 'rules of the game'.

Novelists could be conveniently divided into two groups: the subjectivists and the objectivists. I put the subjectivists first because the father of the novel, Samuel Richardson, was a subjectivist. They write about inner conflicts and problems, and their success depends on persuading you to 'identify' with the hero or heroine. The objectivists are observers, recorders and story tellers – Jane Austen, Scott, Balzac, Tolstoy, Henry James. We note that in this last list, the only true and consistent objectivist is Henry James; all the others occasionally slipped in autobiography, as in Louis Lambert, Edward Waverley, Pierre Bezukhov, and so on. Since Dostoevsky and Hamsun, the modern novel has taken a heavy dive into subjectivism; objectivism has, on the whole, got itself a bad reputation, being associated with Arnold Bennett, John Galsworthy, most Soviet novelists, and practitioners of the modern bestseller; in recent years Capote has tried to revive it as the non-fiction novel.

From the beginning, Isherwood took his stand with the major practitioners of the objective novel – James, Hemingway, Joyce (of *Ulysses*) and Forster. Each one tried determinedly to be a camera.

At which point, the problem arises. A camera is all very well for special purposes – recording a war, or some definite epoch of the past. But if nothing in particular is going on around you, it becomes rather useless.

There are two possible solutions for a novelist. One is to forget the camera and invent, as James did. The other is to point the camera inside yourself, as Proust did. Joyce, who could not see any way out of the problem – having moved from subjectivism to objectivism – found 'extra-literary' solutions and played linguistic games. Hemingway wandered around the world with his camera on his back, looking for wars.

The case of Forster is the most interesting and relevant in the present context. After that one bold attempt to write about his subjective problems in *Maurice*, he chose the Hemingway solution and lugged his camera off to India. In writing *A Passage to India*, it probably struck him that he was again evading the issue, in that the relation between Fielding and Aziz should really have been homosexual, and Adela Quested's weird accusation of Aziz should have been due to her subconscious observation of this – her reaction of jealousy, shock and disgust being transmuted to another level. Forster made one more attempt to write the type of novel for which he had become best known, in *Arctic Summer*, which begins with two young men meeting on a train. At which point, he again saw the impossibility of working it out honestly, and abandoned it – and novel-writing – for good.

In *The World in the Evening*, Isherwood chose a mixture of the two main solutions: he 'invented', and he turned the camera inward. He also decided to avoid Forster's *cul de sac* by bringing the problem of homosexuality into the open. For this is what Forster wanted to write about but never could: the problem of 'the homosexual outsider' – the homosexual as outsider.

All 'subjective' novels are, in their very essence, *Bildungsromans* – that is to say, the hero's problem is to 'find himself'. *The World in the Evening* makes a radical break with all Isherwood's previous novels in that it is about a man trying to find himself – and more-or-less succeeding. Stephen Monk's natural tendency is to be passive and selfish. When he discovers his wife *in flagrante* at a Hollywood party, he runs away, gets involved in an accident that confines him to bed, and spends most of the rest of the book in *recherche du temps perdu*, recalling with particular gloom how he betrayed his novelist wife with his 'adopted' son. The self-examination leads to a kind of renewal, and we are left with the impression that Stephen is now prepared to make a fresh start.

The recreation of the marriage between Stephen and the novelist Elizabeth Rydal is superbly done. Yet the whole novel leaves one with an over-all sense of tremendous effort that has not quite achieved its object. Moreover – and rather surprisingly – there is an air of unreality, of wishful-thinking – about the homosexual seduction scene. Certainly this, in a way, is the core of the book. One suspects that Isherwood even considered making Michael Drummond the legally adopted son of Stephen and Elizabeth, instead of simply a young man they take under their wing; it would add an element of shock, and also emphasise the problem of the divided loyalties of a homosexual. *This* is basically the problem of the novel. Stephen is a passive character, rather feminine, a bit of a gigolo. 'Chris' seems to be fascinated by such characters – Arthur Norris, Otto Nowak, Sally Bowles, 'fabulous Paul' (of *Down There On A Visit*). So now he is writing his first 'true novel' since *The Memorial*, it is to be expected that his hero should be of the same type. The trouble is that most readers do not enjoy identifying with self-proclaimed weaklings (the American word 'fuck-ups' would probably be even more precise here); it was the passages of gloom and futility that made the first two novels so claustrophobic. ('He was weary – weary to the bone.') Moreover, we tend to feel that a real-life Stephen would not be married to a nympho like Jane, and would probably never have got married to Elizabeth Rydal earlier.

In short, while the 'subjective' part of the solution works, the 'inventive' part doesn't ring true. We never believe in Stephen as we believed in Chris. Perhaps this is because we accepted Chris's claims that he was a camera – because he was so careful to maintain the conventions of objectivity – and we can't grant similar credence to a man who seems awash with self-pity.

The World in the Evening is by no means a failure; judged as a totality, it is probably Isherwood's best novel. Its weakness may lie in an attempt to adapt the methods of Aldous Huxley. It is a serious attempt to talk about spiritual renewal, to make fictional use of the lessons he had learned from Vedantism; but Huxley himself never solved that problem, and most of the later novels have an analogous problem with 'focus'. The reader doesn't quite *believe* in them as he believed in *Crome Yellow* and *Antic Hay*. So it is with *The World in the Evening* compared to the Berlin novels.

Down There on A Visit (1962) demonstrates clearly that Isherwood had recognised what went wrong with the previous novel: that there was a faint, but nevertheless detectable, air of *mauvais foi*. He appears to retrace his steps – but this is only an appearance. Only the first part, *Mr. Lancaster*, is a genuine throw-back to the old days. It is less successful than some of 'Chris's' other portraits for a reason that the author recognises: 'When I tried to describe him to my friends, I found I could make very little of him as a significant or even farcical character. I just did not have the key to him, it seemed.' Lancaster is a 'hollow man', a pompous bore who only becomes interesting for a moment when he tries to convince Chris that he composed one of Wilfred Owen's best known lines. If, as one suspects, Mr. Lancaster has created some new and extraordinary form of *mauvais foi* bordering on madness, Chris fails to put his finger on it.

The writing has again the wit and precision of the other 'Chris' books – there were times in *The World in the Evening* when it had become slack. This is from the 'Ambrose' section:

' "How do you do," said the Englishman. I hate the expression "a limp handshake"; it seems to imply the kind of moral judgement which is made by scoutmasters. So I will put it that Ambrose placed his hand briefly in mine and then drew it away again as though it were an inanimate object he was holding by the wrist.'

'Ambrose' describes Chris's stay on a Greek island, 'away from it all', and his own realisation that the 'beat' life (as it might be called now) is no answer to his own problems. 'Waldemar' is, in effect, an explanation of his decision to leave for America when his anti-Nazi friend Waldemar finds England unbearable, and decides to return to Germany. The last part, 'Paul' – to my mind the most successful section in the book – describes his relation with a bisexual gigolo with identity problems. It covers Isherwood's early period in Hollywood – the early days of his Vedantism – and his relation with Gerald Heard. The interesting thing about this story is a kind of ambivalence of motive. Paul is another 'fuck-up', a man who has lacked a centre of gravity too long ever to find one. In that respect, we realise, Chris is lucky; ever since his late teens, he has possessed a centre of gravity – occasionally tenuous, perhaps, but enough to give him a real sense of continuity and identity. Vedantism has been an important stage in his personal evolution; (Carolyn Heilbrun mentions that he was thought to be the model for Larry in Maugham's *The Razor's Edge*). It *ought*, ideally, to be the solution to Paul's problems too. Yet when we see Paul in the midst of the Vedantist group, we find ourselves admiring him for his 'authenticity' – a kind of tough honesty – and getting a little bored with all these high-minded soul-savers. Isherwood plainly feels the same. But Paul never gets anywhere – as anyone who has met his type could predict – and dies of a heart attack. (It could just as well have been a drug overdose.)

Technically speaking, the innovation of *Down There On A Visit* is caught symbolically on Don Bachardy's dust-jacket, showing the middle-aged Isherwood looking at a mirror that reflects back his younger self. That is to say, Isherwood has tried an interesting way out of the camera problem by introducing a form of double-exposure. Instead of 'Chris' – the mirror – we have the action mirrored in a young Chris who is in turn mirrored in the older and wiser Chris. This gives it a greater depth than the earlier Chris novels – and also makes it the ideal conclusion to the series, as Isherwood himself realised at the time.

Yet this in itself means that Isherwood had reached another dead-end. When one looks more closely at *Down There On A Visit*, one can see why. As in *Sally Bowles* and *The Nowaks*, you feel that an essential part of the 'camera' method is to observe people who are either failures or freaks. This suddenly becomes very clear in 'Mr. Lancaster' because – as when he tried recounting the episode to Chalmers – it just doesn't come off. 'Chris' actually copies out a poem by Mr. Lancaster to show to Chalmers, but Chalmers has to be polite and pretend it is much worse than it actually is. Which makes the point that in order to be successful, 'Mr. Lancaster' needs more malice. I am not now speaking of gloating malice, of the kind one finds in the novels of Baron Corvo, but simply of the essential elements of malice – cool superiority. The whole point of *Mr. Norris* and *Goodbye to Berlin* is 'Chris's' superiority to everything that happens to him – rather like Stephen's in *Ulysses*. This is not intended as a criticism of Isherwood's method; a camera is by nature 'superior', since it remains detached from the things it records. 'Paul' is such an interesting exercise because of its ambiguity; 'Chris' *is* superior to Paul, observing him rather pityingly from above, yet is also fond of him, loves him as a fellow human being. But then, Paul is splendid material. Mr. Lancaster and Ambrose are altogether less interesting as people. When Carolyn Heilbrun writes with slight exasperation that all we learn from the 'Ambrose' section is that a chicken can be raped, she reveals her consciousness that Isherwood is not above trying to shock – or at least, that the sordid makes ideal material for his 'camera'.

Now the most significant thing about Isherwood as a novelist is that the driving force behind his work is a genuine craving for truth; there is nothing static or passive about his integrity. The honesty shows on the surface in the 'Chris' books, where he is, if anything, a little too self-analytical. But it runs under the surface in everything he has done; it is the basic recurrent theme of all his work.

It is this honesty that enables him to retreat from another dead-end, and produce one of his most successful novels, *A Single Man* (1964). The remarkable thing about this book is that it starts off by looking like his most resounding failure so far, then gradually gets the reader involved until he is laughing, slapping his thigh, and experiencing the sensation described by Holden Caulfield – the desire to snatch up a pen and write the novelist a letter.

The book sounds autobiographical; it is about a homosexual Englishman in his late fifties, who teaches in a college somewhere on the outskirts of Los Angeles. His boyfriend Jim has been killed in a car crash; George – the professor – is gloomy and lonely. Isherwood has – fortunately – never suffered a similar bereavement, but during these early pages one suspects he has

given way to neurotic daydreams and is trying to exorcise them.
But the tone begins to change very quickly, as George sits on the
lavatory, reads Ruskin, and reflects on his neighbour Mrs. Strunk
and her children. What comes over, like a spring breeze, is
George's essential sweetness – and Christopher Isherwood's own
essential goodness and kindness. This is no sour, nihilistic lament
of a middle-aged man. It has humour – not even 'wry' humour, but
the sunny humour of a man who is at peace with himself. When
George daydreams about kidnapping the members of the local
Purity League and forcing them to act in pornographic movies, the
writing has an unexpected touch of Kingsley Amis.

My own enjoyment of the novel is certainly influenced by
repeated experiences of teaching on American campuses –
Isherwood is here funny and accurate, without ever sinking into
caricature – but friends who have never been to America have
appreciated it just as much. Just as the tone of *The World in the
Evening* is subtly wrong, the tone of this novel is subtly right.
When George and his student Kenny have been swimming in the
sea, Kenny puts his arm around George's shoulders. 'You know
something, Sir? They ought not to let you out on your own, ever.
You're liable to get into real trouble.' And the warmth of this
comment somehow pervades the whole book. As George lies on
the point of sleep, there is a question-and-answer session that has
faint echoes of *Ulysses*. And the final pages of the novel, in which
the novelist speculates on the possibility of George dying in his
sleep, have a calm, peaceful atmosphere – tinged with tragedy –
that makes the perfect ending to the book. If Isherwood had been
more pretentious, and if Hemingway had not already used the
title, he might have called it *The Undefeated*.

Perhaps the most important thing to be learned from *A Single
Man* is that the 'problem of the modern novel' is not purely a
technical problem; on a much more fundamental level, it is a *personal*
problem. If Isherwood had been negative and sour and defeated, the
novel would have provided one more piece of evidence that the
modern novel has landed itself in a *cul de sac* – or on the strand, like
Yeats's post-romantic fish. What is important is that Isherwood has
evolved as a human being since he wrote *All the Conspirators*; his
odyssey has been long and at times dangerous; *A Single Man* is like a
rocket sent up to announce that he has arrived home safely.

In its final pages, one suspects that Isherwood was thinking of it as his valedictory to the novel. Yet the last of the questions in the question-and-answer session is:

'. . . *George is getting old. Won't it soon be too late?*
'Never use those words to George. He won't listen . . .'

To have ended his career as a novelist with George–Chris drifting towards death would have been another kind of failure. The extraordinary thing about Isherwood is his refusal to accept failure or defeat. In one sense, his life has been a series of defeats. At the end of *All the Conspirators*, Philip is apparently exhausted and defeated. And, according to Isherwood, this was just before his disastrous period in Germany with Mr. Lancaster – which ended, in fact, with a 'visitation' – a flash of inspiration for his next novel *The Memorial*. The immense Berlin novel, to be entitled *The Lost*, never got written; instead of a companion to *Ulysses*, *The Man without Qualities* and *The Sleepwalkers*, we have the rough sketches that make up *Mr. Norris* and *Goodbye to Berlin*. The journey to America in 1939 looked like flight – and was so interpreted by the British press; this was followed by ten years of barrenness. (Edmund Wilson has a piece on Auden and Isherwood called 'The Oxford Boys Becalmed'.) And then, from apparently impossible and intransigent material, Isherwood created the novels of the American period, culminating in *A Single Man*. Yet if this had been Isherwood's last word, we might have felt that the whole 'Vedanta period' had been a waste of time, for there is no sign in *A Single Man* of the subject that had been so important in *The World in the Evening*. (And there is a passage in 'Paul' where Isherwood seems to hint that he is now taking Vedantism altogether less seriously.) In fact, one might have argued that Isherwood's excursion into Vedantism had been as much of a mistake as Paul's. He is not an abstract thinker, like Huxley. He sees the world essentially in terms of human beings. The 'Paul' section seems to demonstrate how little he ever really belonged to the Hollywood Vedantists. And after all, what has the artist to do with salvation? 'What theme had Homer but Original Sin?'

As if to reply to this allegation, Isherwood produced a novel specifically concerned with homosexuality *and* 'sainthood' – *A Meeting by the River* – and a life of the Hindu saint Tamakrishna.

The novel is not one of his major works; technically speaking, it is far less successful than *The World in the Evening*, which uses the same form of letters and journals. Yet it is difficult to see how Isherwood could have cast it in the usual novel form without over-weighting it with technique. It could only have been told by one of the two brothers concerned – and each would have given it his own slant – or by a third-person narrator who would need to invent excuses for knowing so much. All things considered, the present solution was the boldest and simplest.

We have a story of two brothers, one a publisher who lives in Los Angeles, the other a Hindu monk about to take his final vows. The publisher has married the girl his brother was in love with – and who was in love with his brother (in fact, still is). And now he pays a visit to the monastery, en route for Japan; he has a heavy emotional problem on his hands. He is bisexual, and has got involved with a young boy named Tommy. He is troubled by guilt, indecision, and a kind of jealousy of his brother, who seems to have solved all his problems by rejecting the world. The only climactic event in the novel is a drunken telephone call from Tommy, which is taken by the wrong brother. There are conflicts; the publisher almost convinces his brother that he ought to return to England. At which point, like Alyosha Karamazov, the monk falls asleep from exhaustion, and has a sudden total conviction of the presence of his dead master, the Swami. It seems to him that the dead man is also deeply concerned about his brother, and intends to help him. (Significantly, the head of the monastery remarks that when a monk takes the final vows, he gains liberation for his whole family.) In fact, the drunken phone call seems to bring the publisher to his senses. He writes to Tommy, offering him only friendship for the future, then writes to his wife, telling her how much he loves her, and explaining that his own emotional immaturity will probably mean that he will continue to have the occasional *affaire*, but that it doesn't meaning anything . . . The two brothers part with genuine affection. And although, in this summary form, it may sound a little too much of a moral parable, its ending carries deep conviction. The publisher's 'conversion' (such as it is) seems a triumph of decency and common sense more than of religion – and this is surely Isherwood's point. He is not suggesting that the answer to human misery and stupidity lies in sainthood or mysticism – only in decency and common sense, and also a certain optimism. For this is the thing that comes over most clearly from *A Single Man* and *A Meeting by the River*: that Isherwood's integrity is born of optimism, of hope.

The Ramakrishna biography may be seen as a postscript to a postscript. It is as if he is saying: 'But please do not imagine that I am somehow dismissing sainthood and mysticism. They still remain the true way – the ultimate way. But the path to them may still lie through decency and common sense . . .'

When I started to write this essay, I piled Isherwood's books up at the side of my typewriter – a sizeable heap – and a letter fell to the floor. It is dated September 1961, and I see that he was living for a time in Squires Mount, Hampstead. He is acknowledging a novel I sent him, and the date – and his comments – provide me with the information that it was my *Adrift in Soho*, heavily influenced by the 'Chris' novels. After some undeservedly kind remarks, he goes on: 'You remember what Wilde wrote: "To be an Egoist one must have an Ego. It is not everyone who says 'I, I' who can enter the Kingdom of Art." '

The comment goes to the heart of Isherwood's own peculiar virtue as a novelist. He is not, in the ordinary sense, an egoist; even the self-effacing 'I' of the Berlin novels is actually a skilfully constructed puppet. Yet on the basis of this refusal to be an 'ego', he has slowly built up a 'true personality', a 'real I'. The interesting result is that he is one of the very few modern novelists I can think of who has escaped the slide into defeat or negation. Because of his own peculiar honesty, a completely undramatic courage, he has succeeded in remaining a living, warm human being, and in imparting this humanity to his novels. His is truly an integrity born of hope.

1976

SEVEN

Some notes on
Graves's prose

I know of only one other modern writer who is as difficult to discuss as Robert Graves – and that one is Henry Miller. Both writers are prolific; both are full of splendid pages; both have a quality of mind which can only be called 'eccentric'. And both are an immense embarrassment if you try to write about them, because their weird mixture of qualities baffles the critical procedure.

I am going to try to be blunt about this – which is not an easy thing for a writer to be about his fellow writers, particularly if he happens to know them. In Miller, you never know what is straight pornography, thrown in for the American tourists in Paris (who pay about five dollars a copy for *Sexus* and *Plexus*) and what is essential to his self-expression. And in Graves, you never know what is the true expression of the Celtic poet, and what has been written with one eye on the best-seller market.

What is worse, you cannot solve the problem simply by asking them. I tried putting the question to Miller one day, and met with an indignant self-defence – a declaration that you cannot treat some of his work as 'essential' and other parts as dispensable pornography.

I also remember the occasion when Graves discomforted a moronic television interviewer on a late night programme. The interviewer – the usual empty headed actor with a big smile and wavy hair – thought he would be brutally direct, and asked Graves: 'I have been told that you consider yourself primarily a poet, but that you write cheap pot-boilers to support yourself and your family. Is this true?' Graves glowered coldly, and retorted: 'Name half a dozen of them.' The interviewer stammered, and hastily changed the subject. And yet, if he had been a little better informed, he might have replied: '*I, Claudius*, *Claudius the God*,

Sergeant Lamb of the Ninth, *Antigua, Penny, Puce*, *Wife to Mr. Milton*' and so on, without raising an eyebrow. Admittedly, only Graves's worst enemy would call a work like *King Jesus* a 'pot-boiler'; and yet there *is* some truth in the remark, for all that.

And yet no one who has read Graves's novels can doubt that he will continue to be read in a hundred years time. Which is to say that, to some extent, Graves can be regarded as a 'classic'. Which is to say that a critic ought to be able to explain what it is about him that makes him a valuable writer. And very few critics can.

There are two other Celtic writers with whom Graves can profitably be compared: W.B. Yeats and John Cowper Powys. (The latter is perhaps not so well known in America as he deserves to be, but his series of novels: *A Glastonbury Romance*, *Porius*, *Wolf Solent*, *Owen Glendower*, will be one day recognised as one of the greatest contributions to the novel in the twentieth century.) And immediately, it becomes easier to grasp what is so important about Graves. Like so many Celts, he is incapable of *not* creating literature; his mind is steeped in the romantic tradition and in the love of antiquity. Unlike so many modern writers, he is never afraid to be subjective. In fact, the problem does not even arise, for he is subjective by instinct. He never has to worry about whether he is creating literature or whether he is too close to the standards and conventions of our society; he does not have to make an obvious effort to transfer himself from the world of money and household worries to the world of 'the poet'. His interest, his centre of gravity, already lies in the world of the poet; unlike so many of his fellow writers – especially in England and America – he has been blessed with total absorption in what he has chosen as his life's work.

It is because Graves is a born writer – because he swims like a fish in his chosen element of literature and the past – that he is also an exasperating and wrong-headed writer. An obvious example – at least one which springs readily to my mind – is his attitude towards his contemporaries in his Clark Lectures on poetry. The breezy, aggressive tone of these lectures is refreshing, but they cannot be condoned for that reason alone. His diatribe against Pound remains a curiosity, like Greene's attack on Shakespeare in the *Groatsworth of Wit*, but there was never less attempt at critical fairness to an important poet. Eliot is attacked as a disciple of

Pound, a 'Poundling' who rewarded Pound for blue pencilling *The Waste Land* with the dedication to 'the better craftsman', and *The Waste Land* itself is dismissed as the first attempt to apply the technique of 'collage' to poetry. More preposterous still, Eliot is attacked as an anti-semite! Now while it is true that Eliot's early poems contain some unflattering references to Jews (which Eliot has confessed to regretting) no one who knows his work could suppose that hatred of Jews is a part of Eliot's 'vision of life' as it was of Hitler's. This kind of criticism, amusingly subjective, would be altogether delightful if expressed to half a dozen boon-companions over a gallon of Spanish wine; but it has no place in a course of university lectures.

But even more extraordinary is his attack on W.B. Yeats. One might imagine that Graves and Yeats had much in common; they appear to take much the same unsympathetic view of *The Waste Land*, and to prefer a poetry rooted in romance and tradition. But Yeats is also dismissed as a borrower, a plagiarist. (Graves once compared Yeats to a man who goes around gathering fragments of wool from briar hedges to make himself a coat – having, Graves implied, no wool of his own.) Graves tells how Yeats once asked Laura Riding to recommend a young poet for inclusion in his Oxford Book of Modern Verse, and then rejected the poet she suggested; whereupon Graves and Laura Riding also refused to be included in The Oxford Book. Graves's motive for telling this story in the middle of a section on Yeats's poetry is obscure; one might almost think that he *wanted* to supply a discreditable personal reason for his dislike of Yeats's work.

It is possible, of course, to sympathise with Graves's amusingly malicious attack. I have discovered that most people who met Yeats thought him an amusing old fake. But how can anyone with an ear for poetry read the work of Yeats's last twenty years without being devastated by the terrible sincerity and the intellectual power revealed in it? If Yeats were fifty times a fake and a charlatan in his personal life (I doubt whether he was – shyness assumes strange masks), nothing could invalidate *Under Ben Bulben and The Tower.*

Possibly Graves and Yeats were too much alike for real sympathy. Add to this that Yeats was very much the older man, and that he was very much the elder statesman of poetry when

Graves was a struggling writer, and it is easy enough to see why Graves might feel a certain impatience with his great contemporary.[1]

One characteristic he undoubtedly shares with Yeats – the desire to be considered a mine of curious and remote erudition. Amusingly enough, this is the feature of Yeats that he singles out for special rebuke in his lecture. Graves quotes a lengthy passage from some old alchemist of the kind that would have delighted Yeats, making the point that Yeats lacked any real knowledge of alchemy. Then Graves adds carelessly that the alchemists made a solvent for gold called muriatic acid. Apparently he was unaware that muriatic acid is only another name for hydrochloric acid, and that gold can only be dissolved in *aqua regia*, a mixture of nitric and hydrochloric acid.[2]

In fact, the strangest similarity between the two poets emerges when Graves's *White Goddess* is compared with Yeats's *A Vision*. (Graves singles this out for attack in his lecture!) Both these books are weird agglomerates of remote and archaic learning, jumbled up to make a kind of 'system' that bears some resemblance to that of William Blake. Both are fascinating reading, and should be kept as bedside books. And in both cases, the reader is never sure whether the book is serious, or whether it is a gigantic leg-pull. Yeats claimed that his book was dictated to his wife by spirits. Graves openly claims a kind of supernatural second-sight for himself that enables him, among other things, to solve the riddle of the number of the beast in Revelation, 666. If you open Graves's book casually, you are likely to assume that it is a learned and closely argued treatise on Celtic mythology and druidic law. But when you proceed to read it from the beginning, you soon realise that it is about as academic as Nostradamus's dream book. In fact, both Yeats's *Vision* and Graves's *White Goddess* are direct descendants of Madam Blavatsky's *Secret Doctrine*; they are attempts by romantic rebels to write a 'sacred book' for the age of machinery. And since the author of a sacred book is necessarily a prophet or visionary, they are also attempts on the part of their authors to claim for themselves the role of priest or mystic lawgiver.

Now in Yeats, there was an interesting contrast between the man who wanted to be wrapped in strange clouds (like Shelley's

Ahasuerus) and the clear-minded, clear-sighted Irish intellectual, who wanted everything in clear, rational terms. The mystic Yeats wishes to be accepted as a lawgiver; the rationalist Yeats wants his readers to go away and think for themselves. The mystic Yeats admires Swendenborg, Blake and Madame Blavatsky; the rational Yeats admires Nietzsche, and his fellow Irishmen Swift, Goldsmith, Burke and Shaw. (Yeats's attitude to the latter was confused, among other things, by sexual rivalry, the lady in question being Florence Farr.)

Now there is no such conflict apparent in the work of Graves, and consequently his work does not contain real tension; it is as undividedly romantic as the work of William Morris. Yet all the same, there are interesting contrasts in Graves. The language of the Claudius novels is as blunt and unpretentious as Cobbett, and it is hardly conceivable that they could have been written by the author of *The White Goddess*. Unfortunately, this contrast never appears in the same work. So the readers of the Claudius novels are aware of Graves as an amusing populariser of history whose chief quality is irreverence.

It is when we come on to the subject of the novels that we become aware of the real problem of Graves's position as a writer. At least three of them – the Claudius novels and *Count Belisarius* – are wholly successful. One is tempted to use that old cliché of reviewers and say they are 'compellingly readable'. Another three – the two Sergeant Lamb novels and *Wife to Mr. Milton* – are excellent books that everyone ought to read once; but they are not on quite the same level. One big novel, *King Jesus*, must be accounted a failure, although it has apparently every element to make it a success; its trouble seems to be that Graves tried too hard, and made it too slow-moving. (I wonder if he was inspired by Mann's Joseph novels; if so, he completely mistook the direction of his own genius.)

The failure of this latter deserves another word. The reader who reads Graves's appendix before he starts the book is absorbed by it. Like *The White Goddess*, this appendix shows wide erudition; but like the Claudius novels, it shows the rebel Graves, prepared to devastate his orthodox readers with irreverence. A combination of the two promises a rare masterpiece: impiety armed with classical learning, a fascinating combination, as Anatole France demonstrated. The book itself is a disappointment. Like *Claudius*, it purports to be a translation of an ancient manuscript; but the device is here used somewhat clumsily. Parts of it read no better than Lloyd C. Douglas or any other popular rehash of ancient history. The 'old manuscript' device is not used consistently, and bits of Old Testament prose alternate with passages that might have been written by any member of the Romantic Novelists Association. For the reader who can persevere, this book has its rewards. Graves obviously meant it to be his masterpiece, and it is a huge and impressive structure. In spite of its slow-motion movement and patches of Lady Novelist writing, it is a remarkable book. But it *could* have been a great novel, and the reader cannot help wondering why it didn't come off. (I should add that there *are* admirers of Graves who regard the book as his masterpiece.)

This sense of 'not quite making it' somehow applies to all Graves's output as a novelist. I mean that Graves obviously has it in him to produce an important body of work; he is a first rate novelist, on a purely technical level, and he is full of interesting ideas; he could also be described as a mystic. And yet the two sets of qualities never seem to combine. Think of any great novels – *Le Rouge et Le Noir*, *Adolphe*, *The Possessed*, *Anna Karenina*, *Bleak House*, *Swann's Way* – and then think of the Claudius novels. Immediately, you become aware that Graves, as a novelist, lacks a dimension of subjectivity, of sincerity. They *are* pot-boilers; probably the best and most brilliant historical pot-boilers of our time, but still essentially commercial novels. You would keep them on the same shelf as *Kidnapped*, *Micah Clarke*, *King Solomon's Mines*, *Quo Vadis* – but not with Stendahl and Balzac and Dostoievsky. All the same, they are, like these other works, classics in their *genre*.

The fact remains that the expert novelist never combines with the Celtic mystic and the classical scholar, and that in the one novel where some kind of effort is made (*King Jesus* – which contains, for example, some of the theories expounded in *The White Goddess*) the two utterly refuse to unite.

Part of the trouble, I have suggested, is that Graves is not a writer of ideas. The unifying emotion of all his work is his love of classical antiquity. It would almost seem that he has evaded the modern world and turned back to the past; consequently, that he has never reached the phase of 'terrible insight' so characteristic of the later Yeats and of Rilke. This must come through facing and accepting the modern world. It is significant that his only two works dealing with the modern world – the autobiography *Goodbye to All That* and the novel *Antigua, Penny, Puce* – fail to reveal any of that 'sense of his own age' that Eliot considered the first attribute of the major writer. The novel is the only total failure among Graves's novels, while the autobiography, significantly enough, looks back to the 1914 war.

I should add that I do not feel that this criticism applies with the same force to the poetry (and this article is supposed to deal only with the prose). Even so, when I casually open a volume of Graves's poems, I am uncomfortably aware of the number of classical references, and also of a curious 'made' feeling about the poems. I mean that a Graves poem is somehow like an article of hand-made furniture, not like an intensely personal outpouring in a personal, magic language (as, for example, in Rimbaud). This, in itself, is no criticism of Graves; some of the best lyrics of the twentieth century have been written in this hard, impersonal language – by Yeats, Synge, Gogarty, M'Diarmid. But although the poetry is undoubtedly Graves's most important work, I cannot feel that it escapes this limitation of the novels – lack of 'a sense of his own age'.

This essay would be incomplete without some comment of the part played by sex in Graves's work. The Claudius books were best sellers because their plots were mainly about sex and murder. Probably the fact that they dealt with actual historical events saved them from being banned as obscene, for they abound in rape, incest and every kind of sexual perversion. (In this, they stay fairly close to their models, Tacitus and Suetonius.) Some of his poetry shows this same Elizabethan zest for the sexual. This also emerges in his volumes of *The Greek Myths*, and even in his translations of Suetonius and Apuleius. Bearing this in mind then, it is all the more surprising that sex plays no central part in Graves's work. In his Clark lectures, he quotes with disapproval Yeats's lines:

'You think it horrible that lust and rage
Should dance attention upon my old age.'

And yet again, Yeats has succeeded, in his later work, in somehow uniting his obsession with sex with the driving force of his poetry, of *personalising* it so that it adds strength to his work. For Graves, sex, like the modern world, seems to be a subject with which he has never come to terms. It must be either draped with a mantle of classical antiquity, or treated in a jocular, Elizabethan manner, as in the poem *Down, Wanton, Down!*

Some modern writers seem to spawn commentators, so that you could hardly count the number of books on Joyce, Kafka and Eliot in the British Museum. Others, like Graves, are unfairly neglected. (Powys and Henry Williamson are another two examples.) Now, a group of English poets, led by John Wain, Kingsley Amis and Philip Larkin, is beginning to find his work an important inspiration. It is to be hoped that Graves now – in his late sixties – finally gains some of the attention he has long deserved.

1962

EIGHT

Valeri Briussov and 'The Fiery Angel'

Russian literature begins in 1820 with the appearance of Pushkin's *Ruslan and Ludmila*, and ends in 1918 with the publication of Blok's poem *The Twelve*.

That is, of course, an oversimplification; but it conveys a general truth. *Ruslan* made Pushkin famous, and it made Russians aware of their great romantic heritage. Russian literature erupted into self-consciousness; the remainder of the century saw the appearance of more masterpieces than at any comparable period in world history – with the possible exception of the Elizabethan age. In 1917 came the Revolution; and Blok's poem – in which twelve Red Guardsmen march through the streets of Petrograd in a snowstorm, with Christ at their head – marks the end of the great era. Jesus had been turned into a symbol of political propaganda. From now on, literary inspiration will be at the service of the State. Self-consciousness is outlawed; only social-consciousness is encouraged by the authorities.

Tolstoy, Dostoievsky and Chekov were the great literary triumvirate of the late nineteenth century; after them, Russia produced no more major writers. Yet that period – from 1900 to 1917 – produced an incredible number of limited but highly individual talents: Andreyev, Artsybashev, Rozanov, Merejkovsky, Sologub, Zamyatin, Bunin, Kuprin, Gorky, Berdyaev, Shestov, Blok, Biely, Mayakovsky, Balmont, Alexei Tolstoy . . . Their works are full of a feverish intensity, a kind of hunger for the absolute. And yet the saddest thing about the generation is that so many writers began superbly, with work that seemed to promise greatness – and then collapsed, as if the creative process had been destroyed from within. In 1910, for example, any perceptive critic might have said that Andreyev, Artsybashev and Gorky were likely to produce masterpieces. In fact, the first two were already in decline; while Gorky, for all his talent, was never to become more than a kind of Russian Jack London.

As to Valery Briussov, the author of *The Fiery Angel*, there were still many critics who would have snorted angrily at the mention of his name. In the 1890s, he had been one of the most controversial writers of his time, arousing the same kind of fury and adulation that Oscar Wilde provoked in England. For the older generation of critics, Briussov was an irritating exhibitionist who tried to substitute showy tricks of style for real talent. No one provoked more fury and derision in the popular press. If *Patience* had been performed in Russia, Bunthorne would have been taken for Briussov.

As in all such cases, the violence of the critics created its own reaction. All the young writers who hated the older generation took sides with Briussov; he became the centre of a 'school'. The young admirers hailed each new volume of poetry as a masterpiece. The older critics, now they were used to the style, were willing to grant that he had talent. *Stephanos*, which appeared in 1906, was a universal success; even his enemies said it was good. In the following year, *The Fiery Angel* appeared, and Briussov was suddenly established as one of the foremost novelists of his age, as well as one of its best poets. His main trouble, perhaps, was that he was too brilliant and versatile; he was also a critic, dramatist, short story writer and translator (he translated Poe, Wilde, Verlaine and D'Annunzio), and the editor of one of the most influential magazines of the day. Although few of his contemporaries noticed it, he was already past his peak by 1910. His second novel, *The Altar of Victory* (1913) is stodgy, and its presentation of fourth century Rome is altogether less convincing than his portrait of the late Middle Ages in *The Fiery Angel*. At the time of the Revolution, he was approaching his mid-forties, and most of his finest work was behind him. He now found it prudent to declare himself a communist, and to constitute himself official spokesman of the new revolutionary literature. An acid note crept into the comments of younger writers who had once been his disciples and admirers (Blok, for example). When he died in 1924, at the age of 51, the Commisar for Education, Lunacharsky, praised his poetry for its vivid language and strange images; the words have rested on

Briussov's reputation like some enormous leaden tombstone.

I first discovered Briussov through a story called *The Republic of the Southern Cross*, printed in B.G. Guerney's *Treasury of Russian Literature* (one of the finest anthologies of Russian literature ever assembled). This is one of the world's great short stories, and immediately convinced me that Briussov was a writer who should rank with Dostoievsky. Written in the first decade of the century, it seems to contain a remarkable anticipation of the future Soviet State. The Republic of the Southern Cross – in the Antarctic – is a worker's democracy. Its capital, Star City, is contained under a vast dome of glass. The houses have no windows because everything is lit by electricity; the city is air-conditioned; all the buildings are exactly the same height. The workers in the steel mills – the chief industry of Star City – all wear exactly the same clothes and live in exactly similar houses. Their working day is short; they are well-paid, and their lives are comfortable to the point of luxury. The city is also full of retired workers living on handsome pensions. Life ought to be idyllic.

Then the citizens begin to be afflicted by a psychological malady called 'contradiction mania', which makes them do and say the opposite of what they intended. A man intending to say yes would find himself saying no; intending to say something agreeable, he will find himself shouting abuse. The epidemic spreads; the streets are filled with dangerous maniacs. The 'sane' try slaughtering the insane; it makes no difference. Criminals descend like vultures. The chief engineer destroys the electricity supply. The story ends with a vision of darkness, violence, bloodshed, universal destruction.

Other writers would explore Briussov's theme – of the soul-destroying effects of universal conformity: Zamyatin in *We*, Huxley in *Brave New World*, Orwell in *1984*. These works are all more complex than *The Republic of the Southern Cross*, but none of them possesses its fierce impact.

Briussov's story could be regarded as an expansion of the theme of Dostoievsky's novel *Notes from Underground*, which is a protest against science and rationalism and Ideal political systems. Dostoievsky's hero feels threatened by science, which (he believes) aims at analysing all human acts, which 'will then be mathematically computed according to natural laws and entered into a table of logarithms'. But if this ever happens, then man will go insane in order to escape this strait-jacket, and to preserve his fundamental freedom.

Notes from Underground is the work in which Dostoievsky introduces his great 'dialectic of freedom', which was to be developed with such power in *Crime and Punishment*, *The Devils* and *The Brothers Karamazov*. I assumed that Briussov's work after *The Republic of the Southern Cross* would develop along the same lines. Unfortunately, it was practically impossible to get hold of any of his works. But I *was* familiar with Prokoviev's opera *The Fiery Angel*, based on Briussov. This work is Prokoviev's masterpiece in operatic form, and a summary of its plot may help to prepare the reader for Briussov's remarkable novel. It opens with the knight Rupprecht entering his room at the inn, and hearing from the next room a girl's voice crying: 'Leave me alone! Disappear!' Rupprecht goes into her room, and discovers the beautiful Renata, who is possessed by demons. She calls him by his name, although she has never seen him before. And when the evil spirit has departed, she tells him the story of her life. When she was eight years old, she says, an angel called Madiël came to play with her. He become her constant companion, exhorting her to become a saint. But as she grew up, she began to desire him physically; one night, she persuaded him to sleep with her, and spent the night trying to induce him to possess her. In a fury, the angel disappeared. But shortly afterwards, she met a young count named Heinrich, and immediately recognised him as Madiël. She ran away with Heinrich, and lived with him in his castle for two years. Then he left her. She returned to her parents, but the demons began their assaults . . . And ever since then, she has searched for her angel of Fire, pursued by evil spirits . . .

Rupprecht falls in love with her and offers to help her find Heinrich – it seems his only chance of persuading her to marry him. He consults the magician Cornelius Agrippa, and they encounter Dr. Faust on their travels. Rupprecht attends a witch's Sabbath and meets the Devil. Finally, Renata allows Rupprecht to possess her. They locate Count Heinrich, and Rupprecht learns that Renata has lied to him. It was she who seduced Heinrich, who had taken a vow of chastity. She has even lured him into practising black magic . . .

Renata's love of Heinrich now changes to hatred; she persuades Rupprecht to challenge him to a duel. But as Rupprecht is about to kill him she screams; it is Rupprecht who is seriously wounded. Renata nurses him back to health and allows him to become her lover. Then she leaves him and goes into a convent. When he finally locates her, she is again possessed by devils, and has affected the whole nunnery. She is tortured and sentenced to the stake, but before she can be burnt, dies in Rupprecht's arms. This opera provided Prokoviev with the opportunity to write some of his most savage and hair-raising music; the last act, with the nuns writhing and screaming and the Inquisitors shouting exorcisms, is a remarkable *tour de force*.

Eventually, I located a copy of Briussov's novel – in the London Library. I found it as absorbing and powerful as I had expected; beyond all doubt, it is one of the masterpieces of twentieth century literature. But I found it hard to connect it with the ideas of *The Republic of the Southern Cross*. It was several more years before I was able to learn enough about Briussov to realise that his closest literary relative is not Dostoievsky but Maupassant.

But since so little has been written about Briussov in English, and since most of this is no longer available in England, perhaps I should, at this point, offer a summary of Briussov's life and literary development.

Briussov's grandfather was a serf who was given his freedom. His father showed remarkable business acumen, and became a rich cork merchant in Moscow. Born in 1873, Briussov spent much of his childhood and teens in European travel. He was slender, with high cheek-bones and Mongolian eyes. Like Turgeniev – and unlike Dostoievsky – he preferred Europe to Russia. He was deeply influenced by Mallarmé, Rimbaud and Verlaine. In his late teens he met a nobleman, Alexander Dobroliubov, who lived in a room with black walls and a grey ceiling, and talked about the occult and demonism, as well as French decadent poetry.

By the age of twenty, Briussov had totally absorbed the gospel of decadence, as encapsulated in Huysmans' *A Rebours* and Villiers de Lisle Adam's *Axel*, with its famous line: 'Live? Our servants can do that for us.' In 1894, when he was 21, he was part-author of a book called *Russian Symbolists*, which achieved a *succès de scandale*.

In the following year came his *Chefs d'Oevres*, which was greeted by the press with sneers and derision. In fact, Briussov was fighting in Russia the battle that Swinburne, Rosetti and the Pre-Raphaelites had fought in the 1860s; and, as in England, there were plenty of conservative critics and journalists to denounce the 'fleshly school of poetry'.

Briussov was, of course, a dedicated sensualist, and this is the real key to his work. In a poem in *Chefs D'Oevres* he speaks of 'voluptuous shadows in an alcove' and of 'bodies intertwined like a pair of avid snakes'. (I am quoting Marc Slonim's *Russian Literature, 1900-1917.*) No biography of Briussov has been published, as far as I know; one hopes that, when it is finally undertaken, the author will belong to the 'revelatory' school which is represented in England by Michael Holroyd; we shall probably discover that Briussov's life was a tangle of love affairs, and that he died of premature sexual exhaustion. His general remarks on literature and poetry suggest a man who was determined to live with Pater's 'hard, gem-like flame', and to treat life as a school for the senses. 'The personality of the artist is the essence of art,' he stated at 22, and: 'I recognise no other obligation save a virginal faith in myself – and that is a truth which needs no proof.' He seems to have meant that he was under no obligation to prove his own greatness to the general public or the critics.

The interesting thing is that, by 1906, Briussov had won his battle. Symbolism was no longer sneered at. He was accepted at one of the major Russian poets, and his disciples regarded him as a great poet. They would have liked him to be a true Symbolist, a kind of religious mystic, like the composer Scriabin, whose music is at once sensual and religious. Briussov declined; he thought of himself as a healthy pagan, devoted to clarity and the delights of the senses. Unlike most of the European decadents, he was a highly disciplined man – as his final triumph shows. I suspect that his personality inspired at least two near-masterpieces: Artsyba-shev's *Sanine* and Alexei Tolstoy's *The Sisters* (the first part of a three volume novel called *The Road to Calvary*). Sanine is a kind of healthy pagan, a cheerful Nietzschean, who loves sex and life, and cannot understand the miseries and moral torments of morbid Christians. Standing by the grave-side of a friend who has committed suicide he remarks: 'One fool less in the world.' In *The Sisters*, Alexey Bessonov (which sounds fairly close to Valery Briussov) is an altogether more sinister figure; he has a 'pale, malignant face', and is the author of 'poisonous' verses that arouse a morbid sexuality in the heroine, Dasha. She actually goes to his room to offer him her virginity; then, when she realises he has already seduced her sister, runs away. Tolstoy obviously dislikes him, but he is nevertheless one of the most interesting characters in the novel; when he disappears, swept away by the Revolution, the novel becomes a rather dreary piece of communist propaganda.

All this enables us to understand *The Fiery Angel*. Briussov had none of Dostoievsky's passionate interest in religion. He seems to have regarded it as a delusion whose chief virtue was that it added to sex an interesting flavour of sinfulness. The underlying emotion of *The Fiery Angel* is decadent. Renata's strange delusions about Madiël and her passion for Count Heinrich only make her more desirable and unattainable. From the beginning, Rupprecht is fascinated by this girl who allows him to spend the night lying beside her – in perfect chastity – and then permits him to accompany her in her strange quest. It is a novel about a man's sexual obsession. I am reminded of two other stories that share the same emotion – of masochistic morbidity: D.H. Lawrence's *The Shadow in the Rose Garden* and Hemingway's *A Sea Change*. Lawrence's story is about a wife who admits to her husband that before they were married, she had a love affair and was the mistress of an army officer. He is convulsed with jealousy. Then she tells him that she has seen the man that morning; he has had sunstroke in the tropics, and become an imbecile. Hemingway's story adds another twist of the knife to the same emotion; a man's mistress is about to leave him to go on a sea voyage with a lesbian; she promises to come back to him – and also to tell him about it. Here again, the emotion is a kind of sick, morbid jealousy. It springs out of a feeling of almost religious adoration of the 'eternal feminine', and the male's inability to come to terms with the fact that these infinitely desirable creatures can reject him and allow others to possess their bodies. Shaw once said that jealousy is one of the most unpleasant of our childish ailments, and this is undoubtedly the healthy view. Lawrence, Hemingway – and

Briussov – wallow in the intensity of the emotion. But compared to Briussov, Lawrence and Hemingway are crude and unsophisticated. By setting his story in the late Middle Ages, by involving his hero with magic and diabolism, Briussov adds an interesting dimension of objectivity to the story. It is the kind of thing he loved to do: a book on two levels: of morbid subjectivity and cool objectivity. He liked to preserve the same double-focus in his poems: feverish sensuality expressed in coolly disciplined language. In a sonnet 'To Form', he says: 'There are subtle but powerful affinities between the shape and the scent of a flower; and the diamond is invisible until it comes to life in the cut of the polished stone. So do images of fleeting fancy, drifting like the clouds of the sky, become as hard as stone, and thereafter live for centuries in a chiselled and finished phrase . . .' And in a poem 'To the Poet', he says: 'Be a coldly dispassionate witness of all things, and turn your gaze to everything . . . Force yourself to be passionless in moments of living embrace, and when you are crucified by agony, glorify your pain.' He is obsessed by the idea of craftsmanship and detachment. He uses them to express what he would call 'the eternal emotions' – passion, agony, pain, death. But it is easy to detect an element of sadism in the 'coldly chiselled periods'. He is obsessed by the 'sex war', and in an oddly irrational way. Patrick Byrne, the Birmingham Y.W.C.A. murderer, explained that he wanted to get revenge on all women for causing his sexual tension. You feel something of this in Briussov. His financial independence has allowed him to develop an almost childish solipsism, a petulant self-absorption. Most of us begin life with this attitude; all children feel they have a *right* to the moon. But life grinds it out of us. In fact, many of us swing to the opposite extreme: from what Robert Ardray calls the 'fallacy of central position', the feeling that the universe revolves around us, to the equally absurd fallacy of feeling that we are totally unimportant in the universal scheme of things, and that life itself is purely arbitrary and meaningless. One of the reasons that people become writers is that they want to maintain the feeling of central position, of being 'somebody' in the eyes of the rest of the human race. (And after all, what better way – if it comes off – than becoming a literary classic who will march down to posterity in the company of Dante, Shakespeare and Goethe?) Briussov was fortunate enough to be the son of a rich man; and in the Russia of 1890, this meant a great deal, for you were either a peasant or a gentleman; and the 'gentlemen' still beat their servants and abused the drivers of the *droshkys* and generally behaved as if the world belonged to them. Briussov had the additional advantage of being brilliant. And he was born into the midst of a great era of revolt – not just social revolt (although Tsars and Grand Dukes were regularly blown to pieces by anarchist bombs) but the deeper revolt of the spirit that so obsessed Dostoevsky: the feeling that 'If man is God, then there is nothing to prevent him from doing what he likes.' Huysmans' Des Esseintes behaves as if he *is* the centre of the universe; so does Wilde's Dorian Grey. The revolt of the spirit was complicated by the feeling that highly sensitive and talented people *ought* to be the centre of the universe – or at least, of society. When Baudelaire contemplated the tragedy of Edgar Allen Poe, he felt that it was appalling that such a genius should burn itself out among people too coarse and stupid to appreciate it; and Baudelaire's sympathy was based on the feeling that he himself was in the same position. Poets and artists were the 'invisible aristocracy' of the earth. This is the feeling that runs through Briussov's early poetry: the conviction that the Artist is the most important person in the world; far more important, in his way, than mere tsars or emperors.

And what is the situation of the artist in this society that has brought him into being? 'His giant wings prevent him from walking' says Baudelaire. He is an outsider and a misfit. Princes and emperors do not recognise his superiority; they do not even recognise the importance of his talents – as they used to in bygone ages. He is alone in a world that he finds boring and vulgar. He has nothing to say to the mob, and the mob ignores his existence. And, unfortunately, he will also lose his battle against time and death. Tolstoy's Bessonov tells a girl he is about to seduce that every night he is overcome by the fear of death, and needs another person close to him. The artist may be an 'invisible aristocrat', but he is also an absurd and tragic figure . . .

In fact, as Alexei Tolstoy points out, Bessonov has condemned himself to death. When Dasha reads his poems she begins to experience 'a morbid feeling of being prompted to let herself go, to relax, to fritter away something precious and yearn for something that had no existence'. A man who deals in such emotions clearly lacks the ability to survive. Tolstoy obviously feels that the solution is to identify with the people, to take part in their struggle – and that conclusion pleased the rulers of the new Russia. It never seems to have struck Tolstoy that Bessonov's real trouble was simply immaturity; emotionally, he is a spoilt child; intellectually, he is a genius. (Or so Tolstoy gives us to believe.) The answer is not to take up the cause of the people, but to shed the basic 'spoiltness' by ruthless self-examination and self-discipline.

What is true of Bessonov is also, unfortunately, true of Briussov. His closest literary relative is, as I have already commented, Maupassant – although I suspect that he would have preferred to be compared to Flaubert. Like Maupassant, he is a sensualist and a romantic; nearly all his work is about women and sex. Maupassant writes of the 'sex war' from the point of view of a confident male who never found it difficult to make conquests. There is a touch of sadism in his attitude towards women – as if, like Byrne, he blamed them for the desires they aroused in him; but he is inclined to picture woman as the victim, man as the conqueror. Briussov also blames women for being so desirable; but he writes as the Artist, who is likely to be rejected and misunderstood. You suspect that the wild adulteries of his poems are largely imagined.

There has been only one collection of Briussov's stories issued in English; that was in 1918, and it was named after the opening story, *The Republic of the Southern Cross*. It clearly reveals Briussov's strength and his weakness. The title story is, of course, a masterpiece; it flows with a kind of impersonal force, like a river. But most of the other stories are highly personal observations; you feel that Briussov could have borrowed a title from Hardy and called it *Life's Little Ironies*. Maugham's *Creatures of Circumstance* would have been almost as appropriate. Like the Italian playwright Pirandello, he enjoys writing about life's ambiguities. In *For Herself or For Another*, a man sees a woman at Interlaken, and is convinced that she is a mistress whom he cast off ten years earlier. When he speaks to her she denies this. But they become friends. He continues to be convinced that she is his ex-mistress, and that this is her way of taking revenge for his betrayal. At which the stranger retorts that if he wants her to be Elizavieta, then she will *be* Elizavieta. And from then on, she 'remembers' their past love affair, or pretends to. Naturally, he finds this even more frustrating. One morning, she goes away, and writes him a letter in which she suggests that although she is not Elizavieta, she had nevertheless heard how badly he had treated his former mistress, and decided to take revenge on behalf of her sex. And the deserted lover is left as puzzled and frustrated as ever. It is a skilful and amusing little story, but basically silly. What is Briussov saying? That we can never know the truth about someone? If so, he is a liar. That we never get what we want until we have ceased to want it? If so, he is a fool. Since the story is about a rather unpleasant and self-indulgent character, it says nothing that applies to mankind in general.

The Marble Bust hinges on this same trick of 'ambiguity'. A tramp is in prison, having been convicted of breaking and entering, and he tells the story of how he came to be there. As a young man, he had a love affair with the wife of a minor government official, a girl called Nina; but after a while he tired of her and cast her off. (This seems to be a recurrent theme in Briussov.) He became a successful and rich man; then things went wrong. He became a bankrupt, an alcoholic, and finally a tramp. One day, he is called to someone's house, as a locksmith, and he sees an Italian Renaissance bust that reminds him of Nina. Now he realises how much he still loves Nina, and how badly he behaved; obsessed by the bust, he breaks into the house – and is caught in the hallway.

It is possible to follow Briussov's thought processes as he wrote the story. The basic emotion is Axel's: 'Live? our servants can do that for us.' The tramp has 'lived'; he has had love affairs, been rich – and now he is poor. He has lived the kind of unexamined life that Socrates condemned. It is a work of art that brings about his 'awakening'. It makes him conscious of what he has lost. And in pursuit of his 'dead life' he is caught and sent to prison. To underline his point, Briussov makes the tramp admit that he is not sure whether he invented Nina as he stood in front of the marble bust, his mind confused by alcohol . . . The work of art is somehow more important than life.

This is also the theme of his longest story – and one that many commentators consider his best, *Rhea Silvia*. It also reads like a 'dummy run' for the novel *The Altar of Victory*. It takes place in Rome after the city has been desolated by the Goths. In the half deserted city, a young girl, Maria, wanders among the ruins all day. As she walks around deserted villas and temples, she comes to love the Rome of the past – or rather, the Rome of her imagination. She lives in a dream world, and becomes little better than an imbecile. Then one day, she crawls through a dark passage and finds herself in a magnificent underground palace that once belonged to Nero. The walls are covered with beautiful works of art. She is entranced by a picture showing a 'sleeping beauty' with a handsome young man standing above her; the sleeping girl seems to be herself. The girl in the painting is the guilty vestal virgin Rhea Silvia, with whom the god Mars fell in love. And one day, as she is dozing in front of the picture and imagining herself in the embraces of Mars, she wakes up to find a handsome young man standing over her. She takes him for the god Mars, but he explains that he is actually a Goth who loves Rome so much that he is risking his life to live there. The Roman general Narses is not fond of Goths.

Maria and the young Goth spend all their spare time wandering around the palace hand in hand. Inevitably, they become lovers. Then one day, he ceases to come. Maria discovers she is pregnant, and believes she is destined to bear a god. Then she overhears a man who describes how the Romans have caught a man who was clambering out of an underground passage. When he insisted that he knew nothing about hidden treasure, he was tortured, and then executed . . . Maria commits suicide in the Tiber.

Here there can be no doubt what Briussov is saying. Maria and Theodat – the young Goth – live in the past and in the world of the imagination. For a long time they are able to live idyllically in this secret world. But sooner or later, the real world demands its dues. Theodat dies cruelly; Maria follows him. And in the last words of the story, Briussov states that she was lucky, because the barbarian Lombards are already advancing on Rome.

Artistically speaking, the story is highly successful; but in terms of content, it is thoroughly 'decadent'; it would have been at home in the *Yellow Book*, sandwiched between Oscar Wilde and Max Beerbohm, and illustrated by Beardsley. Life is crude and nasty; the world of dreams is preferable, but it entails tragedy and ultimate defeat ... One gets the feeling that, for all his craftsmanship and detachment, Briussov is an inadequate romantic, like Yeats's man who dreamed of fairyland. And there is nothing in the short stories that contradicts that impression. They are all rather precious, and they leave a flavour of nastiness. In a story called *In the Mirror*, a beautiful woman admits that she has always been obsessed by mirrors – and it seems to be a confession of the author's fundamental narcissism. Then follows a morbid fantasy in which the woman finds herself being dominated by her image in a certain mirror, until finally her mirror self forces her to change places. Then she herself slowly gains the upper hand, until she has compelled her image to return to the mirror. But as the story ends, she admits that she now feels a compulsion to look into the mirror again, to convince herself that she is a real person, not a mirror image. Similarly, in a story called *In the Tower*, the author describes a detailed dream in which he was a Russian knight held captive by the Teutonic Knights. He falls in love with the daughter of his captor. But when he is ordered to write to the Russian prince to advise him to surrender to the Teutons, he senses that this is only a dream, and refuses, prophesying that the Teutonic Knights will be defeated by Alexander Nevsky. He is thrown into a dungreon ... But, as he records his dream, he wonders whether he himself is not a dream in the mind of the Russian knight, lying in his dungeon ... This is Briussov's constant theme: the notion that life is hardly more than a dream. In *Eluli, Son of Eluli*, two modern archaeologists excavate an ancient tomb; the long dead Carthaginian Eluli returns in a dream to warn the excavators that they will die if they disturb his bones. They ignore him, and are killed when their negro workmen mutiny. It is difficult to see what Briussov intended to say in this story, except that the dead past may be as real as the present. But he is hardly convincing.

A very short story called *The Bemol Stationery Shop* offers an interesting clue to Briussov's artistic processes. It is a rather pointless little story about a girl who gets a job in a tiny stationery shop, and becomes as obsessed by the stationery as Maria had been by Nero's underground palace. She talks to the pens, and caresses the writing paper. One day she is dismissed on suspicion of dishonesty. She is heartbroken. She finds another job in a stationers, but there are two other assistants, and she can no longer enter a dream world. She revisits the shop to buy some stationery, and finds it all changed and 'modernised'. The story ends: 'The October wind penetrated her short, well-worn coat. The light of the street lamps was diffused in large blobs in the mist. All was cold and hopeless.' This comes dangerously close to bathos. We are being asked to shed tears for a shopgirl because she thinks the stationery understands her. It sounds like a bad Victorian melodrama; you can almost hear the violins playing 'Hearts and Flowers'.

Quite obviously, Valery Briussov was not at home in the world of the twentieth century. He could not even write about it convincingly. He sensibly turned back to the world of the past. *Rhea Silvia* is also about a feeble-minded girl, but at least it is not unintentionally funny. And, in *The Fiery Angel*, Briussov made an attempt to write a historical novel worthy of Flaubert.

From what we know of Briussov's temperament, we can predict confidently that the novel will be about sex – particularly in its sensual aspects. We can also predict that it will not be a straightforward love relationship; Briussov never seems to have created a sexual relationship without some off touch of masochism or sadism. What we could not predict, on the basis of the short stories, is that his absorption in the past will produce such a detailed and convincing picture. *The Fiery Angel* is no longer about his favourite theme – the difference between reality and the world of imagination. It is as if the exercise of re-creating Germany in the sixteenth century has allowed him to withdraw confidently into the world of imagination, so that no contrast with the 'real world' is necessary. It is apparent, for example, that he became fascinated by the study of magic and demonology. He has obviously read famous accounts of demonic possession – such as Gaufridi and the Aix-en-Provence nuns, and Grandier and the nuns of Loudun. And now, as he recreates this strange world of cruelty, magic and superstition, his best qualities are able to find expression. He has always been obsessed by the world of the supernatural and the fantastic – one can detect the influence of Hoffman as well as of Poe – but he prefers to remain uncommitted. In the short story *Protection*, a young officer falls in love with a beautiful widow, and one night begs her to give herself to him. She explains this is impossible because she is still in love with the memory of her former husband; moreover, he often returns to her in the spirit. That night, as he is about to sleep in the husband's room, it strikes the officer that he bears a close physical resemblance to the husband; so he puts on the husband's clothes, powders his hair and moustache so they look grey, and goes in to the widow. She takes him for her husband, and faints. But before he can achieve his purpose, he suddenly sees the ghost of the husband standing on the other side of her, gesturing at him to leave the room . . . But the narrator adds that he is now certain that the 'ghost' was actually a tall mirror, in which he saw his own reflection in the half-light. This is typical of Briussov's attitude to the 'supernatural'; and his lack of commitment weakens the stories. (Maupassant's *Horla* is so successful because we believe in the Horla.) But in *The Fiery Angel*, this determination to remain uncommitted is a source of strength which supports the book like a steel backbone. When Rupprecht returns from the Witch's Sabbath, he cannot make up his mind whether it really happened, or whether it was a dream induced by the fumes of the ointment. We are never certain whether Renata is really possessed by devils, or whether she is suffering from delusions. Cornelius Agrippa insists that he is a scientist, not a magician. (In the opera, Prokoviev makes two suspended skeletons dance while they chant 'Liar! Liar!') Briussov is obviously so fascinated as he recreates Agrippa, Faust and Mephistopheles that he is not deeply concerned about whether the demons are real or not. The reader can make his own choice from a number of explanations: that the demons are supernatural beings, that they are 'spirits' of the kind summoned up at modern seances, that they are the product of Renata's own fevered subconscious mind, or that they are simply fakes. The same is true of the shade of Helen of Troy, summoned up by Faust and Mephistopheles. And in the novel, the ambiguity no longer irritates us, as it did in the stories; it is a source of strength.

In fact, the whole novel is such a *tour de force* that it seems incredible that it has been created by the irritating romantic who wrote *In the Mirror* and *Rhea Silvia*. The answer, quite clearly, is that the subject allowed Briussov to overcome that fatal dichotomy that weakens the earlier stories. As in *The Republic of the*

Southern Cross, he can allow his imagination free rein, without feeling called upon to drag in the real world. Even his sexual masochism increases the impact of the narrative, lending it a Freudian realism:

> Not ashamed, as children are not ashamed, Renata quickly took off her dress, then her footwear, and, nearly naked, she laid herself into bed, under the blue canopy, calling me to her . . . So, this second night of our acquaintance, we passed under one coverlet, but remaining as strange as though separated by iron bars. And when it happened that an understandable excitement again overcame my will, and, forgetting my oaths, I strove again for tenderness, Renata quietened me with sad and cold words, so passionless and thereby so cruel, that all the blood became numbed in me, and I fell on my face impotent, like a corpse.

And when, eventually, Renata gives herself to him, he realises that she is thinking of Heinrich:

'But when, in the torture of this unexpected bliss, nearly drunk with the accomplishment of all that had heretofore seemed impossible, I bent, exhausted, over the lips of Renata to thank her with a kiss for my ecstacy, I suddenly saw that her eyes were once more full of tears, that the tears were streaming down her cheeks, and that her lips were twisted in a smile of pain and despair.' And the bridal couch becomes a 'black torture cell'. The masochistic feeling is here reminiscent of Aldous Huxley, and reminds us that Huxley also maintained the same curiously ambiguous attitude towards the 'demonic', and that his *Devils of Loudun* reveals many of the same preoccupations – sexual and mystical – as *The Fiery Angel*.

Russian critics who read *The Fiery Angel* were impressed; but anyone who had followed Briussov's career from the early Symbolist days might have guessed that he had reached a kind of limit. He had combined all his basic obsessions into one magnificent canvas; but where could he go from there? He had 'solved' his problem – of reconciling the real and the ideal – but turning away from the contemporary world that he found so unsympathetic. Now there was no logical 'next step'. Andreyev and Artsybashev had reached the same kind of *impasse*, and for similar reasons. The inner-chaos of their early work is resolved into an apocalyptic vision of meaninglessness, which contained within itself no possibility of further development.

By the time he wrote *The Fiery Angel*, Briussov's poetry had already begun to change its direction; he was flirting with patriotism and the idea of social revolution. The story *In the Tower* contains a patriotic speech ('This sea is Russian; from time immemorial, it belonged to the Varyagi . . .' etc.) that, to my ears at least, strikes a painfully false note. It seems as if Briussov, after all his exercises in ambiguity and decadence, is anxious to show his readers that his heart is in the right place. When symbolism ceased to be an active force in literature, Briussov quickly explained that he had never really been interested in it, and turned to forms of poetry that would strike his readers as more 'contemporary'. Understandably, he was accused of opportunism. When the Revolution came, Andreyev and Artsybashev disowned it with disgust; their work had been an attempt to answer the *lebensfrage* – the question of the meaning of human existence; even if they failed, they at least recognised that a revolutionary socialism based on the concept of the class-war was no answer. Briussov, on the other hand, allowed himself to be convinced by the kind of arguments that Alexei Tolstoy used in *The Road to Calvary*: if men like Bessonov were unhappy, this was because they failed to draw their strength from a great popular movement. Understandably, many people took this to be simply the latest strategem of an incorrigible schemer. In retrospect it is possible to take a more charitable view. During the second world war, Sartre wrote an enormous novel around this problem: whether a man who is rendered impotent by his obsession with the problem of human existence should commit himself to revolutionary socialism. Sartre's Mathieu (in *The Roads to Freedom*) cannot bring himself to take the plunge, but Sartre himself finally took it. His friend Camus remained aloof, insisting that this kind of 'commitment' is no answer. When Camus died in a car crash, there was no sign that he had found his own private solution. But the passage of the years seems to have demonstrated that Sartre's public solution was no more satisfactory. The philosophy and the politics have obstinately refused to combine. Sartre the man continues to distribute revolutionary pamphlets on street corners; Sartre the philosopher admits to a sense of total futility, an increased certainty that 'man is a useless passion'. The flat truth is that revolutionary materialism cannot provide an answer to the central question of romantic idealism: the question of what man ought to do with his life. Briussov's development was poisoned by his inability to answer that question; but *The Fiery Angel* remains a unique expression of his determination to create a universe on his own terms. It is a monument to an artistic courage that has become superfluous in Soviet literature since the Revolution.

1975

NINE

Daniel Defoe and Moll Flanders

Daniel Foe – the real name of the author of *Robinson Crusoe* and *Moll Flanders* – was one of the greatest scoundrels and cheats who ever became a literary classic. Not that he ever committed any real crimes, like murder or highway robbery – he was far too wily for that. But in a lifetime of seventy years, he lied, cheated and swindled with a vitality and effrontery that should have made him a millionaire. Instead, he died in an obscure lodging house, fleeing from his creditors. He is a strange case, and far more interesting that any of the villains and adventurers he wrote about.

Even his name is an example of his shiftiness. In the first of his works to make him notorious, *The True Born Englishman*, he sneers at the people who try to pretend that their families came over with William the Conqueror. But in no time at all, he was changing his signature from 'Dan. Foe' to 'D. Foe', and then to 'De Foe', then to 'Daniel De Foe', in an effort to convince his readers that he was a member of the nobility. (In fact, his father was a butcher in St Giles, Cripplegate.)

The main thing to be said to Defoe's credit is that he wrote the first real novel ever published in English – *Robinson Crusoe*, published when he was sixty. To his discredit, it has to be said that he was the father of modern journalism, the direct ancestor of the opinionated, plausible, name-dropping gossip columnist. It was Defoe who invented the *tone* of the modern newspaper – all the direct, man-to-man stuff; he's always trying to imply: 'I'm honest Dan Defoe, the servant of the great British public, and in spite of all attempts to Silence Me, I Dare to Tell you The Truth in plain, straight-from-the-shoulder language'.

His contemporaries had the sense to throw him in jail and put him in the pillory. They should have made a good job of it and hanged him. But then, of course, we wouldn't have had *Robinson Crusoe* and *Moll Flanders*, so it is impossible to be too dogmatic about this.

Daniel Defoe, then, was born in London in 1660, and he remained a Londoner all his life. Nowadays we look back on these 'good old days' with a certain nostalgia, but in fact it was a pretty vile century, and we can think ourselves lucky to be born in the age of the hydrogen bomb and the moon rocket. London was an enormous sewer, whose stinks and diseases killed about one child in every four. The parish of St Giles, where Defoe was born, was famous for its gin shops and cheap and louse-ridden lodging houses, where you could get a single bed – and fleas – for twopence, or share a double bed for three ha'pence, with an excellent chance of catching the pox. (Naturally, most male vagrants preferred to share, since they got a free female vagrant thrown in.) One reporter who watched the door of a gin shop for three hours one evening counted 1,411 people going in and out, not counting children. As gin was a penny a quart, and cheaper than milk, mothers preferred to feed it to their babies to keep them quiet. The consequences was that anyone walking the streets of St Giles after ten in the evening had to pick his way over the recumbent bodies of men, women and children.

It was an age of barbarous crime and barbarous punishment. The combination of gin, poverty and social injustice made the criminals exceptionally brutal. The following excerpt from the diary of a hangman gives the flavour of the period, although it refers to Germany:

First [Stüller] shot a horse soldier; secondly he cut open a pregnant woman alive in which was a dead child; thirdly he again cut open a pregnant woman in whom was a female child; fourthly he again cut open a pregnant woman in whom were two male children. Sunberg said that they had committed a great sin and that he would take the infants to a priest to be baptized, but Phila said he would himself be priest and baptize them, so he took them by the legs and dashed them to the ground. For these deeds he, Stüller, was drawn on a sledge at Bamberg, his body torn thrice with red hot tongs, and then he was executed on the wheel [i.e. by being stretched so that his arms and legs became disjointed, then having the bones broken with blows from a crowbar].

Another quotation, from Christopher Hibbert's book *The Roots of Evil*, demonstrates that Englishmen of the period were not very different from the Germans:

'Unwanted babies were left out in the street to die or were thrown into dung heaps or open drains; the torture of animals was a popular sport. Cat-dropping (i.e. from a great height, to see if they could land on their feet), bear-baiting and bull-baiting were as universally enjoyed as throwing at cocks.' The English were a patriotic people, so it was perilous to be a foreigner or a Jew in the streets of London. One Portuguese sailor who picked a fight with an Englishman was grabbed by a mob and 'nailed by his ear to a wall. Some time after he broke from there with a loss of part of it, and ran; but the mob was so incensed that they followed out and wounded him with knives till at last he either fell or threw himself into a puddle of water, where he died.' Then again, there were the Mohocks, a society of gentlemen 'whose members were dedicated to the ambition of "doing all manner of hurt to their fellow creatures" ... They employed their ample leisure in forcing prostitutes and old women to stand on their heads in tar barrels so that they could prick their legs with their swords; or in making them jump up and down to avoid the swinging blades; in disfiguring their victims by boring out their eyes or flattening their noses; in waylaying servants and, as in the case of Lady Winchelsea's maid, beating them and slashing their faces.' Another society, the Bold Bucks, went in for rape; and since the age of consent was twelve, it was almost impossible to obtain a conviction for rape unless accompanied by murder or serious physical damage.

All of which should make it clear that we have no reason to sigh with nostalgia for the 'good old days' so artfully recreated in the film of *Tom Jones* and the novel *Fanny Hill*. It wasn't all gleeful fornication and hard drinking. If you were addicted to either, you were likely to die of alcohol poisoning or the pox before the age of twenty. Even the incorrigible James Boswell could show a solid good sense in such matters, as we learn from his *London Journal*:

I picked up a girl in the Strand; went into a court with intention to enjoy her in armour [i.e. a contraceptive]. But she had none. I toyed with her. She wondered at my size, and said if ever I took a girl's maidenhead, I would make her squeak. I gave her a shilling and had command of myself to go without touching her. [Sensible Boswell.]

This was Defoe's world, that he was later to create so vividly in *Moll Flanders* and *Colonel Jack*, his two best novels.

But before he became a novelist, Defoe served a long apprenticeship as a journalist and writer of pamphlets. Defoe wasted most of his life in barren controversies on religion and politics – controversies that have no interest for our age. He was born into a family of Dissenters – that is, people who did not agree either with the Protestants or Roman Catholics. He began his literary career by writing a pamphlet about Dissenters, which angered his fellow Dissenters by declaring that he didn't want the Turks to capture Vienna, even if most of the Viennese *were* Catholics. For most of his life, Defoe was to remain a Dissenter and to enrage his fellow Dissenters by disagreeing with most of their basic ideas.

In those days, if you had something controversial to say, you published a pamphlet and hawked it around the London booksellers yourself. There were no large daily newspapers to pay you for saying it. So there wasn't much money in pamphleteering. Defoe enjoyed writing, but since there was no one to pay him for it, he had to launch into business, trading in textiles with Spain and France. He also took the precaution of marrying an heiress, with whom he collected a dowry of £3,700 – a vast fortune for those days. He married when he was twenty-four, and for the next eight years, business prospered. Then he went suddenly bankrupt, and fled from his creditors. But luckily, William of Orange was now on the throne of England, having thrown out the Catholic James the Second in 1688. 'Dutch Billy' was not a popular king; he was a lonely, introverted man who was generally disliked. The poet Dryden was offered a large sum of money to dedicate his translation of Virgil's *Aeneid* to the king, but he turned down the offer and published it without a dedication. But Defoe, the great opportunist, saw his chance. He leapt in and proceeded to write pamphlets in defence of Dutch Billy, with the consequence that he managed to land a soft government job – Accountant to the Commissioners of Glass Duty – which he held until it was

abolished in 1699. He even, according to his own account, became
a close friend and trusted confidant of Dutch Billy. (But we can
never trust anything Defoe says; he is the prince of liars.) It was in
Dutch Billy's defence that he scored his first notable literary
success, the long poem called *The True Born Englishman* (1701),
which begins with the delightful lines:

> Wherever God erects a house of prayer,
> The devil always builds a chapel there:
> And 'twill be found upon examination,
> The latter has the largest congregation.

With this poem, Defoe could also claim to have started the
English tradition of angry young men who make a living abusing
the English. The point of his poem was that it is unfair to abuse
Dutch Billy for being a foreigner, because *all* Englishmen are
foreigners – Vikings, Normans, Picts and Scots – and England is
the sink and the lavatory of Europe. But Englishmen apparently
enjoyed being called 'offal outcasts', and the poem was a huge
success.

But a year later, Dutch Billy died, and in no time at all, Defoe
found himself in hot water. As I have already remarked, the times
devoted much energy to religious bickering – most of it on such a
stupid and finicky level of dogma that we can hardly understand it
today. The problem of 'dissenters' caused as much trouble as, let
us say, the problem of apartheid in modern South Africa, or the
Negroes in the United States. There was a group of extreme
reactionaries who secretly felt that all dissenters ought to be
suppressed with fire and sword. But most people were more
reasonable. They even allowed dissenters to take public office,
provided they were willing to relax their principles to the extent
of attending an occasional Church of England service. But after
the death of Dutch Billy, the reactionaries began to growl again –
they were known as 'high fliers' because they were so rigid about
their principles – and to demand that dissenters should be banned
from public office (rather as communists are at present banned
from taking public office in England and America). Oddly
enough, Defoe agreed with the high fliers; he thought that the
kind of dissenters who were willing to compromise by attending
C of E services were a poor lot anyway, and deserved whatever

they got. Then he really overturned the apple cart by writing a pamphlet called *The Shortest Way with Dissenters*, in which he ironically suggested that all dissenters should be banished or hanged. He was guying the reactionary case by taking it to an extreme. But the result was more or less what would happen if some American liberal wrote a book arguing that all Negroes should be sent back to Africa, and the ones who refuse to go should be burnt alive, and then signed it 'Barry Goldwater'. The London mobs enjoyed it; they always enjoyed a first-class row and didn't much care who caused it. Many of the 'high fliers' were taken in, and greeted it with enthusiasm. (One clergyman said he valued it above all books except the Bible, and that he prayed that Queen Anne would carry out its suggestions.) The dissenters themselves were at first terrified – they had visions of being burned at the stake. Then, when it leaked out that it was one of Defoe's hard-hitting jokes, everyone was furious. Parliament issued a warrant for Defoe's arrest, on a charge of libelling the high fliers by making them out to be bloodthirsty maniacs. Defoe went into hiding and tried to apologise, but it was no good. He had to give himself up. In July 1703, he was sentenced to stand in the pillory for three days, and to be detained 'during the queen's pleasure'.

It was the best thing that could have happened to him. Overnight, he became a popular hero. It was the making of him. The crowd who usually gathered to jeer and throw rotten eggs shouted 'Good old Dan' and threw bunches of flowers. There was to be nothing quite like it for another fifty years, when John Wilkes found himself a popular hero through a similar accident.

Even more important, Defoe was then confined in Newgate for a year, and spent his time mixing with pickpockets, prostitutes and footpads. He made excellent use of his time, and the result can be seen in *Moll Flanders*, *Captain Singleton* and *Colonel Jack*. It was Newgate that turned Defoe into a novelist.

Things were going better than he realised. Admittedly, his imprisonment ruined his business – he owned a brick factory at Tilbury – but then, there are those who say that the brick factory was on the point of bankruptcy anyway because Tilbury has no decent clay. He was a national hero and martyr. And his influence was now so great that the government did not dare to silence him, and he continued to write books and pamphlets in jail at a greater pace than ever. He even started his first newspaper in jail. It was called *The Review*, and it was not a newspaper in our modern sense. It was more of an eight-page magazine, entirely written by Defoe, with gossip column on current scandals, lively interviews with thieves and murderers, and lots of political commentary. With his reputation, it could not fail to be a success, even if he'd been a bad writer. And he wasn't. He was a first-rate writer, one of the most brilliant controversialists that England has ever produced, with the exceptions of Swift and Shaw. It is a pity that most of his controversial writings are now quite meaningless to us; they were essentially day-to-day journalism.

I should mention that the *Shortest Way with Dissenters* affair gave us the only physical description we have of Defoe. (It must be remembered that nobody thought of Defoe as a great writer; he was generally rated a pretty low journalist, and none of his contemporaries thought it worth while writing about him.) 'A middle-sized spare man about forty years old, of a brown complexion and dark brown coloured hair, but wears a wig; a hooked nose, a sharp chin, grey eyes and a large mole near the mouth.' He was also, apparently, less than five feet tall. This is from the 'wanted' notice.

For the remaining twenty-five years of his life, Defoe was famous, or at least notorious. But the rest of his career is not particularly edifying. In his *Review*, he struck his pose of 'honest Dan Defoe' and never ceased to assault his opponents and praise himself. He professed to be a Whig, but when the Whig government collapsed in 1710, he succeeded in publicly changing sides and becoming a Tory supporter, all the time yelling that he was Honest Dan Defoe, and daring his opponents to prove that he was being inconsistent. He managed this difficult trick by declaring that he cared for his country more than party principles – 'We must all sink or swim together'; meanwhile he sneaked off to the government with his cap in his hand, trying to obtain some 'connection'. He was a useful ally, so his affairs continued to prosper. Things became slightly embarrassing a few years later, when Queen Anne died, and the Whigs came back into power. But again Defoe managed to brave the storm with loud shouts of 'honest Dan Defoe'. And this time he managed to save his neck by becoming a kind of government spy. The Whigs forgave him, but they decided that it would be useful it everyone assumed that Defoe was still in disgrace. A spy in the enemy camp was just what they needed. But in this case, the enemy was not the Tories, but the Jacobites – the supporters of the house of Stuart. An innocent gentleman called Mr Mist ran a Jacobite paper, *Mist's Journal*. Defoe became his assistant. He was a first-class journalist, and Mist had no reason to complain about circulation. But he also made sure that nothing offensive to the government got into the paper, and the government was kept closely informed about Jacobite conspiracies. (It was to be another twenty-five years before Bonnie Prince Charlie made his unsuccessful attempt to restore the house of Stuart.) Poor Mist was Defoe's dupe for eight years. Then he found out, and tried to knock Defoe down. Defoe, as usual, set up a loud screech of 'honest Dan Defoe', and wailed about ingratitude. But Mist was sick of being a dupe. He went around and told everybody what a sneak and turncoat Defoe was. Everyone had known this for years, but they had not realised he was quite such a scoundrel. The consequence was that Defoe's credit began to collapse. It was the beginning of the end for him. He was sixty-three, and had seven more years to live. He had a large country house and ran a coach. But he was always a spendthrift, and debts began to engulf him. Newspaper editors would no longer accept his articles. (Newspapers had begun to flourish by this time – partly thanks to Defoe.) It was a blow to his pride more than his pocket – but the life of a day-to-day journalist was beginning to tell on him anyway, and the old energy was flagging.

And yet it was this tired, much-abused Defoe who now produced the novels that have made him a classic.

First came *Robinson Crusoe*, published in 1720, while he was still working with Mist. It should have made him a millionaire – or at least, comfortably off for the rest of his life, for it was a tremendous success. Nothing like it had ever been known before. There had been no English novels up till then, unless you count *The Pilgrim's Progress*. It immediately went into half a dozen languages and sold thousands of copies. Unfortunately, Defoe received very little from all this, as most of the editions of the book were pirated.

The plot of his most famous book was not original: it was based on the story of a ruffianly pirate named Alexander Selkirk, a somewhat unlikeable character. (On one occasion, Selkirk beat up his mother and father.) Selkirk had quarrelled with the captain of his pirate ship and told him furiously that he would stay behind on the island of Juan Fernandez; he soon found the solitude more than he had bargained for, but became so fleet of foot that he was able to catch goats by outrunning them. When he was finally picked up and returned to London, he became something of a celebrity. Defoe actually travelled all the way to Bristol simply to interview him, and bought his 'papers' for some fairly low sum.

It is worth mentioning this because it demonstrates that Defoe was no inventor. He could not create a story out of his imagination. Twenty or thirty years ago, Defoe suddenly became fashionable – after two centuries of neglect – because of the 'realism' of his narratives, and critics seemed to regard him as a kind of seventeenth-century Hemingway or Steinbeck. But the truth is that Defoe is realistic because he is a journalist with very little imagination. It is true that his work is refreshingly straightforward, particularly if you have had an overdose of great American epics like *Gone with the Wind*. But this is not because Defoe is obsessed by a need to tell the truth, like the Hemingway of *A Farewell to Arms*. It is because he has stolen most of his material from contemporary books of travel and memoirs. Defoe's story *The Apparition of Mrs Veal* was for years cited by critics as the ideal of what a ghost story should be – plain, realistic, convincing – until someone discovered that it wasn't fiction at all, but a rehashed account of a story that had already appeared in newspapers. In the same way, if you really want to compare the difference between journalism and the imagination, read Defoe's *Colonel Jack* and then Dumas's *Three Musketeers* – and then turn to Courtilz de Sandras's *Memoirs of D'Artagnan* and *Memoirs of the Count de Rochefort* – from which both Defoe and Dumas stole liberally. Dumas has stolen and transformed; Defoe has merely stolen.

It is certainly its journalistic realism that makes *Moll Flanders* attractive to the modern reader. Its full title also gives a fair outline of its plot: *The Fortunes and Misfortunes of the famous Moll*

Flanders, who was born in Newgate, and during a life of continued variety, for threescore years, besides her childhood, was twelve years a Whore five times a Wife (whereof once to her own brother), twelve years a Thief, eight years a transported Felon in Virginia, at last grew rich, lived honest, and died a Penitent. Written from her own Memorandums.

The real name of Moll Flanders was Moll King, and she was a pickpocket whom Defoe had interviewed in Newgate. Defoe published many interviews with criminals in his *Review*, and later, in *Mist's Journal*, he wrote at length about Moll King. It is a careless, breezy, shapeless kind of novel that shows Defoe at his best. In places, you suspect that he has done little more than transcribe the words of Moll King:

> Going through Aldersgate Street, there was a pretty little child had been at a dancing-school, and was going home all alone; and my prompter, like a true devil, set me upon this innocent creature. I talked to it, and it prattled to me again, and I took it by the hand and led it along till I came to a paved alley that leads into Bartholomew Close, and I led it in there. The child said, that was not its way home. I said, 'Yes, my dear, it is; I'll show you the way home'. The child had a little necklace on of gold beads, and I had my eye upon that, and in the dark of the alley I stooped, pretending to mend the child's clog that was loose, and took off her necklace, and the child never felt it, and so led the child on again. Here, I say, the devil put me upon killing the child in the dark alley, that it might not cry, but the very thought frighted me so that I was ready to drop down; but I turned the child about and bade it go back again, for that was not its way home; the child said, so she would. . . . The last affair left no great concern upon me, for as I did the poor child no harm, I only thought I had given the parents a just reproof for their negligence, in leaving the poor lamb to come home by itself, and it would teach them to take more care another time.

This is a beautiful piece of psychology – the final words about teaching the parents not to let the 'poor lamb' come home alone, after the confession that she thought of murdering the child. But you get a glimpse of Defoe's cloven hoof when he writes primly about 'my prompter, like a true devil'. He always puts in some of this stuff about the devil and true repentance, by way of keeping his pious readers happy. And you only have to read twenty pages of any of his novels to realise what a lying old scoundrel he was. He writes these novels about pirates and criminals for exactly the same reason that certain Sunday newspapers specialise in scandal and murder – because people have a gloating interest in the subject. His motto was 'The customer is always right' – give the public what it wants. This is why he is no great writer. He has no vision of his own, and his books have no centre of gravity; they are collections of anecdotes. There are long sustained passages of first-rate writing – like Captain Singleton's voyage across Africa – but upon investigation we usually discover that these have been lifted from other people's books. Defoe was a crook, and he took a delight in writing about crooks. If he had had the courage of the Marquis de Sade, he would have made it quite clear that he was an anarchist who enjoyed crime for its own sake. You can always tell when he is being honest, and when he is putting on his 'honest Dan Defoe' act. When he tells how Moll and Jemmy the highwayman tricked one another into marriage by each pretending to be wealthy, you can almost hear him chortling and rubbing his hands. On the other hand, when she later describes how Jemmy became 'as sincere a penitent, and as thoroughly a reformed man as ever God's goodness brought back from being a profligate', you become aware of Tartuffe Defoe wearing his slimiest look of piety. (Especially when you learn that this change of character is brought about by the sudden acquisition of a large plantation: 'reformation by cows and hogs' as one critic calls it.)

No, Defoe was a miserable old rogue, and as nasty a piece of work as journalism has ever produced – in spite of heavy competition. Two centuries later he would have made the ideal henchman for William Randolph Hearst or Alfred Harmsworth. Still, a writer doesn't have to be a man of genius to deserve survival; in fact, it is often a disadvantage. Who nowadays reads Carlyle or Ruskin – both men who were bursting with genius? On the other hand, our greatest classic of autobiography is written by James Boswell, a man without a single idea between his two ears – and one of the most irritating weaklings of the eighteenth century. Defoe is not a great writer, but he is a great reporter. Take him for what he is worth, and you will find him an excellent companion on a long train journey.

1965

TEN

A personal response to *Wuthering Heights*

In 1900, George Smith, of the firm of Smith Elder, published in the *Cornhill Magazine* his own account of the discovery of *Jane Eyre*, and of the subsequent visit to London of the two sisters 'Ellis and Currer Bell'. It might have been written with one eye on Hollywood. 'After breakfast on Sunday morning I took the MS. of *Jane Eyre* to my little study and began to read it. The story quickly took me captive. Before twelve o'clock my horse came to the door, but I could not put the book down. I scribbled two or three lines to my friend, saying I was very sorry that circumstances had arisen to prevent my meeting him, sent the note off by my groom, and went on reading the MS. Presently the servant came to tell me that luncheon was ready; I asked him to bring me a sandwich and a glass of wine, and still went on with *Jane Eyre*. Dinner came; for me the meal was a very hasty one, and before I went to bed that night I had finished reading the manuscript.' Which, in the best Hollywood tradition, went on to become a best seller. Then came the Saturday morning when Mr Smith was told that two ladies wished to see him and declined to give their names. 'Two rather quaintly dressed little ladies, pale-faced and anxious-looking walked into the room,' and one of them presented him with his own recent letter to 'Currer Bell'. He asked sharply how she came by a private letter to one of his authors; to which, of course, she replied that *she* was 'Currer Bell Esq'. Astonishment, excitement, invitations to dinner and the theatre . . . to all of which the little ladies responded with embarrassment and alarm.

And our chief regret, of course, is that it was Anne, and not Emily who accompanied Charlotte to London. (She was presumably too ill to travel.) That 'mysterious genius', who has inspired such extravagant cults since her death, is as much a mystery now as she was a century ago. George Smith could scarcely have described her as a 'little' lady; she was taller than her sisters. Branwell's paintings of her seem to suggest that she was the best-looking of the three – almost pretty in her mild, introspective way. Smith said of Anne's manner that it was 'curiously expressive of a wish for protection and encouragement'. It is doubtful whether he could have said the same of Emily; she emerges from Charlotte's descriptions as stubborn, determined and rather formidable. But unfortunately, that is about all we *do* know of Emily. As Margaret Lane remarks: 'The experiences which formed her unique personality are out of our reach; we can never know what they were, or what it was that so early turned her imagination inwards and caused her to refuse the ordinary demands of life'. A comment I shall presently dispute.

When I recently read *Wuthering Heights* for the third time, it was mainly with the intention of noting Emily's use of 'the occult'. And certainly, it could be argued that the supernatural element is vital to the book's total effect. What would it be, without those closing pages about the ghosts who walk the moor, and can be seen from the chamber window on rainy nights? The only comparable effect I can call to mind is the appearance of the ghosts of Rafi and Pirvaneh in the last pages of Flecker's *Hassan*. 'This music is successful with a dying fall', Eliot remarks, 'now that we talk of dying. . . .' Yet my final impression – and it is only an impression – is that Emily did not believe in ghosts. She made use of them, in her strange, detached way; but the intellect remained cool and sceptical. She would have regarded belief in ghosts as some kind of excuse for self-pity. And one of the most salient features of her character is her rejection of self-pity. It was her almost morbid loathing of self-pity that made her decline to see a doctor when she was dying.

Yes, one speculates what would have happened if it had been *Wuthering Heights* that absorbed George Smith from breakfast to bedtime, and that had become the success of the London season. . . . But then, it wouldn't have been. As Mrs Gaskell remarks, *Wuthering Heights* 'revolted many readers by the power with which wicked and exceptional characters are depicted', and one old schoolfriend who read *Jane Eyre*, *Agnes Grey* and *Wuthering Heights* one after the other concluded that the latter had been written to deliberately shock a certain class of reader. The critics found it a nasty, repellent book, and many of them thought it to be piece of juvenilia by the author of *Jane Eyre*. And we, of course, condemn the critics as idiots who couldn't recognise a work of genius when it stared them in the face. Or make patronising remarks about change of taste, implying that no modern reader could be so obtuse.

And yet I have to admit that, as I re-read the book a few weeks ago, I found myself sympathising with those critics. And it struck me as a matter of some interest to realise how much my attitude had changed over the years since I first read it. That was some time during the war, and I must have been about twelve. My mother was reading it, in that poky little Reader's Library edition, with its tiny print on cheap paper – I think she had seen the film with Olivier – and she told me the plot as she went along. I remember being rather shaken by the cruelty of the scene in which Lockwood sees the ghost of Cathy, and rubs her wrist against the broken glass to force her to let go of his hand. My mother found the whole thing totally absorbing, and I think I can understand why. She often said that she liked books about 'real life'; in practice, this meant books with a fair quantity of unhappiness; *Sons and Lovers* and Cronin's *Hatter's Castle* came high on her list. Life in a provincial town can be dull for a working class housewife with three children, particularly when food and clothes and coal are rationed. But at least we weren't as poor as the Morells; and if my father was bad tempered, he was never as tyrannical as Cronin's Mr Brodie. Reading these books made her feel life wasn't so bad after all. As to *Wuthering Heights*, I doubt whether the romantic interest held her as much as the general bleakness and emotional harshness.

I read through most of the book, although I found it hard going. It struck me as cruel and frightening and wholly real. A few years later, when I was about seventeen, I bought the World Classic edition and read it again. At this time I was reading *Paradise Lost*, and I could appreciate Heathcliff as a sort of Lucifer figure. The complicated family relationships no longer bewildered me. And the last pages, with the quiet graves blowing in the wind, produced 'an effect like music', so that it suddenly seemed to me one of the most tremendous novels ever written. And this was how I remembered it for some three decades.

In between 1948 and 1975, I have written a dozen novels myself, which at least places me in a good position to appreciate literary skill. When I came back to *Wuthering Heights*, the first thing that struck me was the technical achievement. It seems astonishing that a young girl brought up on the novels of Scott and the epic poems of Southey should write with this kind of economy and terseness:

> We came to the chapel. I have passed it really in my walks, twice or thrice; it lies in a hollow, between two hills – an elevated hollow, near a swamp, whose peaty moisture is said to answer all the purposes of embalming on the few corpses deposited there (III, 28).

Here even the punctuation, the semi-colon and the dash, give the impression that she knows exactly where she is going and what she means to say. And although she is never 'clever', there is an epigrammatic quality worthy of Jane Austen: of the detestable Joseph: 'He was, and is yet, most likely, the wearisomest, self-righteous pharisee that ever ransacked a Bible to take the promises to himself, and fling the curses on his neighbours' (V, 42).

But from the technical point of view, perhaps the most impressive thing about it is the way she has somehow brought a credibility to a narrative method that sounds – in theory – hopelessly implausible. We are asked to believe that Nelly Dean can remember long conversations word for word – including the expressions on everybody's faces – and repeat speeches that sometimes last for a page and a half. We are also asked to believe that the narrator Lockwood recalls every word of Nelly's story. A more accomplished novelist would have used the device of letters and manuscripts found in drawers – and spoiled the whole effect. For in fact, it is not at all difficult to believe that a gossipy and lonely old servant *would* enjoy dwelling on the past and embellish her memories with all kinds of invented detail. And once Lockwood has also become established as a kind of irritating busybody, like one of those tirelessly curious narrators in Henry James, you find it easy enough to believe that he would add his own embellishments when re-creating Nelly's monologue. The nett result is that the authoress manages to side-step the blame for the implausibilities – which is essential if the reader is to place himself entirely in her hands. All this seems to have been accomplished by a combination of luck and literary instinct – although, since *Wuthering Heights* was her only novel, it seems probable that instinct played the smaller part. I think that most writers are inclined to believe that some god of literature occasionally makes a direct intervention, using the author as a mere amanuensis; *Wuthering Heights* seems to be a plausible example.

Having said which, I must state that I did not enjoy my third reading of *Wuthering Heights*. Like its original critics, I found it repellent, morbid and rather sadistic. The first fit of revulsion came in the scene where Heathcliff throws the tureen of hot apple sauce in Edgar's face. A page later, Heathcliff tells Nelly he is trying to decide how to pay back Hindley for the beating: 'I don't care how long I wait. I hope he will not die before I do!' And when Nelly points out that punishment is God's business, he answers: 'No, God won't have the satisfaction that I shall . . . while I'm thinking of that, I don't feel pain' (VII, 57). And suddenly you are back in an older and crueller world, where tyrants have men skinned alive, or force them to eat the hearts of their own children. It would be melodramatic to call it a breath of hell. It is a breath of sheer stupidity and childishness. Joyce Cary's Gulley Jimson remarked that no one ever really gets his own back, because when you get it, it's not yours any more; it's moved on. It seems odd that Emily Brontë, with all her intelligence and sensitivity, never found this out. For there can be no doubt whatsoever that the basic emotion underlying her novel is a kind of vengefulness. 'Life being what it is, one dreams of revenge,' said Gauguin – a remark that Graham Greene has often quoted with approval. It is the kind of sentiment you might expect from a painter of genius whose work is ignored, or from a novelist obsessed by Original Sin. But it is unusual to find it pervading the work of a young girl who has spent most of her life as a member of an affectionate and closely-knit family. One feels like paraphrasing Gosse's remark about Thomas Hardy, and asking what Providence has done to Emily Brontë that she should shake her fist so furiously in its face?

It is, of course, always dangerous to assume that a writer is expressing his, or her, convictions through the mouths of the characters. But in the case of *Wuthering Heights*, I would have thought there was little room for doubt. Heathcliff may be 'black browed' and insulting, but it is fairly clear that Emily Brontë admires him. He is her equivalent of Byron's Childe Harold or Manfred. Lockwood is a fop who treats seduction as a game; Heathcliff is a 'real man', rough, strong, brutal – but honest, and totally unswerving in his affections, a 'true heart', as the Victorians put it.

Yet when one looks at him objectively, declining to accept him at Emily's evaluation, he is pathetically stupid. Anyone can daydream of sweet revenge; if daydreams could kill, most traffic wardens would die fifty times a day. But what kind of a man would actually go to such dreary and nasty lengths to soothe his wounded ego? Victorian alienists sometimes used the phrase 'morally insane', and there is no better instance in literature than Heathcliff. To deliberately ruin Hindley is perhaps comprehensible; Hindley is male, and a childhood rival. But Isabella Linton is neither. There is more than a touch of De Sade in the elopement scene, where Heathcliff hangs her dog.

Yet Emily Brontë obviously continues to find him rather magnificent. She makes no attempt to 'cover up' his nastiness. And this in itself is curious. Byron announces that Childe Harold is weighted down by his sins, but you never actually *see* him doing anything that would shock you. On the contrary, he remains consistently pale and sensitive and noble. This is even true of Dostoievsky's Byronic villain Stavrogin in *The Devils*; in the suppressed chapter we see him sexually assaulting a ten year old girl (although apparently with her co-operation) and stealing money from a poverty-stricken clerk; but Dostoievsky leaves us in no doubt that these actions are a cry of desperation, a frantic groping after meaning. Heathcliff is driven by sheer childishness, and his actions have the predictable effect of ruining his life and everyone else's. He spends two hundred and fifty pages cutting off his nose to spite his face.

My capacity for gloating on self-inflicted torture is limited. After the dog-hanging scene, I gave it up, and turned to Daphne du Maurier's book about Branwell. That raised the interesting possibility that *Wuthering Heights* might have been a collaboration between Branwell and Emily. Which would certainly go far towards solving some of the mysteries. *Wuthering Heights* is a half-masculine, half-feminine book. In most novels written by males, you can sense the writer's attraction to the heroine; in novels written by women, the hero exudes more than his fair share of maleness. In *Wuthering Heights*, the author seems to be equally attracted to Cathy and Heathcliff. On the other hand, there is absolutely no evidence that Branwell had a hand in the book – even in its planning. And the few things we know about Emily suggest that she had a touch of masculinity in her character. When her father asked her what he ought to do with Branwell when he was naughty, she answered: 'Reason with him, and when he won't listen to reason, whip him.' Charlotte's friend Ellen Nussey described Emily, 'half reclining on a slab of stone', and how she 'played . . . with the tadpoles in the water, making them swim about, and then fell to moralising on the strong and the weak, the brave and the cowardly, as she chased them with her hand. . . .' Am I, perhaps, allowing my imagination to run away with me in supplying a Nietzschean discourse on survival of the fittest? Perhaps Nietzschean is the wrong word in this context, for it evokes images of the superman. But the young Nietzsche was very much a stoic; he once set a pile of matches alight on his hand to prove he could bear pain like Mucius Scaevola. *He* could well have written a poem beginning: 'No coward soul is mine.' (Neither do I find it difficult to imagine Heathcliff uttering the famous sentiment: 'Are you going to woman? Don't forget your whip.') There *is* a Nietzschean touch in Emily.

And when I finally turned back to *Wuthering Heights*, armed with a bundle of theories and speculations gleaned from Daphne du Maurier, Margaret Lane and Mrs Gaskell, I found the moral revulsion had vanished, pushed aside by the purely psychological interest of the problem presented by Emily's creative drive. It is not, I think, a question of 'the experiences that formed her unique personality' – in Margaret Lane's phrase – so much as the personality itself. There is one very obvious difference between *Wuthering Heights*, *Jane Eyre* and *The Tenant of Wildfell Hall*. In the novels of Anne and Charlotte, there is the predictable element of wish-fulfilment that you might expect in novels by intelligent but inexperienced young ladies. You could go on to draw interesting parallels with the novels of Jane Austen or Daphne du Maurier. Modest and sensitive young girl meets dominant male; after two hundred pages of complications, they are united and live happily ever after. . . . But Emily is not one to daydream by the open window. She knows the kind of man she would find physically attractive, and he is not necessarily the romantic lover. And, for some reason, her fantasies are filled with resentment: 'Life being what it is, one dreams of revenge.'

In a book about the American psychologist Abraham Maslow, I mentioned his researches into the question of dominance in women. After several years of study, Maslow came to the conclusion that women – and men too – fell into three clear groups, which he labelled high dominance, medium dominance and low dominance. High dominance women were an extremely small percentage. Sexually speaking, they were inclined to promiscuity and experimentalism; many of them had tried Lesbian experiences. They liked dominant males – unsentimental men who would make love violently. Medium dominance women were 'romantics', inclined to settle with one man, although they might experiment under propitious circumstances. They liked the kind of male who would bring them bunches of flowers and take them to restaurants with soft lights. Low dominance women were scared of men in general; they thought sex was rather nasty, strictly for the purpose of producing children; they liked the kind of man who would admire them from a distance for years without daring to make an advance. All women, in all the dominance groups, preferred the male to be slightly more dominant than themselves, but not too much so. Medium dominance women were scared stiff of the kind of male who appealed to high dominance women.

I apologise for dragging in the subject of experimental psychology, and promise that I do not intend to try to explain Emily in terms of her sexual inhibitions or repressed guilt feelings. Maslow's findings strike me as basically sound, and my own observation seems to confirm them. On the basis of their novels, it is fairly clear that Emily was high dominance, Charlotte medium-to-high, and Anne medium-to-low. And so, as you would expect, the hero of *Wuthering Heights* is a brutal roughneck; of *Jane Eyre*, a gloomy, temperamental man who actually turns out to be a faithful lover and ideal husband; of *The Tenant of Wildfell Hall* and *Agnes Grey*, a fairly conventional suitor with no obvious drawbacks. (Margaret Lane speculates that the hero of *Agnes Grey* was based on Patrick Brontë's kindly curate, William Weightman.)

A common theme of the three major novels is the ill-treatment of the heroine; but here the first major difference emerges. Helen Huntingdon, the tenant of Wildfell Hall, is treated with indifference by her drunken husband; Jane Eyre is bullied by everybody; Catherine Earnshaw is bullied by Joseph and Hindley. But on the whole, Cathy emerges unscathed; she is definitely an 'alpha' (the term Maslow often used for highly dominant individuals). It is Heathcliff who takes the real brunt of the cruelty in *Wuthering Heights*, and who repays it all with interest. Unlike her sisters, Emily had little self-pity in her nature, and what there was she firmly suppressed. Jane Eyre overcomes the injustice of fate with her gentleness; Emily's male alter-ego fights back murderously, and drinks his revenge to the last drop. This also means that Emily can shift the blame for the moral stupidity involved. She was too bright not to know that Heathcliff's whole outlook is self-destructive, and that a world full of Heathcliffs would be a nightmarish place. But since the authoress of a novel is expected to identify with the heroine, that is hardly her affair. . . .

'Her view of mankind was, for some reason that we shall never know, profoundly pessimistic,' says Margaret Lane; and again, it seems to me that Maslow can answer the implied question. Maslow rejected the notion that human beings are driven by purely biological or sexual – or even personal – drives. Of course, these drives are among the basic motivations of all human beings. If you are born in a poor country where you suffer permanent malnutrition, the craving for food will remain a basic pre-occupation – until it is satisfied. This is, of course, a simple 'deficiency need'. If such a child were asked to write a school essay, it would almost certainly be about food. And – to extend the speculation – if an intelligent adolescent in such a situation took it into his head to write novels, their ultimate 'value' would be food. The hero would live happily ever after in a land where sausage rolls grow on trees and the rivers flow with double cream. But readers who had never known hunger would find it curiously pointless; and they would be right. Our novelist himself would change his point of view if the book brought him enough money to get used to eating in good restaurants.

There is obviously a level at which the desire for sex and love, for security – a roof over one's head – or for the respect and admiration of one's neighbours, can all be deficiency needs that motivate a human being to the exclusion of everything else. But on the whole, we are inclined to agree that such deficiency needs should *not* play a central role in a work of art – for example, a novel. The artist should attempt to *transcend* the need and move towards some wider horizon. *Romeo and Juliet* and the latest trashy romantic novel are 'about' the same deficiency need; but Shakespeare's play is about so much more. According to Maslow, the basic human desire is not merely to satisfy needs, but to transcend them, to move beyond the personal towards the impersonal. The craving for beauty, harmony, goodness, knowledge, is just as 'basic' as the need for food or sex; but it cannot operate freely until the need for food or sex has ceased to be a deficiency need.

Towards the end of his life, Maslow had to acknowledge sadly that his picture of a 'hierarchy of needs' was not as universal as he had at first assumed. Some people satisfy the need for security, sex and self-esteem, and then stop short. There seems to be no evidence whatever of a need for beauty, harmony, knowledge. Conversely, in other people, the need for beauty, harmony and knowledge is so powerful that it can override the need for sex or security, or even food. He never had time to explore these inconsistencies. But one might have thought that they are not too difficult to understand. Surely dominance fits into the picture somewhere? I do not know whether the kind of people who 'stop short' are non-dominant. But I *am* reasonably certain that the kind of person who grinds on, refusing to be deflected by deficiency needs – even trampling them underfoot – is highly dominant. In short, when you combine 'self-actualisation' with a high degree of dominance, you have a dangerously explosive mixture. Such a person is violently impatient of his 'deficiency needs' and human frailties. In the Middle Ages, he might have become a monk and gone in for self-flagellation. In the nineteenth century, with no obvious role to play in a materialistic civilisation, he became an 'outsider', a misfit who detested society and probably detested himself. Most of the great tragic artists of the nineteenth century, from Coleridge and Schiller to Nietzsche and Rimbaud, were dominant and frustrated self-actualisers. For Emily Brontë the problem was further complicated by the fact that she possessed a female body.

But in speaking of Emily Brontë, there is another important factor to take into account. The year 1740 was a turning point in the history of civilisation; it was in that year that the first volume of Samuel Richardson's *Pamela* appeared. There *had* been novels before *Pamela*, including *Don Quixote* and *Robinson Crusoe*; but they were mainly about *events*, about 'things happening'. In *Pamela*, nearly everything that happens takes place *inside* the heroine. The plot is slight: a rich landowner tries to seduce a virtuous servant girl and ends by marrying her. But Richardson's contemporaries discovered that they could be absorbed by Pamela's thoughts and feelings in a way they had never been absorbed by the adventures of Moll Flanders or Gil Blas. In short, they could 'identify'. It was a kind of do-it-yourself play, in which the reader became the chief actor.

I would contend that the change that took place as a result of *Pamela* was wider and deeper than historians have realised. European man – and woman – learnt the use of imagination. They learned how to forget their own lives, to enter an imaginary world and stay there for hours.

To grasp the magnitude of the change, we have to imagine that contemporary scientists stumble upon some new variety of plant that can grow under any conditions, and that can provide unlimited quantities of highly nutritious food to the world's starving millions. This is a precise parallel; for before Richardson, imaginative people had to make do with gossip, sermons, broadsheets about crime, and an occasional visit to the theatre. (This explains the central role of the preacher in the age of Dr Johnson; for millions of people, the Sunday morning sermon was their only 'escape' from material reality.) The novel provided easy, cheap and nutritious food for the imagination. You could commit adultery with Rousseau, die of unrequited passion with young Werther, explore Hell with 'Monk' Lewis, visit the past in Scott's time machine. . . .

If Emily Brontë had been born in 1718 instead of 1818, the outward circumstances of her life might have been much the same

– the lot of the country parson remained fairly constant over the centuries. But she would probably have remained as emotionally undeveloped as Richardson's Pamela. As it was, she absorbed Scott, Byron, Wordsworth, Southey, and probably Rousseau, Mrs Radcliffe, Maria Edgeworth, Jane Porter and Charles Maturin. From *Wuthering Heights*, it is clear that her imagination was drawn to ghosts, goblins and horrors. (The editor of my acquaintance was kind enough to send me a list of references to the supernatural in *Wuthering Heights*; it ran to sixteen typed pages, with an average of a dozen references per page.) By the 1820s, there were hundreds of Gothic romances – from Walpole's *Castle of Otranto* to Maturin's *Melmoth the Wanderer* – that would have been easily available, even to the daughter of a Yorkshire parson.

A propos this taste in horrors, I am indebted to Mr Patric Dickinson for pointing out to me the following quotation from Baudelaire: 'As for the ardour with which Poe often treats horrifying material, I have observed in a number of men that this was often the result of a large fund of unused vital energy, sometimes the result of an unyielding chastity and of vital feelings kept repressed.' In short, of frustrated vitality and sexual frustration. I have argued the view at some length in *The Strength to Dream* (1962), citing 'Monk' Lewis, Hoffmann, Poe, Gogol, Le Fanu, M.R. James and others. This seems to me to explain Emily Brontë's Poe-like absorption in death and corruption. If Maslow is correct about dominant women, then Emily's interest in Byronic males was not purely emotional and romantic; she herself probably recognised a strong physical component – and was shocked by it. (Half a century later, we can recognise this same almost demonic chastity in Nietzsche.) Is this not the explanation of the curiously chaste relations between Cathy and Heathcliff? Unlike most young lovers, they do not kiss and hold hands. In actuality, a couple like Cathy and Heathcliff *would* have become lovers – even in 1830. Emily Brontë does not even hint at such a thing; one feels she would have rejected the idea with disgust. The closest they come to normal sexual contact is when Heathcliff holds her in his arms as she lies dying in bed. The novel is permeated with sexual passion. It crackles in the air like electricity. Yet the thunderstorm never breaks. Emily cannot even imagine a sexual relation between Heathcliff and Isabella without a shudder of disgust; it has to be transformed into bitterness and sadism.

There seems to be one curiously paradoxical element in Emily's character: her capacity for contentment. Ellen Nussey commented on her buoyancy and happiness as a child; and even in the last years, when she was dying, she often seemed to be the most contented member of the family. Margaret Lane sees the answer in her 'mysticism'; but I am inclined to feel that is putting the cart before the horse. All self-actualisers have what Maslow calls 'peak experiences', moments of deep contentment, a feeling of being undeservedly lucky. On a quiet evening, the frustrations suddenly die down; the soul becomes still, as if a wind has dropped; and then an enormous peace seems to spread upwards, bringing a deep inner certainty that all is well. I doubt whether it brings us any closer to the nature of such experiences to call them 'mystical'. On the contrary, it makes them sound unearthly, when in fact they are no more abnormal than a sexual orgasm or the pleasure of drinking when you are thirsty. In short, they are a perfectly natural part of the self-actualisation process. Emily writes:

> But first a hush of peace, a soundless calm descends;
> The struggle of distress and fierce impatience ends;
> Mute music soothes my breast – unuttered harmony
> That I could never dream till earth was lost to me.

This certainly *sounds* like 'mysticism', particularly when she goes on: 'Then dawns the Invisible, the unseen its truth reveals. . . .' And in the next stanza she writes:

> Oh dreadful is the check – intense the agony
> When the ear begins to hear and the eye begins to see;
> When the pulse begins to throb, the brain to think again,
> The soul to feel the flesh and the flesh to feel the chain!
>
> (Hatfield, 190)

At this point, if there was space, I could insert a lengthy comparison with T.E. Lawrence: with his hatred of his own body, his dislike of the 'thought riddled nature', his feeling that his personality was his 'gaoler', his admiration of the Arabs with their mystical love of freedom and longing for the abstract. Yet I doubt whether any reader of *Seven Pillars of Wisdom* would describe Lawrence as a mystic. Like Emily Brontë, he was a highly frustrated self-actualiser, who never succeeded in clearing away the obstacle that lay between himself and self-expression. Recent biographical researches have revealed that Lawrence was a masochist who was morbidly ashamed of his craving to be flogged by vigorous young men. This guilt presented the greatest obstacle to self-realisation. But as far as we know, Emily Brontë had no perverse desires. The sadism in *Wuthering Heights* is emotional, not physical, an inverted expression of the masochism that springs from self-disgust. Which suggests that if Emily had ever met her Heathcliff, the relationship would have been healthily sensual, and the ghosts and goblins would have ceased to haunt her imagination. (In fact, I suspect she would have found a real-life Heathcliff intolerable, although she might have been head over heels in love for a few weeks; she was too self-disciplined to approve of a man who was a slave to his emotions. I am inclined to believe that her ideal would have been closer to George Henry Lewes, the man George Eliot settled down with: intelligent, kindly, and capable of making her feel like a normal human being.)

In *The Outsider* (1956), I commented in a footnote on the relative scarcity of female 'Outsiders', particularly in fiction. Until the re-reading of *Wuthering Heights* I have recently been provoked into making, it had never struck me that Emily Brontë is an almost archetypal female outsider, and that Catherine Earnshaw represents the same thing in fiction. Catherine is not intended as an autobiographical self-portrait – or if she was, Emily's indirect method of narration made it impossible for her to realise her intention. This is a pity. In Emily Brontë, I see the fundamental drama of the dominant self-actualiser, placed in an unsympathetic environment, wracked by frustration, inclined to wonder if the fate that placed her in the world is entirely malevolent – or at least, possessed of a sardonic sense of humour. She fought with astonishing courage, and never realised how close she came to winning her battle – for I believe that if she had held out for another year or so, the tide would have turned in her favour.

Yet I have to admit that my own final judgement on *Wuthering*

Heights is that it is not a great novel. Perhaps my critical faculties are being warped by my distaste for Heathcliff; but it seems to me that *Wuthering Heights* should be classified with *Le Grand Meaulnes*, as a piece of brilliant juvenilia. Curiously haunting, perhaps, but only a rough sketch for the masterpiece that should have followed. I suspect that it is so often taken for a great novel because it makes one feel clearly that Emily Brontë could have *been* a great novelist – her powers are so obviously extraordinary. But even this could be an illusion. Great novelists – like Scott, Balzac, Dickens – are interested in people, and they have a certain attitude of indulgence towards people. Emily Brontë, like Nietzsche, found the majority of people 'all too human'. Like Nietzsche, she believed that lack of pity is a virtue. And she may not have been entirely wrong. The only trouble is that lack of pity ceases to be a useful virtue when it is directed against oneself. Particularly if it kills you off at the age of thirty.

1976

ELEVEN

George Bernard Shaw:
A personal view

In November 1919, the composer Busoni described a meeting with Shaw in a letter. 'Yesterday afternoon GBS came to tea. He talks too much and cannot cloak his vanity.' And when Busoni remarked that he would like to write music for the hell scene in *Man and Superman*, Shaw told him it wouldn't bring in any profit. 'That is not what attracts me,' said Busoni. 'Oh, but you *must* reckon with that,' said Shaw. 'Everybody has to reckon with it. Of course, I am now a famous artist' (he added half jokingly), 'and I can allow myself to ride hobby horses.' To a man who had been a world-famous pianist for more than three decades this was a singularly tactless remark.

It helps to explain why Shaw aroused such curious hostility during his lifetime – a hostility that is still remarkably widespread, considering that he has been dead for more than a quarter of a century. Edmund Wilson, a thoroughly sympathetic critic, remarked: '. . . egoism like Shaw's was a disability like any disability – which you had to carry with you all your life. When he was young, it had been amusing, he had carried it off with panache; but it had become disagreeable with his later years, and one saw then that it was compulsive, incurable.'

The interesting consequence was that most of Shaw's contemporaries regarded him as an irritating egoist who also happened to possess talent – rather, I think, as most people still feel about Salvador Dali and Cassius Clay. In the first decade of his fame – from 1905 to 1915 – the British were impressed; after that, there was a widespread feeling that he was rather a 'cad', a self-advertiser, and they did their best to show their disapproval by ignoring him. Impossible, of course, but they tried.

The attitude still persists among those who actually recall Shaw as a contemporary. In 1956, the centenary of Shaw's birth, I wrote a memorial article for the *Sunday Times* in which I expressed my feeling that Shaw was a major writer who had been strangely underrated by his contemporaries. When the pieces appeared, I found that *The Times* had also commissioned an article from A.J.P. Taylor, in which Shaw was dismissed as an outmoded exhibitionist whose works would soon be forgotten. The difference in attitude can be explained by noting that A.J.P. Taylor is some quarter of a century my senior, and was old enough to remember Shaw at the height of his fame; whereas I was born in 1931, and knew next to nothing of the Shaw personality when I went to see the film of *Caesar and Cleopatra* in 1946. I came to know Shaw purely through his work.

It was not until some time after the publication of my first book, *The Outsider*, in 1956 that I fully understood the nature of the trap Shaw had fallen into. Because the book became a freak 'bestseller', because I found myself bracketed with the 'Angry Young Men' of the period, I found myself carried to 'fame' on a wave of publicity – only to discover that this kind of fame is one of the subtlest forms of obscurity. Everybody knew who I was, and nobody knew what I stood for. The public image meant that nobody was interested in what I had to say, for everybody was convinced that they already knew. I could talk until I was blue in the face about my attempt to revise the pessimistic existentialism of Heidegger, Camus and Sartre; as far as most people were concerned, I was an autodidact who was angry about something or other.

It took me only a few months to realise that the sensible thing was to get out of London and avoid publicity; even so, it took well over a decade to live down the Angry Young Man image. Shaw never had the opportunity to live down his own miscalculation about publicity. The first night of *John Bull's Other Island* in 1904 made him a celebrity at the age of forty-eight – exactly twice the age at which I published *The Outsider*. He had been waiting far too long. He fell upon fame like a starving man on food; he repeated in the limelight all the tricks he had developed as a defence against neglect. Oblivious of the rising tide of irritation – or incapable of grasping its implications – he continued doing this until 1914, when his attitude to the war caused the British public to express its contempt so violently that even Shaw was taken aback. By that time it was too late to back-pedal – although *Heartbreak House* seems to me an attempt to acquire a new personality. From then on, every literate contemporary thought he knew all about Shaw without the necessity of finding out what he really stood for. Like 'Professor' Joad of the Brains Trust – a devout Shavian – he had become a self-caricature. The only way to discover the essential Shaw was to read his works without knowing anything about him; and Shaw's innate exhibitionism meant that few people were in this position.

In this respect, I was incredibly lucky; I still regard my own discovery of Shaw as the most important single event of my early teens. My background was working class; my parents probably knew nothing of Shaw except that he had a beard. I had heard of Shaw – everybody had – but had no idea whether he was a writer, a politician or an inventor. My training was scientific rather than literary; from the age of ten I wanted to become an atomic physicist; all my adolescent hero worship was directed at Einstein. This preoccupation with atoms and stars turned me into a pessimist. The more I thought about the nature of life, the more I became possessed of the conviction that our human values are trivial and parochial, mere expressions of biological needs. The scientist seemed the highest type of man; yet even his 'love of truth' struck me as an illusion; human beings have no more need for absolute truth than a baby has for a table of logarithms. At fifteen I had passed beyond pessimism into a kind of nihilism; I felt that no one had ever fathomed the appalling truth of Koheleth's 'All is vanity'.

The worst thing about it was the feeling of total aloneness, of alienation from the rest of the human race. It lasted until the evening in 1946 when I came home from the cinema, switched on the BBC's new Third Programme, and heard the opening words of Act 3 of *Man and Superman*, spoken by a narrator: '*Evening in the Sierra Nevada. Rolling slopes of brown with olive trees . . .*' At first I was amused and excited – it was more witty and intelligent than anything I had ever heard on the radio. And then as Don Juan began to speak about the purpose of human existence, I experienced a sensation like cold water being poured down my back. 'Life was driving at brains – at its darling object: an organ by which it can attain not only self-consciousness but self-understanding.' It was as if a bubble had burst; that deep underlying sense of detachment and futility disappeared; someone else was talking about the problem that I thought incommunicable. When I went to bed, after midnight, I felt exhausted and slightly stunned; yet underneath the confusion, there was a deep certainty that my life had changed.

Later that week, when the play was repeated, I listened to it from beginning to end – all five hours of it. Then I borrowed the book from the library and read it over and over again until I knew whole passages by heart. It confirmed that my original insight had not been a misunderstanding. Shaw was saying that to regard most human existence as futile is not necessarily a disadvantage – only the first step in becoming a philosopher. 'No: I sing, not arms and the hero, but the philosophic man: he who seeks in contemplation to discover the inner will of the world, in invention to discover the means of fulfilling that will, and in action to do that will by the so-discovered means.' In which case, it seemed clear that my business in life was not to become a scientist, but one of Shaw's 'artist-philosophers'. Accordingly, I pushed aside my textbooks of physics and chemistry, and began writing plays instead. The result was that I failed to pass the examination that might have opened the way to a career in science, and so became an educational 'drop out' at the age of seventeen.

The next two years were the worst of my life – I still wince when I look back on them. I worked hard at jobs I hated, and felt myself to be trapped on a treadmill. I experienced intense depressions, and once came close to suicide. I read a great deal of poetry, listened to a great deal of music, and envied writers like Henry James who had been rich enough to spend their lives as detached observers. I brooded on the fate of poets who had been destroyed by this 'real world' that I detested so much: Keats, Schiller, Beddoes, Poe, James Thomson, and was inclined to accept the notion that I would end the same way. And again, it was Shaw who kept me basically sane and optimistic. This was because it seemed obvious that his starting point had been the same as mine – as a world-rejecting romantic. His comments on Shelley, on Poe, on Wagner, reveal that Shaw understood the romantic mentality because he shared it. In *Candida*, it is the Shelleyan poet, not the crusading social reformer, who comes off best. In the preface to *Misalliance*, Shaw distinguishes between two types of imagination: the romantic imagination, that would like to escape into a realm of fairy tales ('from a world more full of weeping than you can understand'), and the realistic imagination that can grasp things as they are 'without actually sensing them' – the imagination that can change the world. And since Shaw had managed the transition from one to the other, it no longer seemed impossible that I might succeed in doing the same. . . . This was the basic theme of *The Outsider* (a term I also borrowed from Shaw): that the 'alienated man' has to rouse himself out of his self-pity and set about transforming the society he finds so uncongenial. (Later still, Shaw's concept of the realistic imagination was developed into my notion of 'Faculty X' – the mystic's ability to grasp the reality of other times and places.)

The odd thing is that although I had read every Shaw play by the time I was seventeen and most of the novels and prefaces, I never became a 'complete Shavian'. I felt that after *Man and Superman*, Shaw had made no real effort to analyse the central problem of *what human beings are supposed to do with their lives*. Don Juan could speak about the need to 'help life in its struggle upward', about 'Life's incessant aspiration to higher organisation, wider, deeper intenser self-consciousness and clearer self-understanding' but how does the individual actually go about it? Shaw's political solutions always aroused my deepest scepticism. Shaw once remarked that Jesus's miracles were irrelevant because it would be absurd to say: 'You should love your enemies; and to convince you of this, I will now proceed to cure this gentleman of a cataract.' It seemed to me equally irrelevant when Shaw said: 'Life aims at deeper self-awareness, therefore we must abolish capitalism.' Then, as now, Shaw's socialist dogmas struck me as largely fallacious. Similarly, the intellectual content of most of the major plays seemed to me oddly disappointing. I wanted him to talk about ultimate problems of philosophy, and he insisted on talking about politics and education and marriage and the iniquities of the medical profession (another matter on which I felt he was mildly cranky). The result was that in my first book on Shaw (*The Quintessence of Shavianism*, written at sixteen) I remained more than a little critical, and ended by implying that I would one day do better.

But then, the moment I actually opened a volume of Shaw, this hypercritical attitude vanished; I found it impossible not to keep on reading with a kind of excited approval, like a spectator at a boxing match who has to shout his enthusiasm. Johnson once told Boswell that when he first read Law's *Serious Call* he expected to find it rather beneath him, 'but Law proved to be quite an overmatch for me'. When it actually came down to it, Shaw always proved an overmatch for me. Within a few lines, I was chuckling, then shouting with laughter – not so much because I found it funny as because it was so exhilarating. It made no difference whether I opened the *Collected Plays* at *Widowers' Houses* or *Farfetched Fables*; the effect was always the same: a sense of revitalisation, of excitement, like setting out on a holiday.

Oddly enough, it never struck me to try and analyse the source of this effect until I was asked to write the present essay. And then I found it fairly easy to track down. It is the fact that, embedded in its very syntax, Shaw's prose has an irresistibly *optimistic* forward movement.

> Then there was my Uncle William, a most amiable man, with great natural dignity. In early manhood he was not only an inveterate smoker, but so insistent a toper that a man who made a bet that he would produce Barney Shaw sober, and knocked him up at six in the morning with that object, lost his bet. But this might have happened to any common drunkard. What gave the peculiar Shaw finish and humour to the case was that my uncle suddenly and instantly gave up smoking and drinking at one blow, and devoted himself to the accomplishment of playing the ophicleide. . . .

As I now read these words, I find myself beginning to smile halfway through the first sentence: 'a most amiable man, with great natural dignity' – for I know this is going to be the prelude to some anticlimactic absurdity. And then there is an element in the prose which in a comedian like Groucho Marx would be called perfect timing. If Shaw had written: 'my uncle suddenly gave up smoking and drinking, and devoted himself . . .' etc., it would not be funny; to say: 'suddenly and instantly gave up smoking and drinking at one blow' produces a kind of shock effect, like a clown walking into a custard pie.

All Shaw's prose produces an effect of determined clarity, and it is this clarity that causes our ears to prick up: he is obviously saying something important or he wouldn't be making such an effort. And the air of optimism is a consequence of the directness. Inability to express ourselves makes us feel depressed and defeated – a gloomy conviction that the world is too complicated for our limited powers of assimilation. Kafka's effects of nightmare are produced by piling up dreamlike ambiguities and complications until the mind is hypnotised into a sense of helplessness. Shaw's clarity produces exactly the opposite effect, for it is obviously inspired by a conviction that any problem will yield to a combination of reason, courage and determination. 'The brain will not fail when the will is in earnest.' No matter what Shaw happens to be saying – whether he is talking about human evolution or municipal trading – it is this underlying tone of sanity and optimism that produces the exhilarating effect.

All this helps to explain why the inevitable period of devaluation and neglect that followed Shaw's death was shorter than usual, and why his plays are now more popular than ever. It is a case of rediscovery in the most precisely literal sense. When *Man and Superman* and *John Bull's Other Island* burst in London in 1904, his contemporaries were dazzled; it was like a firework display. But even in those early years, there must have been admirers who were worried that a man of Shaw's genius could present a piece as feeble and silly as *How He Lied to Her Husband* on the same bill as *The Man of Destiny*. During the next ten years or so, Shaw repeated the offence with pieces like the atrocious *Shewing Up of Blanco Posnet*, *Overruled*, *Press Cuttings*, *The Fascinating Foundling* (he even enjoyed giving them defiant sub-titles like 'A Piece of Utter Nonsense' and 'A Disgrace to the Author'). And plays like *Getting Married*, *Misalliance*, *Fanny's First Play* revealed the odd streak of complacency that Busoni noted later. By 1920, as far as the public was concerned, the Shaw genius had been completely over-shadowed by the Shaw silliness and egoism – that is, by the posturings of the puppet called GBS. Before Shaw could be truly appreciated again, he had to shut up for a long time – in short, to die. When that happened, it was only a matter of time before the genius of his plays could once again compel the respect and enthusiasm of audiences. And this had happened by 1961.

And what about Shaw as a thinker? Shaw liked to regard himself as an artist-philosopher. Most of us will concede that he was an artist, but we have our doubts about the philosopher. Again that could be due to our lack of perspective. We think of a list of typical philosophers – Plato, Spinoza, Locke, Hegel, Whitehead – ask if Shaw belongs on it, and decide he doesn't fit. But philosophers cannot be judged simply as abstract thinkers; what is equally important is their place in the history of ideas. And here Shaw undoubtedly qualifies. He was born in the middle of the Romantic era, the century of pessimism. The materialist philosophers announced that man is a machine and that free will is a delusion; the idealists said that mind undoubtedly exists but that matter may be a delusion. And all the romantic poets from Shelley to Yeats agreed that life is a dim vast vale of tears and that the human condition is tragic. When Shaw came on the literary scene, in the early 1880s, the romantics had decided that mankind can be split into two groups: the stupid go-getters and the sensitive world-rejectors. You were either a shallow-minded optimist or an intelligent pessimist. (Thomas Mann made this antimony the basis of all his work.)

Shaw's revolt was instinctive. If he was a romantic, it was not of the self-pitying variety that regards the universe as cruel and meaningless because it refuses to treat them as exceptions. And it was Shaw's intuitive intelligence that made him aware that no healthy civilisation can embrace a philosophy of pessimism. In *Man and Superman* he points out that man is the only animal who can be nerved to bravery by putting an *idea* into his head: that is to say, that man's inner strength depends on his beliefs; in *Back to Methuselah* he shows the other side of the coin when Pygmalion's two human creations lie down and die when they feel discouraged. It follows that a civilisation that believes that Darwin and Freud are right about human nature is going to deflate like a tyre with a slow puncture. Shaw was not capable of analysing the history of philosophy since Descartes, the history of science since Newton, the history of religion since Luther, the history of romanticism since Rousseau and writing his own *Decline of the West*, yet he recognised that all have converged into the conviction that made Sartre write: 'Man is a useless passion.' He knew only one thing: *that somehow, sooner or later, the trend will have to be reversed.* His own age was not ready for that insight, and a younger generation of writers – Proust, Eliot, Joyce *et al* – continued the tradition of romantic pessimism as if Shaw had never existed. Most of them took the opportunity to denounce Shaw for failing to recognise the seriousness of the situation. Yet as this century of confusion and anxiety enters its last decades, it becomes clear that Shaw's instinct was correct. Somehow, whether we like it or not, we have to start believing in the future, and in man's power to transform it. At the end of *Too True to be Good*, the rascally clergyman declares: 'We have outgrown our religion, outgrown our political system, outgrown our own strength of mind and character. . . . But what next? Is NO enough? For a boy, yes: for a man, never. Are we any the less obsessed with a belief when we are denying it than when we are affirming it? No, I must have affirmations to preach. . . .'

The affirmations are still in the painful process of being born. When it finally happens, we shall recognise that Shaw did more than any other man to bring them into being.

1979

TWELVE

Ronald Duncan:
a self-revealing poet

'An autobiography cannot give an accurate picture of a man's life if it is to be readable,' says Ronald Duncan in the opening sentence of *How to Make Enemies*. Having made which discouraging disclaimer, he proceeds to write one of the frankest, most detailed and self-revealing pieces of autobiography since Rousseau. That is somehow typical of Ronald Duncan. Unlike most poets, he is much given to self-underestimation. He writes at the beginning of *The Solitudes*, in a parody of Whitman:

> To my essential self – I sing –
> Not to the I,
> Man of the hat, coat and tie:
> But to the me,
> coffee, muddle and misery.

Anyone who knew him only through the two volumes of autobiography might be inclined to accept that description as more-or-less accurate. But you have only to turn from the autobiographies to the verse dramas, or to that remarkable epic poem *Man*, to realise that this is only one of the many characters who bear the name Ronald Duncan. One is a religious mystic, one a scientist, one a lover – who is inclined to wear his heart on his sleeve – and one a farmer and countryman. There are at least half a dozen more, including an extremely shrewd psychologist. And all these are held together by a Ronald Duncan who is an excellent literary craftsman. The sum of these many aspects adds up to one of the strangest and most complex personalities in modern literature.

In the literary sense, this has been to his disadvantage. There are, it seems to me, basically two kinds of writer: personalities and non-personalities. Dr Johnson was a personality; so were

Hemingway and Dylan Thomas and Brendan Behan and W.B. Yeats. Walter Pater was a non-personality; so were T.S. Eliot, Aldous Huxley and W.H. Auden. The main difference is that in order to appreciate the writings of the second group, you do not need to know much about them personally. On the other hand, if we knew about Dr Johnson only through his writings, we would hardly know him at all. And Dylan Thomas achieved his belated fame largely through Brinnin's *Dylan Thomas In America*, which suddenly *added a dimension* to poetry that had previously been counted rather esoteric.

Now Ronald Duncan undoubtedly belongs to the 'personality' group. And by this, I mean that it seems probable that he will not be appreciated until some literary historian, probably an American professor, writes a book about him and shows all the other professors of literature how he should be approached. All Duncan's work springs out of his complexity as a human being. And, fortunately, he has handed us the key to some of this complexity in those two magnificent and wholly delightful volumes of autobiography. *All Men Are Islands* and *How to Make Enemies*. (I trust there will be a third.) However, there is a sense in which the autobiographies are thoroughly misleading. His peculiar kind of almost masochistic honesty drives him to try to tell the worst about himself. And the personality that emerges is simply not the poet who wrote *This Way to the Tomb* and *Man*. There is a dimension missing.

To some extent, of course, this is inevitable. An autobiography is rather like a TV talk show. It is supposed to be a presentation of 'salient facts' – preferably scandalous – not an attempt to express your deepest responses to existence. Yet in another sense, the two dimensional effect *is* Duncan's own fault. In his determination to be honest about the 'coffee, muddle and misery' (he is a coffee addict), he deliberately scales himself down. It is rather as if Swinburne had written an autobiography emphasising his lifelong obsession with flogging, and failed to mention any of the factors – his love of the sea, of ancient Greece, of mediaeval England – that make him a great poet. But then, Swinburne didn't write an autobiography, because he was one of the non-personal poets – reading about his drunkenness and taste for flagellation adds nothing to our appreciation of his poetry. Duncan is as intensely personal as Yeats or Rilke. And to mention him with these poets emphasises a certain element of perverseness about him. Yeats's autobiographies projected the character he wanted to be, the other-worldly poet, slightly larger than life. People who actually met Yeats are inclined to call him Willy, and describe him with a touch of comedy. Now Duncan, on the other hand, deflates himself. There is the typical episode where, tormented by his secretary's display of her legs and breasts as she takes dictation, he orders her to come to the beach and take off her clothes. She lies on a sun-warmed rock: he undresses and flings himself beside her – and lands on two jellyfishes. 'My screams perforated the still air . . .' It is as if a scene written by D.H. Lawrence had been completed by Charlie Chaplin.

This kind of thing makes the book hilarious reading. But you would not even suspect the existence of the poet who wrote in *Man*:

> Then once upon a dream, a nightmare of nights ago,
>   the seas cooled, the clouds of steam dispersed,
> And the sun daggered the horizon again, and the light,
>   the light entered its inheritance,
> Walking with white feet over the silent waters . . .

Now with another poet, this might not matter so much. You can turn from Brinnin's book on Dylan Thomas to Thomas's own *Fern Hill*, and discover the extra-dimension for yourself. But this is because the two are only casually connected. All Duncan's work is deeply autobiographical, and what makes him such a remarkable poet is his capacity to *use* weakness or self-indulgence as a springboard for pure impersonality. He is a dramatist whose most interesting creation is himself. The autobiography is in the nature of a deliberate red herring. But, for the benefit of those who have not read the autobiographies, let me offer an outline sketch of his extraordinary life.

He was born in 1914, the day before war was declared. His father's name was Dunkelsbuhler; he came from a rich family, and the misunderstandings began before Ronnie was born. When his father decided to marry a Miss Cannon, his family assumed she was an actress who was playing in *The Merry Widow* and threatened to disinherit him. Instead of assuring them that the girl was just out of a convent, his father married her without their consent, and was disinherited. As the autobiographies show, Duncan himself has inherited some of this odd tendency to allow misunderstandings to persist, when a few words could remove them.

His mother was charged by a bull – they were now in Rhodesia – when seven months pregnant. Ronnie was removed by a Caesarian operation. He was undersized and had a large head. At school, later, his lack of inches worried him, and he has described himself as 'an animated ink blot' (he also has a dark complexion). At the outbreak of war, his mother decided it would be safer to return to England; his father remained behind in Africa, and died of influenza four years later. His family would still not receive her – she could still not be bothered to explain that she was not an actress – but allowed her twenty-five pounds a month. Ronnie and his sister grew up in a working class – or lower middle class – environment in Clapham. But at least, there was money in the background.

He claims that an incident at the age of four gave him a deep fund of self-confidence. He became obsessed by fishing. His mother waited until he was looking the other way, then put a fish – purchased in the normal way – on the end of his line. 'I have gone through life always sublimely confident that whenever I flung my hook an obliging fish would swallow it.' And for the most part, the confidence has been justified.

To be honest, I am a little suspicious of this story. I don't doubt it happened. But he is inclined to attribute personal characteristics – which may well be genetic – to specific incidents. He tells how his sister made her first cake, and hid under the table while he was offered a slice. Unaware of her presence, he said it was horrible. She sobbed, and he explains that the incident 'has turned me into a vacillating creature, unable at times to speak my mind to anybody I am fond of'. It doesn't seem to strike him that he may just be a rather gentle, considerate character.

He undressed his first girl at the age of five. She was six, and they were in a cupboard at a party. It is worth mentioning the incident, because sex plays a vital and central role in all Duncan's work. He later became deeply interested in his own dreams, and kept a dream diary. When he first read Freud, at 17, he was disappointed to realise that many of his own conclusions were not original. He had hoped to devote his life to the science of dreams.

The basic characteristics were emerging. He mentions that 'I always had access to experiences which I had never experienced. As a child I was constantly told things which I already knew.' At a public school in Yorkshire, he was known as a rebel. He was virtually expelled – not for any fault, but for having had a homosexual master dismissed. Then there was a period of illness – anaemia and bronchitis – and he admits thoroughly enjoying the holiday, and his mother's exclusive attention. The Proustian pattern was emerging. He was too naturally fond of girls to develop homosexual tendencies – another thing that was later to separate him from most of his own generation of poets and artists – but the almost morbid sensitivity was there.

A visit to Johannesburg awoke the moral reformer in him; he was disgusted by the treatment of the blacks. Then he went up to Cambridge, and realised he was a poet. His definition is typical: 'It is to bleed when you are not wounded; it is to be wounded when you are not hit; it is to enjoy so intensely that enjoyment is unbearable, another kind of pain.' That is to say, it is a rather dangerous form of oversensitivity.

His first ambitious poem seems to have been a three thousand line epic describing a trip from Calais to Constantinople – on horseback – which he had intended to make with a girl. The girl's parents forbade it; he stayed at home and wrote the poem, whose detail seemed so authentic that a publisher offered to bring it out as a 'travel poem'. Unfortunately he sent the only copy to the girl, who failed to return it. This conclusion of the story is fairly typical. Such things happen several times in the autobiography, and it is often difficult to draw the line between poetic abstraction and imbecilic incompetence.

At Cambridge, he studied with F.R. Leavis – who is the first of many sharply etched and fasinating literary portraits in the autobiography. Leavis introduced Duncan to the poetry of Pound and Hopkins – the latter moved him so deeply that he was unable to make any comment. He acknowledges fully the extent of his debt to Leavis. But the relation ended strangely. One day, Duncan showed some of his own poems to Leavis. Leavis became very cold, as if he had been betrayed. A later comment suggested he had found something to admire in the poems – by which time, Duncan had destroyed them – but he seemed to resent the notion that one of his students had decided to go in for creation rather than criticism. There was an abortive love affair with a girl called Laura, who was apparently determined on marriage, when Duncan's intentions were less honourable. What seems to emerge is that he was less than adept at human relations – a fairly normal state for young poets. But what reveals the quality of his mind – and will – is that he made a determined attempt to slough off his old skin by becoming a coal miner. He had written the words to a protest song for the Rhondda miners, who were marching to London. Now he tramped to Holmwood, near Chesterfield, and got a job looking after the pit ponies. In a half-hearted way, he became involved with a local girl called Maureen, 'a dull-looking girl of about twenty, with large eyes, large breasts and a listless air of unwanted virginity'. His skill in human relations hadn't improved much: after a walk in the woods, it seemed to be assumed that he intended to marry her. One day, he fell asleep by the roadside, and was awakened by policemen who assumed he was a gypsy. When he produced his union card to prove his identity, one of them pocketed it, and told him to get out of the area. He seems to have been glad to take advantage of the misunderstanding to sever his connection with coal mining. He moved to London, became a pacifist, and began a friendship with a young composer named Benjamin Britten. He also began to correspond with Mahatma Gandhi, and one day decided to go and see him in India. He stayed at Gandhi's ashram for several months. One incident stands out. Gandhi took Duncan to a village that was ridden with disease. Villagers were squatting in front of their huts and excreting near the only well. Gandhi did not lecture them. He began to clear up the excreta and bury it with his own hands. Duncan helped him. Soon, the villagers, seeing their Mahatma engaged in this undignified activity, joined in and helped bury it. This is was Gandhi called teaching by example.

Duncan also skips quickly over another episode that seems to me of immense interest. On his way back to England, via Calcutta, an Indian doctor offered to cure him of a bad cold. He was strapped rigidly to the upright frame of a bed: then the doctor pulled a lever so the bed fell with a crash. He was unstrapped,

furious and shaken, but without the cold. The implication seems
to be that the cold was driven away by shock, and by the sudden
surge of vitality it produces In some of the episodes he describes
later, I suspect that Duncan's subconscious mind is trying out the
same shock treatment to cure the emotional equivalent of a bad
cold.

On his way back to England he called to see Ezra Pound at
Rapallo – a meeting that was to have far-reaching consequences.
Not only did it confirm Pound's stylistic and critical influence; it
also gave Duncan a kind of passport to the contemporary literary
scene; for Pound, although in retirement, was still something of an
eminence grise to the younger generation of poets. Pound took an
immediate liking to Duncan – which, to anyone who knows
Ronnie, is understandable. Apart from his obvious intelligence –
always a beguiling quality – there is a touch of the child-like about
him, an air of being 'in need of care and protection', which would
appeal to a naturally generous character like Pound. Duncan, for
his part, was captivated; his loyalty to Pound has been fierce and
unswerving.

He came back to London to meet his fate – in the form of an
attractive film starlet named Rose Marie Hansom. An old
Cambridge friend named Spottiswoode was in love with her. The
three of them had lunch at a vegetarian restaurant; Spottiswoode
had to return to work. Ronnie and Rose Marie found one another
so congenial that they exchanged shoes as they left the restaurant
and staggered side by side through central London, roaring with
laughter. It was a spirit that characterised much of their future
relationship. Together with Spottiswoode they went to Devon for
a weekend, and the men ended by sleeping – chastely – on either
side of her in a double bed. Halfway through the night, Ronnie
found a soft hand and squeezed it, the pressure was returned. It
was only when Rose Marie got up to go to the bathroom that
Ronnie and Spottiswoode realised they had been holding hands
half the night.

Still, Spottiswoode could not match the glamour of the poet
from India. Rose Marie moved to Devon with Ronnie – into West
Mill, a cottage he had rented for thirty shillings a year. He bought
forty acres of land – mostly weeds – and became a farmer. He had
utopian dreams – a Community Farm, self-supporting, publishing

its own literary magazine (*The Townsman*), writing and performing its own plays . . . But it was not to be. The Community drifted apart – and the war came. The locals were suspicious of the poet in their midst, and suspected him of being a German spy. This seems to be something of a tradition in the English countryside – D.H. Lawrence and Henry Williamson had the same trouble. Duncan's account of his war years is one of the most amusing parts of *All Men Are Islands*, but it is too long to summarise here. Suffice it to say that the play he began to write for the Community – *This Way to the Tomb* – was eventually accepted for production at the Mercury Theatre, Notting Hill, where Eliot's *Murder in the Cathedral* had startled everybody by drawing packed houses for a year. Britten wrote the music for *This Way to the Tomb* – his *Peter Grimes* had just been the great success of the opera season – and in return, Duncan began working on an opera libretto, *The Rape of Lucretia*. It was a time of anxiety; Rose Marie had overworked, and now collapsed with consumption; for a while, it looked as if her chances of recovery were slight. *This Way to the Tomb* was received politely, but without wild enthusiasm; everyone concerned assumed it might run for a couple of weeks, then close. However, Beverley Baxter gave it new momentum with a rave review in the *Evening Standard*. It was all it needed; it also went on to run for a year. And, to his amazement, Duncan realised suddenly that he was a famous playwright. His anxieties about Rose Marie were so wearing that he hardly noticed it at first. Then she began to recover. *Lucretia* was presented, and was also a success. At this point, Duncan was asked to adapt a play by Cocteau. His adaptation was, to put it mildly, rather free; in fact, it was more Duncan that Cocteau. But *The Eagle Has Two Heads* brought fame to its unknown star, Eileen Herlie, and made Duncan the most successful playwright in London. Like Somerset Maugham half a century earlier, he had scored a hat trick, three plays running simultaneously in the West End. And, fortunately, Rose Marie began to recover. At last, Duncan had time to relax, and to take in the incredible fact that he had become, in every sense, a 'Man of the Theatre'.

Most of the critics had assumed, understandably, that Duncan was a religious dramatist, like Eliot. The first part of *This Way to the Tomb* consisted mainly of a long soliloquy by Saint Anthony on the island of Zante. The second part, using jazz and satire, is a criticism of the modern world. The influence of Eliot is strong throughout – of *The Waste Land* as well as of *Murder in the Cathedral*, *The Rock* and *Sweeney Agonistes*. The only Eliot work of which there is definitely no trace is *The Hollow Men* – for Duncan was no life-denier. In fact, my own view – for which I claim no authority – is that *This Way to the Tomb* is something of a divagation. Duncan understands religion, but he is not fundamentally religious. He is a lover, a poet, a philosopher and something of a scientist. And he is a romantic, not – in Eliot's sense – a classic.

These comments are necessary as an introduction to the next part of the story, which he has recounted with characteristic frankness in *How to Make Enemies*. He had fallen in love with a teenage art student named Petra. She reciprocated the feeling; they had an affair. Stated baldly, in this way, this could easily be misunderstood; it sounds like the kind of thing that the biographer ought to overlook, or refer to obliquely in a footnote. But in the case of Ronald Duncan, this would be to miss something important about the man, and therefore about the poetry. In the course of *How to Make Enemies* he describes a number of love affairs – with an Italian actress, with his secretary Antonia, with Petra – and when the book ends, he is about to launch into another affair with Virginia, the actress who played the lead in *The Catalyst*. The last sentence of the book is: 'I haven't the strength now, or the courage, to write the rest.' But he has both the strength and the courage to write a great deal about himself and his emotions, both here and in *The Solitudes*. In *How to Make Enemies* he writes:

> It is a platitude of literature and the false assumption in life that a man falls in love with one person because he has tired of or fallen out of love with another. This convention may be convenient. But it is a simplification without reality. My feelings [for Petra] could not conform to it . . . I suppose I was a born bigamist . . . Monogamy was invented by a woman. If a man doesn't find at least two women who attract him, he's unlikely to find one . . . Of course I was emotionally insecure. Is there a man who isn't? . . .

Shelley would agree with him; D.H. Lawrence would disagree. And an ordinary overworked writer like myself might feel that, while it is true that one might love several women at the same time, it is less emotionally wearing to stick to the same one. As *The Catalyst* and *The Solitudes* make clear, Duncan has not avoided the emotional wear and tear. No one can accuse him of having his cake and eating it. Some of his friends, including Eliot, have regarded his views on these matters as regrettable. Which may be so; but they are as much an integral part of his poetic personality as Shelley's were of his. Eliot also disapproved of *Epipsychidion* and *Julian and Maddalo*.

What is quite plain, from *How to Make Enemies* and *The Catalyst*, is that the interest in other women was not due to any loss of interest in Rose Marie. It seems perfectly clear that he was as much in love with her as ever. The explanation that suggests itself is simple. Until he was in his mid-twenties, there had been something of a conflict between poetic and sexual development, so that his sex life had been rather frustrating. Then he met Rose Marie, became the father of two children, and spent the next five years farming in a remote part of the country, and slowly maturing as a poet and dramatist. Shelley, by the time he was thirty, had been married twice, lived all over Europe, and written most of his poetry. By the same age, Ronald Duncan had written very little, and lived like a recluse for almost a decade. Then, suddenly, he achieved success as a playwright, and found himself in constant contact with a world of poets, writers and musicians. Then, one day, he realised that a pretty girl of eighteen was in love with him. Understandably, he seized the experience. 'This first kiss with this girl of eighteen whom I expected to rebuff me, was the most passionate surrender I ever experienced.'

And Rose Marie – who is a complex character who deserves a biography to herself – not only accepted the new situation, but seems to have encouraged these *amours* with a certain amount of amusement. She certainly seems to have been more tolerant and understanding than Mary Shelley. It seems she recognised the affairs for what they were: part of the development of her husband's romantic and turbulent personality. Ronnie was no Don Juan, in the ordinary sense. In this respect, his play *Don Juan* is highly revealing. The Don is no philanderer; he is, in spite of his infidelities, a constant lover, cast in the romantic mould of the nineteenth rather than the twentieth century. Duncan's lifelong theme has been love and the varieties of love. His Don Juan has less in common with Byron's than with Shelley's Alastor – the poet seeking the 'eternal feminine'. Like Dante, Ronald Duncan is obsessed by the possibility of a transfiguration of earthly love into a form of religious experience; the figure of Dante seems to hover constantly in the background of *Heloise and Abelard*. And when he writes of love, one is always aware of him as a divided man: the realist who observes it with a cynicism akin to Arthur Schnitzler, and the romantic idealist, who dreams of love as a force that will ultimately transform reality. This self-division explains the tension and misery of so much of his love poetry.

The literary success was soured by a number of setbacks. Andre Obey sued Duncan on the grounds that *Lucretia* was a free adaptation of his *Viol de Lucrecs*. In fact, the only similarity between the plays lies in the subject; but, for the sake of peace, Duncan agreed to add the words 'adapted from the play by Andre Obey' on the liberetto of *Lucretia*. Some kind of quarrel with Cocteau blew up; Cocteau re-titled his play *Azrael* (from which *The Eagle Has Two Heads* was adapted) *L'Aigle a Deux Têtes* and went around telling people that Duncan had mistranslated his title. These trivialities would hardly be worth mentioning, except that problems of this sort seem to recur in Duncan's life. He is less accident-prone than misunderstanding-prone. And this again is so typical of his personality that it requires some comment.

The misunderstandings seem to occur on all levels, from his war-time clashes with the authorities to fairly trivial and amusing incidents. He tells how, one day, a family of tourists strolled into his farm sitting room and ordered tea. Duncan went quietly to the kitchen and made them tea. When they left, they asked how much they owed, and he said 'Nothing'. 'Why?' 'Because we don't do teas.' Instead of thanking him, the visitors stamped off indignantly, implying that it was his fault – which, in a way, it was. It would have been simpler to tell them so when they walked in. On the other hand, the dramatist in him – and perhaps the small boy – wanted to carry out the situation to its absurd conclusion.

Closely allied to this tendency to involve himself in

misunderstandings is a rather odd kind of absent-mindedness. I say rather odd because ordinary absent-mindedness is easy to understand, and Duncan's seem to be of an altogether more exalted order, related to the trances of the Delphic oracle. He tells how, for example, when driving in his car, he switched on the radio and heard a few sentences of a parlour game of the kind that usually drove him from the room. Automatically, he opened the door of the moving car and tried to climb out. Travelling on a train one day, he observed with irritation that the man opposite was about to eat a packet of smoked salmon sandwiches. Ten minutes later, the dining car attendant announced lunch, and the man booked for the first session: Duncan said he would go to the second session, and the man muttered audibly 'Thank God'. Enraged, Duncan asked him what the hell he meant. The man then pointed out that Duncan had eaten all his sandwiches; he said that every time he opened the packet, Ronnie's hand snaked out from behind his newspaper and took one. Ronnie indignantly denied it – then tasted the smoked salmon on his lips. He apologised and took the man to lunch . . . There are a number of other stories of a similar nature that would suggest to most people that he is absent minded to the point of dottiness. W.B. Yeats tells a story of how a policeman assumed he was mad because he walked along muttering to himself – until a neighbour explained that he was a poet. 'Oh, is that all . . .' said the policeman. But Duncan's absent mindedness seems to be so much more bizarre that one can only assume it has some subconscious origin – that the romantic in him rejects the everyday world so completely that he sometimes behaves as if it did not exist.

Possibly the combination of misunderstanding-proneness and absent-mindedness may explain how such a gentle and diffident character has managed to get himself involved in so many quarrels – as suggested by the title *How to Make Enemies*. Although capable of waspishness, he is not basically a malicious man. I have known many examples of his goodness and generosity. Yet, out of some spirit of perverseness, he often deliberately gives the impression of rudeness or bile. It is as if he is convinced that a poet is bound to be misunderstood by the world, and is determined to compound the misunderstanding.

At this point, I should describe how I became acquainted with Duncan. In 1956, George Devine, the director of the Royal Court Theatre (which was Ronald Duncan's brainchild) asked me to write a play. My first book *The Outsider* had made me an overnight reputation; I was classified with John Osborne and Brendan Behan as an 'Angry Young Man', so it seemed logical that I should write a play. Devine said that I could hear it read aloud by a cast of actors, and then work with him, licking it into shape. It took me a year to write *The Death of God*, a play set in a monastery. I sent it to Devine; after a silence of two months, it came back with a printed rejection slip.

I wasn't entirely unprepared for something of the sort. For some months I had heard rumours that I was regarded with distaste by the Left-wing literati at the Court. I was aggressively non-political, and there was a tendency to refer to me as a fascist. Still, the printed rejection slip smarted. I wrote a letter to Devine, protesting – not only on my behalf, but on that of a number of other playwrights who had been treated shabbily, including Stuart Holroyd, Michael Hastings and Sandy Wilson. As an afterthought I sent copies of the letter to various newspapers. That was a mistake. The newspapers rang Devine, who was unobtainable. So they rang Ronald Duncan, who was still on the board of directors. Wakened by the *Daily Express* in the middle of the night, Ronnie commented irritably that the play read like a child's TV serial, and that I ought to be a soap advertisement salesman. These comments appeared, with my letter, the next day. Another newspaper rang me to ask what I had to say. 'Who is Ronald Duncan?', the reporter asked. I said I didn't know. All I knew about him was that I had seen his name in the collected letters of Ezra Pound, and that Pound had expected him to become a major poet. I said that as far as I knew, this had not happened. The reporter asked helpfully: 'Would you say that if you *were* a soap advertisement salesman, you'd send him a packet to wash his mouth out with?' I said hastily that I *wouldn't* say this. But the comments about Ronnie and Ezra Pound duly appeared in the next day's paper, together with more comments obtained from Ronnie.

When the newspaper rang me back to ask for my comments on Ronnie's latest comments, it struck me that we were being used. All the newspapers wanted was a story with plenty of bitchery. So

I wrote Duncan a letter, saying that I felt we both ought to decline to co-operate further. I think I expected a rebuff – the newspaper comments made him sound bitter and aggressive – but it seemed worth a try. To my surprise, his reply was reasonable, charming and good-tempered. He even said some nice things about the play, and told me how much trouble *he* had had getting some of his work on in the theatre. A few weeks later, on my way over to see Negley Farson, who lived near Woolacombe in North Devon, I stopped at Welcombe and introduced myself. I found Mead Farm a mile beyond the village, and a pretty blonde girl outside churning butter – his daughter Briony. Duncan shook hands and invited me in. He was a short man, whose dark complexion suggested that he was a southerner. The manner was shy, slightly awkward at first. I suspected he might find the meeting embarrassing. But as soon as he began to talk about newspapers, critics, the theatre, he became voluble; the shyness disappeared. He is, I think, basically a shy man, who can hurtle himself out of his shyness as soon as he is interested in an idea – and who can retire back into it just as quickly. At the beginning of my first book, I had defined an outsider as someone who is not at home in the world. I could see immediately that he was one of them.

I noticed with surprise that he had a copy of my second book *Religion and the Rebel* on his desk; it had recently been slaughtered by the critics. When I asked him if he bought it, he said it had been sent to him for review by the editor of a London newspaper. It was to be his first assignment as the book critic. A note accompanying the book said that the editor felt it deserved a bad review, and that he trusted that Duncan would produce something suitably scathing. Ronnie read the book, decided he liked it, and told the editor so. He lost the job as book critic. I was greatly concerned when he told me this. From what he had told me about his finances – and those of poets in general – I realised that the job would have been useful. I said that I felt one more bad review would have made no difference. He didn't seem concerned. He said he didn't want to write for a newspaper whose editor told him what kind of a review he wanted anyway.

Subsequently, I saw a great deal of him – and his family: Rose Marie, and the two children, Briony and Roger; together with my wife, I often stayed at Mead Farm or West Mill. He is a generous man with his hospitality. He and his family have also stayed with us in Cornwall. We have seen one another fairly constantly, on and off, since then, and in recent years have also met regularly on the literary panel of the South Western Arts Association.

The first thing I noticed about him was that he arouses a certain protective urge in most people. There is something vague, slightly lost, about him. But then, I became aware of the truly paradoxical nature of his personality. He is *not* basically accident-prone or a born loser. On the contrary, as he says, he has the curious ability to toss his line into the water and catch a fish. Shortly after the success of *This Way to the Tomb*, Beaverbrook sent for him and offered him a job as theatre critic. The first review he wrote was scathing: then he had pangs of conscience – since he knew what it was like to be pounded by critics who have thought out their witticisms before they walk into the theatre. He scrapped it and wrote a kindly review. Beaverbrook told him that a kindly review was no good: malice made better journalism. So after a month or two, he ceased to be a theatre critic. But Beaverbrook, instead of dropping him, made him farming correspondent, and Jan's Journal bacame a regular feature in the *Evening Standard* from 1946 onwards. The autobiography makes it clear that his life has been full of this kind of serendipity. Yet he can write 'Anger consumes me. There is one word which describes my experience, indeed, my life. It is "waste".' This is hardly true – although it *is* true, as he says, that most of that original success in the theatre has evaporated. Eliot made poetic drama fashionable, briefly, with works like *The Cocktail Party*. Duncan and Christopher Fry consolidated the gain, and for a few years, it looked as of poetic drama might be here to stay. But Fry's particular vein of comedy was quickly worked out, and audiences were altogether less interested in the serious plays. Duncan's second major play, *Stratton*, strikes me as one of his finest, demonstrating a sustained dramatic power that is only hinted at in *This Way to the Tomb*. But the success of *This Way to the Tomb* had been nothing to do with the merit of the play; it had been the Beverley Baxter review that had drawn attention to it, and, in effect, launched it. *Stratton* was altogether less lucky; in fact, downright unlucky. It was poorly acted and directed, and the play's backer actually wrote in a final scene without bothering to consult the author. It was a sad and frustrating experience. And as he talks about this – and similar experiences – it becomes clear that Duncan has never reconciled himself to this aspect of theatrical life. He rages against it. 'Only mediocrity can possibly survive where mediocrity alone flourishes, where fashion parades as taste, and cynicism and indifference cover all.' Unfortunately, this kind of denunciation has never made the slightest difference. And perhaps there is no reason why it should. Mediocrity will not be persuaded to improve its taste by being told that it is mediocre. It might just conceivably, with enough plays like *Stratton* and *The Cocktail Party*, begin to acquire a taste for them, and be improved in spite of itself. All the writer can do is to keep on producing good work, and hope it will eventually make its impact. Duncan produced one of his finest poetic dramas, *Don Juan*, while still borne onward by the wave of success and hope for the future – as well as the admiration of a beautiful Italian actress who saw herself as Dona Anna. But Olivier, who had initially encouraged him to write the play, lost interest (in fact, worse still, forgot that he had ever expressed interest). Duncan then decided to found his own theatre to present this and its sequel, *The Death of Satan*, a satirical comedy. He decided upon the disused Royal Court Theatre. Ironically, its first major success was Osborne's *Look Back in Anger*, which inaugurated the new trend away from poetic drama – the kitchen sink school. Devine filled the Royal Court with leftists and their sympathisers; a few more excellent plays emerged – *Sergeant Musgrave's Dance*, *Roots*, *Cards of Identity* (my own favourite of all the 'Court plays'). Duncan, the proponent of the poetic, subjective drama was as out of place there as I would have been myself. Bitter disagreements followed, and he left the committee. Just before he left, I found him one day reading the manuscript of a new play by Osborne, *Luther*. I asked him what he thought of it. 'Excellent, the best thing he's done.' This was typical of his detachment and generosity; *Luther* is totally remote from his own interests and preoccupations, yet he appreciated its quality.

In the face of discouragements, Duncan turned to 'chamber drama' – *Heloise and Abelard*, for two players, and *The Catalyst*, for three, exploring the possibilities of a three-cornered love affair between the husband, the wife and the mistress. There was also a

novel, *Saint Spiv*, an abortive novel based on the same theme as
the play *Nothing up my Sleeves* and two excellent volumes of short
stories, *The Perfect Mistress* and *A Kettle of Fish*. The title story of
The Perfect Mistress is perhaps one of his most typical works.
Bratton is a lawyer whose wife has become pathologically
suspicious – with some reason, since he has had two clandestine
love affairs. Finally, her jealousy begins to make his life a misery.
So he invents a mistress. He behaves as if he is having an affair,
then moves to a country cottage. Finally, his wife storms in – and
finds him alone. This time, she leaves him, saying that she can
compete with real mistresses, but not with someone in his
imagination. Bratton then goes on to live out his fantasy of the
mistress, becoming mildly insane; the narrator calls on him and
finds him repainting the front door because his mistress wants it
changed . . . The story should be read, perhaps, as an epilogue to
The Solitudes – a volume that contains some beautiful love poems,
but which goes to almost masochistic lengths in describing 'coffee,
muddle and misery'.

> Betray me utterly. For that you'll need
> Some new device: a mere fuck or two won't do.
> Even when you admit that lapse was not
> From weakness but deliberately done;
> That your vow was false as the groans you faked for
>   him. No any cunt
> Can do that trick. Try something more: Much more!
> It's not enough! Do more!

The Solitudes contains some of the best and worst of Duncan: it is
completely typical, completely personal, the poet using himself as
his material, without disguise. There has been very little love
poetry like this in English; to find a parallel, we need to go back to
Sappho and Catullus. At times, it moves dangerously close to the
line that divides self-dramatisation from self-pity. Yet, at the end,
it is the 'essential self' that stands out. He ends:

> Words are a net;
> Feeling, the water, escapes through the meshes
> I fish for silence.

The poet is always aware that, in spite of the torments he

suffers, a detached part of himself looks on and records, using the pain to galvanise himself to new insights. The personal blends into the impersonal.

All of which brings me to the central paradox of Ronald Duncan. There are poets who set out to convey a larger-than-life image of themselves to the reader – Byron, Whitman, Mayakovsky, Brecht. And there are poets who, like Poe, Dowson, Verlaine, dramatise their misery and despair, and end by projecting a simplified image which is, in effect, larger than life. There is an honesty in Duncan that makes him determined to avoid this kind of simplification. Like all real poets, he knows that he is, in most respects, like other men, and that in a few basic respects, he is unlike them. A poet is a man who, like the Lady of Shalott, is condemned to see life through a mirror, and always to be aware of his separateness. And although he may get a great deal of pleasure from his privileged position, he also envies 'normal' human beings for the directness of their perceptions. T.E. Lawrence envied a soldier walking with his girl or a man patting a dog. Hemingway envied bullfighters for living their lives 'all the way up', and did his best to emulate them – without success, for the writer is condemned to be an observer. Before a man recognises that he is a poet – and that this is both his burden and his fulfillment – he is aware of himself mainly as a maladjusted individual, a misfit. The recognition that he is a poet endows him with a new range of possibilities; the future suddenly becomes fascinating, if rather frightening. With surprise – a kind of spiritual vertigo – he realises that he may be one of Shelley's 'unacknowledged legislators of the world', and have a right to regard himself as a member – no matter how humble – of the same company as Dante, Shakespeare and Goethe. And, unlike most of the human beings around him, he may still be remembered five hundred years from now . . . Later, as he lives out his destiny as a poet, he comes to realise that it also involves separateness – that instead of living, he is condemned to a kind of partial-living, the magic-mirror. Rilke compared the moment of recognition to taking a monastic vow. But in some ways, it is less like taking a monastic vow than selling your soul to the devil. Unlike a monastic vow, it cannot be broken once it is made. The devil insists on his bargain, and there is no way back to primal innocence.

This, I think, explains why those pages in *All Men Are Islands* – in which Duncan describes his own recognition that he is a poet – have a moving quality that goes beyond their obvious content. He had been more of misfit than most – which was due equally to his size and his temperament. His schoolfellows teased him about his lack of inches. When he complained about this to his mother, she said: 'Tell them that poison always comes in small bottles' – which suggests that he had aleady begun to develop the acid wit that can be found on every other page of the autobiographies. He was lonely, introverted, subject to disturbing emotions. And now, suddenly the ugly duckling suspected he was a swan . . . No doubt the moment of recognition must have been equally startling for Shakespeare, Goethe, Tennyson: but they were less misfits to begin with. It is Byron whose childhood suggests the closest parallels with Duncan: the fatherless, undersized child with the crippled foot and the passionate temper. It is also significant that Byron also developed a lifelong obsession with love. Duncan's rise to fame was as abrupt as Byron's, and his subsequent repudiation by the critics was equally traumatic. Under the circumstances, it is not surprising that both Byron and Duncan developed a penchant for satire, and a talent for making enemies.

But, for all his Byronic tendencies, Duncan is a more serious character than Byron. Or perhaps, to be fair to Byron, one should say that Duncan's fame came at a later age, that he has outlived Byron by a quarter of a century, and has been able to develop beyond the *Don Juan* stage. (Significantly, both wrote their respective *Don Juans* in their mid-thirties.) It is interesting – but fruitless – to speculate whether, if Byron had lived to be sixty, he would have been capable of the tremendous imaginative detachment and sheer creative stamina required to produce an epic like *Man*.

And what would have happened if it had been Duncan's *Don Juan* that had brought him fame, rather than *This Way to the Tomb*? In a sense, as I have suggested, *This Way to the Tomb* was a false start. It gave Duncan the reputation of a follower of Eliot, and suggested that he is a far less turbulent and complex character than he is. *Childe Harold* established Byron as a kind of nineteenth century Rudolph Valentino, a combination of lover and sinner:

and for the sake of the expectant public, he simplified his literary persona, and became a combination of Childe Harold, Manfred and Don Juan. This may have been his ruination as a serious poet (the point is debatable, but I think it is arguable), but it simplified his life. By comparison, Duncan started off on the wrong foot. *This Way to the Tomb*, *Lucretia* and *The Eagle Has Two Haeds* suggested a neo-classic intellectual; only with *Stratton*, *Don Juan* and *The Death of Satan* did it become clear that he was, in fact, a romantic rebel. It looked as if he had changed direction in midstream. He hadn't. He had only found his direction. This had one supreme advantage, and one considerable disadvantage. It meant that he had no false *persona* to impede his development; he was able to develop the Rousseau-like complexity and introspection that are so typical of all his best work. But he also had no easy, comfortable self-image to live-up to – or, more important, write-up to. His only certainty was his identity as a poet. It becomes possible to see why he called his most self-revelatory volume of poetry *The Solitudes*. It produces the impression of a shipwrecked man, naked, clinging to a rock in a rough sea. The lover who has been dreaming of some ideal relationship – a Beatrice, a Heloise, a Dona Ana – finds himself caught in a whirl-pool of neurosis and tied to a hellcat. (At least, this is the impression the poetry produces.) She tells him he is insignificant, that his last play's a bore; she betrays him with his friends and borrows his money. All this might not matter if he *was* a cynical Don Juan; but he is an idealist who remains obsessed by the idea of some ultimate union of souls – Dante and Beatrice, Heloise and Abelard. The poem *Heloise and Abelard* seems to be an attempt to restore himself, and his belief in the possibility of this healing and fulfilling relationship.

At a time when most poets have established a reputation and are living on past experience, Ronald Duncan was, in effect, starting all over again. In the early Sixties, I attended the first night of a revival of *This Way to the Tomb* at the Arts Theatre Club. I felt that he set a great deal of store by this production. His last play, *The Catalyst*, had only confirmed that the critics had no understanding and no liking for what he was trying to do: they were not interested in his odd metaphysical obsession with the love relationship. I felt he wanted to go back to the beginning, to his first major success, and see whether *this* would meet with more comprehension. If it had, it seems possible that he might have experienced some temptation to retrace his steps, to revert to the earlier style and preoccupations. (I suspect he also wanted to thumb his nose at the kitchen-sink generation and the critics who supported it.) In fact,the reviews were as hostile as ever, suggesting that Saint Anthony and everybody else should have been left entombed.

For a while, he seemed uncertain what to do next. He wrote the first volume of autobiography, tinkered with a novel based on the same subject as *The Catalyst*, and wrote short stories. Then, in 1964, he had a curious experience in a new London flat, whose bare walls he had daubed with colours. Glancing up at these daubs from his writing, he realised that he had drawn a bison and matchstick men. Later, he saw similar drawings in the caves at Lascaux. Once again, his unconscious mind had come to the rescue. It struck him suddenly that 'I was not 47; some parts of me were possibly 20,000 years old'. This, he was convinced, was an experience of Jung's 'racial memory'.

I have never asked him how long it took for this germ to become the origin of *Man*. But it does strike me that this insight was, in a sense, his 'salvation'. Suddenly, after the intensely personal hell of *The Solitudes*, the disappointing *cul de sac* of the theatre, he had stumbled upon a theme that liberated all his imaginative energy, and that allowed him to direct it into his most ambitious creative enterprise.

Man is undoubtedly Duncan's greatest work, the work by which he will be judged. It must also rank as one of the most ambitious poems ever written, in this century or on any other. Its range dwarfs even Pound's *Cantos* or Olsen's *Maximus Poems*. It could be regarded, quite simply, as an attempt by a twentieth century man to write a new *Divina Commedia*. Dante tried to take in the whole cosmology, as it was known in his day. He raised the question: what is man? what is his place in the universe? and he attempted to answer it with all the resources – theological, scientific, philosophical – then available. Dante stood at the crossroads of European thought, both spatially and temporally. Historians of the future may say the same of Ronald Duncan. He is not only post-romantic and post-existentialist; he is also one of the first poets to grasp the fact that he is writing at the end of the age of scientific materialism. In the nineteenth century, science literally became a religion for those who loved it. Reading Davy, Faraday, Huxley, Tyndall, Lyell, we become aware that they felt about science as St Theresa or St Francis felt about religion; they saw it as the answer to all humanity's questions. This spirit can still be found in Freud, Einstein, Planck. Through the philosophy of Husserl, Wittgenstein and Bertrand Russell, it has dominated much of mid-twentieth century philosophy. It has also been responsible for a great deal of philosophic despair, since it insists that man is a purely accidental product of a mechanical universe. The late Fifties and Sixties saw the beginning of a revolt against this attitude *in science itself.* An eminent scientist, Michael Polanyi, winner of a Nobel Prize for chemistry, argued in *Personal Knowledge* that scientific creativity is as 'inspirational' and 'irrational' as artistic creativity. Poincaré had said the same sort of thing half a century earlier; but his remarks had been accepted simply as interesting psychological observations. It was Polanyi who, together with Karl Popper, insisted that what it all meant was that science has been too narrow, and that it must recognise that not only are science and art both attempts to grasp reality, but that their methods are fundamentally similar. Or, to put this more straightforwardly: nineteenth century science regarded mysticism with detestation, as something that ought not to exist; in the past decade or so, science has become increasingly 'mysticised'. It is learning that it must broaden its boundaries.

At the time of writing, the extent of this revolution has scarcely been grasped, even by scientists. But Duncan has grasped it, and made it the starting point of *Man*. *Man* could not have been written before the mid-1960s; the 'anti-reductionist' revolution had not yet taken place, and the question 'What is man?' would have been largely rhetorical. As it is, Duncan can attempt to answer the question both as a poet and a scientist, and produce an answer that is valid both for poetry and science.

Man is still incomplete; I received my copy of its third volume only a few weeks before writing this essay. Any comments on it are therefore bound to be provisional. But one thing seems clear: unlike Pound's *Cantos*, it will eventually form a coherent whole with a beginning and an end. The poem starts with the origin of the solar system, and examines the theories of scientists, philosophers, theologians, to explain the creation of life. Part two deals with life on earth, from its first appearance to the arrival of man. Part three deals with the evolution of man, the slow evolution of his mind and imagination, the discovery of fire, the development of language (which, as one might expect, Duncan sees as the most important experience of all). Man learns to see himself objectively through language, to understand his needs, to think and speculate – and, finally, to ask himself the question of his own identity. This third part of *Man* culminates in man's first act of creation, the scratching of pictures on walls. So, after forty-two cantos, Duncan has arrived at the point from which the whole thing started: those matchstick men and prehistoric animals that he unconsciously daubed on his walls. . . .

In some ways, this third canto is the most exciting and satisfying so far; Duncan's imagination is more deeply involved. The remaining cantos should be more exciting still, covering the evolution of human intelligence. And, presumably, the long voyage into time will end with Duncan himself, since it was the recognition of his own 'permanence' that formed its starting point.

I am unwilling to write more fully of *Man* until I have read its final cantos; they may alter the whole perspective. But even if they should, against all expectation, fail to bring the poem to a satisfactory conclusion, *Man* would still remain one of the most exciting and boldly conceived works of modern literature.

Perhaps the most amazing thing about it is that it should have come from a poet like Duncan, who, like Kierkegaard, has always regarded the abstract as a betrayal of the personal. He has written about himself, as Villon or Whitman did, and attempted to transform the personal into the universal. In *The Solitudes*, the personal seemed to threaten to strangle him. It was difficult to see in which direction he could advance. But *Man* is less an advance than a creative leap. Read in the context of his other work, it has an element of the miraculous, the totally unexpected. It is a proof of the incredible vitality of the creative imagination.

What it suggests is that the whole estimate of Duncan that I have put forward in this essay could be false, or at least, incomplete. If, by some mischance, Duncan had died before he had written *Man*, then I think it would have been accurate to say of him that he is a 'personal' writer, in the sense defined earlier: that the personal life and the work are so closely interwoven that one cannot be understood without the other. And I think it would have been true to say that his work reveals a dangerous underestimation of himself. In *The Outsider*, I had argued that men like Nietzsche, Van Gogh, T.E. Lawrence, were ultimately destroyed by lack of self-belief – failure, as it were, to see themselves through the eyes of posterity. All of them lived according to Kafka's advice: 'In the struggle between yourself and the world, always take the world's side.' I suggested that it might be better to have a wildly exaggerated idea of your own genius – like Keats's friend Haydon, or Philip James Bailey, the author of that pathetic masterpiece *Festus* – than to lack the vital core of self-belief. I would have said that Duncan fits this basic 'outsider' pattern, and that this lack of a definite self-image can be seen in *The Solitudes*.

Man demands a complete revision of this estimate. It reveals that he has brought under control and learned to utilise the enormous subconscious forces that seemed to threaten to destroy him. The work has the vitality of a volcanic upheaval; images, ideas, visions, pour out of its pages like lava. And it is already clear that he has succeeded where Pound and Charles Olsen failed. The casualness, the formlessness, of their work often seems to be the result of lack of inspiration, as if they are publishing first-draft notebooks instead of a finished poem. *Man* is equally rough-cast, but the technique here seems inevitable, part of the crude, violent process of creation.

For more than two decades now, Duncan has been largely ignored. Pound had a similar period of eclipse from about 1930 onward; and obviously, he was thinking of himself when he makes Elpenor describe himself as 'a man of no fortune, with a name to come!' Publication of *The Pisan Cantos* in 1948 re-established him as a major literary figure. *Man* should do for Duncan what the later *Cantos* did for Pound: reveal him as one of the most interesting and important writers of his generation. I think it would amuse him to become a Grand Old Man of letters. It will surely be the most unlikely disguise he has assumed so far.

1975

THIRTEEN

Crimes of freedom – and their cure

First of all, we have to clear our minds of nonsense on this matter of the increase in violence. No figures exist for earlier centuries, but it seems probable that if Vidocq or Sir Robert Peel could be transported by time machine into the twentieth century, they would be impressed that the world has become so law-abiding. Social misery has always been the great incubator of violence. In the East End of London throughout the nineteenth century, murder was so frequent that the newspapers did not even bother to report it. Jack the Ripper's crimes were not reported until he had killed and mutilated two women – and only then because of his odd habit of removing some of the inner organs. This kind of poverty-motivated violence is steadily vanishing. We are now concerned because the murder rate has risen from an average of 130 a year in the 1930s to 160 a year (or thereabouts – 150 is a closer figure for the past four years) in the 1960s. A hundred years ago Whitechapel alone could probably have equalled our new national average.

Again, we are concerned with juvenile violence, with teddy boys committing all kinds of crimes from slashing railway seats to kicking people to death. It would be salutory to remember that in previous centuries hooliganism was not the prerogative of the young. In his book *The Roots of Violence* (1963), Christopher Hibbert describes a society of gentlemen called the Mohocks who flourished in the eighteenth century, and who were dedicated to 'doing all manner of hurt to their fellow creatures'; they used to beat up servants, gouge people's eyes out, and make old ladies dance by swinging swords under their feet. Again, in Chapter 17 of his *Memoirs*, Casanova tells how he became a fiddler in a theatre orchestra, and joined a band of madcaps whose idea of a joke was to beat up prostitutes, send doctors and midwives on false errands in the middle of the night and overturn statues in public squares; Casanova describes without shame how eight of them kidnapped a girl from a tavern where she was having a meal, and all raped her. If this happened today in London, it would get headlines for a week. The adult of the twentieth century *is* more adult; we would nowadays find it very difficult to imagine members of a theatre orchestra behaving in this manner. The teddy-boy at 25 is usually a married man with a good job and a couple of children. The same point could be made about robbery. We hear every week of some cashier being robbed of the wages; but in the eighteenth century it would have required a special newspaper to chronicle all the robberies that took place in different parts of England in a day. (Let anyone who doubts this read Gordon Maxwell's *Highwayman's Heath* (Thomasons Ltd, 1949), a history of Hounslow Heath, and simply count up the number of highway robberies that took place in this relatively small area in the eighteenth century.)

So the first thing to recognise in a discussion of twentieth century violence is that modern police methods have reduced violence to a fraction of the figure for earlier centuries. It is possible to foresee a time when nine criminals in ten will be caught within an hour of the crime. This means that organised crime is bound to diminish. If England devoted the money spent on defence in one year to fighting crime – that is, to increasing the number of police and equipping police forces everywhere with the latest scientific equipment – the crime rate could be halved instantaneously.

On the other hand, this also means that many unstable personalities will respond to the new conditions by exploding into violence, the violence of neurotic protest. This, in fact, is what has happened, and this is certainly the point most worth discussing. Twentieth century violence differs from that of previous centuries in being definable largely in *psychological* terms. In previous ages, the causes were largely sociological. I do not mean simply that most murderers today are psychotics. (To begin with, this is not true, if we are talking about the whole world; most murders today take place in the under-developed countries, and their causes are usually sociological. Mexico still has the world's highest murder rate.) I mean that, in order to understand them fully, one must grasp something about the psychology of man in the twentieth century.

In *The Transcendence of the Ego* Sartre cites an interesting case of a young married woman who was terrified of being left alone because she experienced a powerful desire to go to the window and summon passers-by like a prostitute. There was no obvious reason for this desire, except that it horrified her. Sartre speaks of a 'vertigo of possibility'; 'she found herself monstrously free'. Goethe had also investigated the same psychology of freedom in his story of the honest attorney (*Der Prokurator*), in which a virtuous wife, whose husband is on a journey, finally becomes obsessed by the need for an affair because she is bored and thinks about it too much; her very resistance to the idea drags her towards it. The 'honest attorney', whom she approaches to become her lover, makes her 'snap out' of her morbid state simply by persuading her to undertake a fast; the effort of will involved pulls her together. What has happened here is that the wife has found herself drifting towards infidelity out of excess of mental energy and a lack of psychological resources. It is worth noting that her horror of infidelity propels her towards it more quickly than ever; someone who believed in the devil would probably explain that the devil was using *her own strength* against her, in the manner of a ju-jitsu wrestler.

All this is only to say that there are crimes that are the outcome of leisure and freedom just as there are crimes that are the outcome of social misery and lack of freedom. It is also worth pointing out that this 'excess of freedom' is likely to lead to suicide too; as many people have observed, it is significant that the highest suicide rate in Europe is to be found in one of the most highly developed welfare states – Denmark. (The only two countries with a comparable suicide rate are Austria and Japan – both small countries with a high degree of 'paternalism'.) This leads to another interesting statistic: that about 40 per cent of murder suspects commit suicide in England. (In 1962 it was 45 out of 129.) Again, no earlier statistics are available, but I would be very surprised indeed if the figures for the eighteenth century were anything like as high. (I can find no reference to murderers committing suicide in the *Newgate Calendar* or the *New Newgate Calendar*.) This, I think, would seem to support the notion of 'crimes of freedom'.

The problem, then, is one of freedom. Whitehead wrote:

DETERIORATION NO RISK =

'Without adventure, civilisation is in full decay.' But then, Chesterton pointed out that adventure is only an inconvenience rightly considered, and the whole aim of civilisation is to remove inconveniences. Therefore civilisation aims at the destruction of adventure, and it is difficult to see how this can be otherwise. In that case, bored people with a sense of adventure will continue to turn to crime. This, I think, focuses the problem fairly clearly. The typical crime of the twentieth century is sadistic, because sadism is a disease of 'monstrous freedom'. (We sometimes refer to a robber as 'sadistic' because he has beaten an old woman to death with an iron bar, but this is a misuse of the word. Strictly speaking, sadism means to derive *sexual pleasure* from an act of violence, and should not be confused with stupid brutality.) We can see this if we consider some of the murder cases that have made a sensation in England in the past 20 years – Heath, Haigh, Christie, the A.6 murderer; there is a powerful flavour of abnormality about them all when compared with the *causes célèbres* that excited our grandparents – Crippen, Mrs Bravo, Charlie Peace. It is impossible to conceive of a crime like that of Leopold and Loeb taking place in the nineteenth century. The Dusseldorf mass-killer, Peter Kürten (in many ways a highly intelligent and likeable man) admitted that his sadism developed in long periods of solitary confinement in prison. Sartre's young married woman tempted to be a prostitute has something in common with these criminals.

In short, the cause of most Western violence in this century is mental, not sociological. But before considering this more closely, there is one point worth making: the violence of the twentieth century is not yet 'out of hand'. It is true that it has been rising steadily since the war; crime is *always* high after wars. Still, the crime rate today is very reasonable compared with a century ago, because social reforms have removed many of the causes. Further social reforms and more scientific ways of crime-fighting will make it still lower. The problem that will then remain – the violence that comes from neurosis – will still be serious; but in actual figures, it should not be too great.

At first sight, this problem of 'mental crime' seems insoluble; the very idea of solving it seems to lead in a vicious circle, since it would require an enormous *organised* effort, and such crime is often a rebellion against the very idea of organisation. Extreme examples of this type of crime are child murders, often involving sexual assault. In the case of Derek Edwardes a few years ago, there was something of a public outcry because Edwardes had been under a psychiatrist for some time before his murder of Edwina Taylor, and had actually told him that he would murder a small girl one day. But on reflection, it is difficult to see how psychiatrists could take precautions in such cases; there is no known test to distinguish a murderer in advance. The only way of attacking this problem would seem to be for the public health service to provide far more psychiatrists, and then to hope for the best.

But murder is only a small part of the problem. It would be interesting to know how many of the men involved in the great train robbery were in some way driven to crime – by social causes – and how many *chose* it in the same way that Leopold and Loeb chose to murder Bobby Franks, as an obscure gesture or rebellion or bravado. For in any kind of highly organised and fairly affluent society, a kind of mental strain based on boredom and unfulfilment is bound to result in various criminal acts. One of the major problems of our society is that so many people are too intelligent to accept religion, but not intelligent or strong-minded enough to look for acceptable alternatives; in the same way, many people are strong-minded enough not to want to be 'organisation men', but incapable of seeing beyond an act of protest. These situations produce a sense of being 'between two stools', lacking real motive; a sense of mental strain is produced that may find its outlet in violence, or in organised anti-social behaviour. Periodically, some appalling case involving hooliganism or sadism makes us aware that there is a great deal of this state of mind to be found in our society – as in the A.6 murder, or the case of the teddy boys who kicked a man to death for a few shillings. We then realise that there are thousands of young people who feel no kind of responsibility towards society, but only a kind of slow-burning resentment. *This* is the problem, and it is hard to see how it can be attacked.

In the terms in which it has been stated above, it is certainly almost impossible to see a solution. But I think that more than a glimmer can be obtained by considering some of the work done over the past few years by the American psychologist Abraham Maslow, of Brandeis University. Maslow was trained as a Freudian in the pre-war years, but became increasingly dissatisfied with the Freudian mechanistic explanations of neuroses. One of his early cases was a girl who had hoped for a college career, but who had been forced to take a rather dull job to support her family; she developed all kinds of neuroses that would have given Freud a field day. Maslow took the astonishing step of simply advising her to take night classes – which completely cured her! Maslow came to conclude that there is an active 'need to know' in most highly developed human beings that has to be fulfilled; this need cannot be reduced to any simpler Freudian terms. That is to say – I am not now using Maslow's terminology – that there is an active *evolutionary* component in many human beings that demands satisfaction just as much as the social or sexual urges. But this was only half the discovery. Maslow felt that Freud had made a mistake to lay so much emphasis on sick and sub-normal people, and to use material derived from such cases as the basis for a general psychology. Maslow took the curious step of deciding to investigate *healthy* human beings; he deliberately looked around for the healthiest and best-adjusted people he could find.

The result was interesting. Maslow discovered that nearly all of these exceptionally healthy people had experiences which he decided to call 'peak experiences'. A peak experience is a sudden flare of intense life-affirmation. It would be a mistake to confuse it with 'mystical experience', but equally a mistake to imagine there is no kind of connection. A mother described a 'peak experience' watching her husband and children eating breakfast together; a hostess described one after a successful party. There is nothing very mystical about this; but it indicates that this evolutionary sense may be the basis of the psychology of health. We do not hear much about it because sick people talk about their sickness while healthy people never talk about their health; yet it might not seem premature to say that Maslow has discovered an important new dimension in psychology.

Having decided to investigate carefully the role of the peak-experience, Maslow went into the whole question of the drives of ordinary healthy people. His researches are still incomplete, but

the picture that emerges differs in many ways from the static
Freudian picture of man as a creature who seeks security and
adjustment. One of the most interesting experiments, conducted
by a colleague of Maslow's, concerned the 'will to live' in chronic
alcoholics. The alcoholics were given lysergic acid or mescalin,
and then 'peak experiences' were induced by means of art or
music. The result was better than anyone anticipated; about half
the alcoholics were cured.

The interesting question, of course, is why. If Charles Jackson's
picture of an alcoholic in *The Lost Weekend* (1945) has any general
validity, the answer is not far to seek. The alcoholic may be the
more-than-averagely sensitive man who is particularly susceptible
to boredom, to dissatisfaction with what life offers him. Now any
form of satisfying mental experience, aesthetic or purely
intellectual, demands two things: a certain idealism or sense of
purpose, and the energy to devote to the pursuit of the purpose.
Satisfying experience is not a *passive* affair; it demands as much
work, let us say, as learning a foreign language in order to get the
best out of a holiday in that country. The energy usually follows
the vision, the sense of purpose. Once a sense of defeat has set in,
the vision is lost; the senses seem to 'close up' – to use Blake's
phrase. Maslow's experiment worked on all the 'Lost Weekend'
type of drunks by restoring the feeling – which most of us possess
in youth – that the quality of one's experience can be improved
indefinitely by making the mental effort: that is to say, it restored
to these men their 'evolutionary dimension' without which they
were incomplete.

The implications of all this are enormous. It should be
emphasised at this point that Maslow is by no means a solitary
pioneer in this new field: 'existential psychologists' all over
Europe and America are working along parallel lines. Hadley
Cantril of Princeton is also doing some equally absorbing work in
the theory of perception that supports Maslow's conclusions;
unfortunately, there is not space here to talk about this.[1]

Now the alcoholic and the criminal have much in common.
This has always been so; in the days when crime was mostly social
in cause, the same strains produced both crime and alcoholism.
Nowadays, when so much crime is 'psychological' in cause, the
same is true of alcoholism. I am not now proposing that Maslow

should establish an enormous clinic to try to give criminals peak experiences; it would obviously be absurd and impractical. But it seems to me that Maslow and others like him are at last probing to the very root of the problem of violence in our society, and that they have taken an important step – the most important step – in recognising the evolutionary factor in the human psyche, the need to know, the need to create, the need to achieve a richer quality of experience.

CF: BRADSHAW 1964
AGAIN

FOURTEEN

Introduction to *The Dark Gods*

On the morning of 2 June 1973 a boat containing four men rowed out into Loch Ness in Scotland. One of the four was the Rev. Donald Omand, author of *Experiences of a Present Day Exorcist*. His purpose: to exorcise the loch, to try to rid it of its famous monster. For Omand had written:

> The explanation for these extraordinary appearances (like the Loch Ness Monster) lies not in the field of science, but in the realm of the supernatural. What has been seen . . . is not a concrete, present-day monster but a projection into our day and age of something which had its habitat in Loch Ness . . . millions of years ago.

A 'projection'? How could a monster from the Jurassic Age be projected into twentieth-century Scotland? The answer to this question involves a theory that is widely held by dowsers and other believers in the 'fringe' science of radiaesthesia. This is the notion that everything that has happened in the past has somehow left a 'recording' – very much like a photograph – imprinted on its surroundings. It is well known that flashes of lightning can occasionally 'photograph' objects or people, by some process that is still not understood by science. Moreover, in the mid-nineteenth century, two American scientists, J. Rodes Buchanan and William Denton, conducted a series of experiments that convinced them that many people have the ability to 'pick up' details of the history of an object merely by holding it in their hands; Denton found that some of his students could give remarkably accurate accounts of the history of volcanic rocks, meteorites and other specimens that were wrapped in thick brown paper. They called this curious ability 'psychometry', and Denton believed that it could provide a kind of magic peepshow into the history of the earth. 'From the first dawn of light upon this infant globe,' writes Denton, 'Nature has been photographing every moment. . . .'

Let us return to the Rev. Donald Omand, who is standing upright in the boat, repeating the powerful rite of exorcism. One of his companions was the well-known 'monster hunter' F.W. Holiday, author of *The Great Orme of Loch Ness* and other books. He reports that, although it was a warm and sunny evening when they dragged the boat across the beach, it had become grey and choppy by the time Omand had completed the exorcism and thrown the last of the holy water into the loch. Holiday writes: 'As we paused under the squat tower of Urquart Castle I saw a change had come over Donald Omand. Suddenly he looked very old and very cold. I was afraid he was going to faint. . . .' The following day, as Holiday was having drinks with friends in a house on the edge of the loch, there was a sudden loud crashing sound from the garden, and through the window Holiday saw a pyramid-shaped column of blackish smoke about eight feet high. His hostess shrieked. Yet, oddly enough, her husband, who was pouring the drinks, saw and heard nothing. When they again looked in the garden, all was quiet and peaceful.

This curious little episode is typical of a certain type of 'psychic' occurrence. Holiday's host was not deaf; he simply failed to hear the loud crashes and sudden turmoil – which went on for a quarter of a minute, and which terrified the other two. The explanation would seem to be that what Holiday and his hostess heard were not physical sounds – vibrations in the air – but some telepathic phenomenon that sounded inside their heads, so to speak. And occurrences of this sort are so widely reported in the annals of psychical research that most investigators would accept that man seems to possess some 'sense' of faculty that is quite distinct from the other five senses – which is why one of the early investigators, Professor Charles Richet, coined the phrase 'sixth sense' to describe it. It is presumably this 'sixth sense' that operates when someone is able to describe the history of a chunk of volcanic rock or meteorite.

All of which brings us to a most interesting problem. Let us, for the sake of argument, accept the notion that there *is* a 'sixth sense' which can pick up information that is not normally accessible to the other five. Let us, also for the sake of argument, accept that, in some sense, nature has been taking 'photographs' since the beginning of time, and that every object contains its history somehow encoded in its atoms. In that case, the sixth sense would simply be a kind of decoder. We need not even think of it as something paranormal or supernatural. Sherlock Holmes could read the history of Dr Watson's alcoholic brother in his watch. Indian trackers can read minute signs on a completely rocky terrain that tell them that a man or animal has passed that way recently. When a sense is developed to this point of intensity, it seems to deserve a different name. . . .

But *if* this sixth sense exists, would it be confined to reading – or picking up – purely natural events – i.e. that a watch has been owned by a drunkard, or even, conceivably, that a desperate man has committed suicide in a certain room? ('Emotional' events are supposed to 'imprint' themselves with unusual intensity on their surroundings.) The answer to this would seem to be No. Probably nine out of ten people have known some relative who 'knew' when a letter would be arriving with bad news, or when cousin John was killed in a car accident in New Zealand. . . . It is difficult to stretch the word 'natural' to cover this kind of thing. And what about that thoroughly disturbing – but, again, convincingly documented – phenomenon, glimpses into the future? Precognitions *should be* impossible, because the future has not yet taken place, and is completely undetermined. Yet, as Martin Ebon reports in a volume clled *Prophecy in Our Time*, 'The American Society for Psychical Research in New York has collected close to two thousand cases of "spontaneous phenomena" which include specifically detailed precognitive and telepathic experiences. . . .'

Let us not, however, be side-tracked into a discussion of the nature of time. For the important question that now arises is this: Does that world upon which the sixth sense operates contain only objects and events? Or is it conceivable that it also contains living entities? That is to say, life-forms that are invisible to our ordinary senses?

I have deliberately chosen to present the question in this roundabout – and rather abstract – way, because it lies at the centre of the present book. And the authors themselves have not tried to lead the reader into their subject by this relatively gentle and uncontroversial route. Instead, they have plunged in at the deep end, with flying saucers, 'men in black', conspiracies, and sinister non-human entities which might conceivably cause trouble (at least) for the human race. I am reasonably certain that various scientific friends of the sceptical persuasion – like Dr Christopher Evans, Martin Gardner and Professor John Taylor – would dismiss this as a 'crank', work, aimed only at the lunatic fringe. I partially sympathise with this attitude, and agree that Messrs Roberts and Gilbertson *are* inclined to take much for granted. Yet I cannot agree that what they have to say can be entirely dismissed as a manifestation of modern romanticism – a kind of twentieth-century Gothic Revival. Whatever the explanation, it is not as straightforward as that. Perhaps the simplest way of explaining this point is by referring back to the story of Donald Omand and Ted Holiday (which Mr Holiday has written up in a remarkable manuscript called *The Goblin Universe*, which he has been kind enough to allow me to quote). Holiday's purpose in going to Scotland was not simply to see the exorcism of Loch Ness, but also to investigate a curious story concerning a Swedish journalist named Jan-Ove Sundberg. In August 1971 Sundberg was in England writing a story on the Loch Ness Monster for his Swedish magazine *Lektyr*. Taking a short cut through the woods near Foyers early one morning, he suddenly encountered a strange-looking machine in a woodland glade, resembling a large black metal cigar. Then three creatures in 'diving helmets' emerged from the bushes, got into the black cigar and 'took off'. Sundberg had a camera round his neck and had the presence of mind to take a picture as the machine lifted off. Back in Sweden, Sundberg began to be persecuted by a strange man dressed in black, who kept making unexpected appearances and leaving footprints in the garden. As a result, Sundberg had a nervous breakdown.

Ted Holiday discovered that three other reliable observers also claimed to have seen a UFO in the Loch Ness area. And he was discussing these manifestations with his host and hostess when the loud crashes took place. He slept very badly that night. Early the next morning, as he walked down towards the caravan where Donald Omand was sleeping, he saw a man who was dressed entirely in black leather or plastic. He walked past him and turned. The man had vanished, although there was nowhere for him to vanish to. It was the last Holiday saw of him. But one year later, close to the spot where he had seen the man in black, Holiday was struck down with a heart attack. . . .

My natural scepticism suggests that there was, in fact, no connection between Donald Omand's exorcism of Loch Ness, the strange bangs, the man in black and the heart attack (which fortunately was not fatal). The notion that the exorcism had stirred up hostile supernatural forces sounds absurd. But – as readers of this book will discover – a large number of people who have seen UFOs have encountered 'men in black' who have warned them to say nothing. More often than not these 'men' explain that they are from some government department or military intelligence; but the government departments invariably deny all knowledge of such agents. Another UFO investigator, John Keel, has not only chronicled dozens of cases of men in black but encountered them himself. If Ted Holiday's 'man in black' was really one of these weird visitants, then the rest of his story would begin to sound altogether more plausible. . . .

The authors of this book argue that mankind has always been plagued by certain 'dark forces', and that in our own time these forces have reappeared in the form of UFOs, weird-looking aliens and men in black. This is not to say that they believe that all UFOs are hostile or malevolent. The basic position has been stated by the doyen of modern Ufologists, Brinsley le Poer Trench (Lord Clancarty), who believes that there are two types of UFO phenomena: one is benevolent, and has been around throughout human history; the other is more recent, and seems to be either hostile, or at least non-friendly towards human beings – perhaps feeling about us as our scientists feel about laboratory rats.

In the past century, we have become aware of at least one piece of evidence that fails to fit the rationalist picture. I am speaking of poltergeist phenomena. The poltergeist – or noisy spirit – seems to be the Till Eulenspiegel of the spirit world, causing loud bangs and crashes, and various other annoying, but seldom dangerous, phenomena. In the second half of the nineteenth century, it began to dawn on psychical investigators that such phenomena nearly always occurred when there was a disturbed adolescent in the house. And the explanation that finally emerged was that, when certain people are thoroughly frustrated, some 'unconscious' part of the mind releases violent energies to create a diversion – in the same way that a vandal smashes telephones or slashes seats. No one has a clear idea of what energies are involved, or how they operate. But at least we are now beginning to understand how the child at the 'focus' of the disturbance can be unaware that he or she is to blame. Modern brain research has revealed that we have virtually two different people inside our heads. The left cerebral hemisphere controls language and ideas – the 'rational self'. The right hemisphere is concerned with recognition and with intuition. These two halves are joined by a knot of nerve fibres called the *corpus callosum*. If this is cut, the patient splits into two different people. If the left half is shown an orange, and the right half an apple, and the patient is asked what he has seen, he replies: 'An orange.' If he is asked to write down what he has seen with his left hand (which is connected to the right side of the brain), he writes: 'An apple.' *Asked* what he has just written, he replies: 'An orange.'

What this shows clearly is that, when 'I' reply to a question, it is the left half of my brain that is replying. Yet the right half also has its own identity and feelings. For example, if an obscene picture is shown to the right hemisphere of a split-brain patient, he may blush; asked why he is blushing, he replies truthfully: 'I don't know.' Because it is the *other* person in the brain who is embarrassed.

Common sense suggests that this 'other' person could be also responsible for poltergeist activity. At least, it is the obvious suspect. So while we still have no idea *how* a frustrated adolescent can cause objects to fly through the air, we begin to have an inkling of 'who' might be responsible.

A similar point has been made by Suzanne Padfield, an eminent investigator of paranormal powers. She herself possesses powers of 'psychokinesis': that is to say, she can quite deliberately, with an effort of will, deflect a very light needle in the labratory by concentrating on it. She discovered that most people who possess such powers seem to experience a need to believe that 'somebody else' is doing it – some supernatural entity or unknown force. In order to 'summon' her powers, she had to imagine she was invoking some 'space intelligence'. Then one day she decided to try making them work 'on her own', without imagining this hidden support; they worked as well as ever.

The point that emerges here is of enormous importance. Let us, for a moment, assume that the 'person' who is responsible for psychokinesis (or poltergeist activity) *is* that 'unknown self' in the right cerebral hemisphere. Of course, it is not really 'cut off' from the left – as with split-brain patients; yet for some reason, its activities are unknown to the rational self. Yet it *will* respond to a request by the rational self, just as my hand will respond to an order to pick up an object from the table. Now imagine a person who has been suffering from some form of paralysis of the hands, and is just beginning to regain his powers. You can easily imagine his reaching out slowly and painfully, and talking to his hands: 'Come on now, steady does it, don't be afraid.' And this act of talking actually makes it easier – or, at least, succeeds in damping down the self-consciousness that might make it twice as difficult. (For we all know that when we *think* too much about something we do it badly.) As the man slowly recovers the proper use of his hands, the talking becomes unnecessary; they now respond easily, and there is no need to bridge the gap between 'the desire and the response' (where, as Eliot points out in 'The Hollow Men', there falls 'the Shadow').

We might extend the analogy, and say that our psychic powers are at present in a state of paralysis, but that we can, under certain circumstances, persuade them to operate. The easiest way, to begin with, is to address them as if they are separate entities – to pray to them, so to speak. If we could become accustomed to using them, this would become unnecessary; they would begin to respond immediately. . . .

In my book *The Occult*, I pointed out that the science-fiction writer W.J. Stewart had anticipated such a theory in *Forbidden Planet*, which became one of the classic SF films. His scientist, Dr Morbius, is investigating an alien civilisation on a remote planet, and has learned to use certain machines that amplify the powers of the brain. What he does not realise is that the same ancient machinery has amplified his *unconscious* powers too. And since he has a deep unconscious resentment of any other human beings who visit his planet, a kind of monstrous poltergeist from his subconscious destroys every expedition that lands there. Yet he himself is unaware that 'he' is the monster.

I have now been involved in fairly constant study of the 'occult' for the past ten years, and I have to admit that the notion of the 'hidden side' of consciousness plays an increasingly important part. The average person hears too little about psychic phenomena to feel the need for any serious adjustment to his way of thinking. Occasionally they force themselves on the attention; but they can be regarded as 'exceptions' to the usual order of nature. For example, at the time I write this, an extraordinary trial is taking place in Chicago. A Filipino nurse was found murdered – stabbed to death – and there was no clue to the identity of the killer. Then the wife of a doctor went into a trance, and the voice of the murdered woman spoke from her mouth, using the correct Filipino dialect, and identified a fellow worker in the hospital as the killer. The police made a routine check, and the accused man confessed to the murder. Now, in September 1978, he has been brought to trial. Such a case simply contradicts most of the basic assumptions of 'normal life'. The voice of a murdered woman cannot identify someone as her killer. . . . Yet I have to admit that someone sent me a press cutting about the case soon after the accused man was arrested, and *I* totally forgot about it until I heard the item on the news yesterday. I accept the reality of many paranormal phenomena; but this particular one failed to 'fit in' to my present interest in the 'hidden side' of the mind, so I pushed it aside and forgot it. . . . This tendency to 'forget' facts that contradict our usual patterns of thinking is universal.

And it explains why I have agreed to write an introduction to *The Dark Gods*. I have to admit that I am not entirely happy with it. I feel rather as T.H. Huxley might have felt if he had been asked to introduce a volume of Cardinal Manning's sermons. Anthony Roberts and Geoff Gilbertson are convinced 'Ufologists'; they are also admirers of the late H.P. Lovecraft, and of the 'occult tradition' in literature. They are firm believers in the 'objective' reality of their Dark Gods. I am not accusing them of being unduly credulous; there are few things in this book that I cannot accept myself, considered in isolation. But because they have studied so much of the evidence, they are inclined to write as if everyone knew about it and shared their views. In short, a book like this would arouse little dissension among readers of the *Flying*

Saucer Review or the *Fortean Times*; but it is bound to strike most unprepared readers as romantic and speculative. And this is a pity, since the general public *ought* to be aware of the thinking of these unconventional individuals and groups. Whenever they appear on television, the commentary is usually slanted so that they appear to be cranks. And, of course, many of them are. But this is like judging the Church of England by the beliefs of some extreme salvationist sect. The beliefs of Anthony Roberts and Geoff Gilbertson are shared by an enormous number of quite sane and normal people who happen to have seen a flying saucer, or have met someone who has. They feel that *something* is going on, although they are by no means sure what it is. The inhabitants of UFOs may be creatures from another galaxy; they may be creatures from another dimension; they may be – as Jung believed – some kind of product of the human mind. They may be a mixture of all these. But anyone who takes the trouble to look into the subject will end by agreeing that they arc *not* pure fantasy. It is therefore my feeling that, even if you end by dismissing this book as an exercise in morbid imagination, it will be a salutary exercise to read it. You may not agree with all the answers; but you may come to feel that some of the questions are worth asking.

It may also be worth mentioning at least one possible answer to the question: where do poltergeists etc., get their energy? There is a certain amount of evidence – by no means conclusive, but nevertheless suggestive – that it may come from the earth itself. This thought occurred to me during the great drought of 1976, when our local (West Country) television news ran an item about a farmer who had been locating underground springs for his neighbours. This 'dowser' made no use of the normal forked twig; he simply locked his hands together in front of him. When he stood over a hidden source of water, his hands began to move up and down as violently as if he was working a pump handle. After a few seconds of this, he was breathless and sweating. I can dowse myself, but I need a forked twig or a plastic dowsing rod; and the results are unimpressive. And what surprised me the first time I used a dowsing rod was that it seemed to twist in my fingers of its own accord; I felt nothing. But certain dowsers – particularly those who specialise in finding water – react far more violently. A famous French dowser discovered his powers because he felt sick or fainted when he stood over underground streams.

It seems, then, that some force from the earth can cause these violent convulsions in dowsers. And the 'forces' are not necessarily associated with water. I discovered I could dowse around a group of ancient standing stones near Penzance. Two weeks ago, my wife and I visited the Clava stone circle near Culloden in Scotland; this also contains three immense cairns or ancient burial chambers. I obtained only slight reactions – perhaps because I was using a makeshift twig cut from a tree – but my wife found the 'force' in the stones so powerful that she said she felt dizzy afterwards.

Having examined many such sites, I am inclined to accept the notion that the stones were placed there because there was an unusual vortex of magnetic force in the ground. The ancients almost certainly attached some religious meaning to the force, and regarded the earth as a great mother. It seems also conceivable that such stones were used for healing. Legends certainly recount such miraculous occurrences.

Magnetism, as we know, runs in 'lines'. Nowadays, the lines of earth magnetism are usually referred to as 'leys', a word invented by the late Alfred Watkins. There is much evidence to associate various 'psychic occurrences' with ley lines – particularly with the crossing point of two or more leys. (Again, there is no space to give examples; I have given many in my book *Mysteries*.) That is to say that *if* a highly disturbed teenager lived in a house at the crossing point of two leys, he would be more likely to trigger poltergeist activity than if he lived in a place with low magnetic intensity. A house at the crossing point of leys would also be more likely to 'record' some tragic emotion, which might manifest itself to later occupants as a 'haunting'.

So, altogether, it seems possible to explain many of the 'dark forces' of the past – and present – by a reasonably scientific theory. But once we accept the notion of a 'hidden' side of the mind, which can respond to certain forces of the earth – and perhaps even make use of them – we have also created, so to speak, another *realm* of phenomena. It may, indeed, be possible to measure the earth forces with an ordinary magnetometer; but there seems to be no obvious way of measuring what happens in the brain of a disturbed adolescent who is *causing* poltergeist effects. There is a shadowy realm of interaction between the earth and the right side of the brain – this, at least, is a reasonable hypothesis. And it also seems conceivable – indeed likely – that this is also the 'realm' in which Richet's 'sixth sense' operates. But once we have admitted the possibility of this new phenomenal realm, we have also opened to door to all kinds of astonishing speculations. Anyone who looks at a large body of water has the uneasy – and perfectly accurate – feeling that there could be all kinds of creatures swimming in it depths. The same applies to this shadowy realm of the paranormal. Why should this particular world be sterile, devoid of its own indigenous life-forms?

Which brings us to perhaps the most basic question raised by *The Dark Gods. If* there are such things as disembodied entities – spirits – could some of these be 'evil'? The very title of this book implies that the answer is Yes. But such a belief raises basic philosophical problems. It is true that 'dualism' is one of the world's oldest forms of religion – the belief that there are forces of evil as well as good in the universe. I find myself inclining more and more to the notion that there are such things as 'forces of good'. (The cybernetician David Foster believes that this can be demonstrated through the basic laws of cybernetics – as I have explained in the introductory chapter of *The Occult*.) This seems to invite the reasonable question: If there are forces of good, then why not of evil?

However, it is not as simple as this; for our human experience tells us that good is not the genuine 'opposite' of evil, any more than female is the genuine opposite of male. (Biologically speaking, they are very close together.) Religions tend to make arbitrary distinctions, which seem to justify the concept; but there is no general agreement about what is evil. For a Buddhist it is evil to take life; but ritual slaughter of animals is a part of orthodox Judaism. . . . Still, all of us have a basic feeling about what is good. 'Good' is anything that makes us feel more alive, which offers a possibility of development and evolution. And if a robber was about to pull the trigger of a gun, we would feel it to be evil, not because the Christian religion forbids killing, but because his act threatens to put a sudden end to our possibilities of development. Nietzsche remarked that happiness is the feeling that obstacles are vanishing, and this also defines our basic intuition of what is good. Conversely, 'evil' is a reversal of this forward movement, a blockage. And it is basically a form of narrowness, of blindness, of stupidity.

A recent American murder case presents me with an example. In February 1976, a teenage couple from Fontana, California, decided to run away from home. They were picked up by five youths who were cruising around in a car, who took them to a remote spot and started to assault the girl. The boy managed to kick one of them, which so enraged them that they told him they would 'show him what it was really like to have a girl raped'. Two of the youths then held the boy and forced him to watch as the other three had sex with the girl simultaneously, using her vagina, anus, and mouth. Then the couple were shot and the bodies abandoned. San Bernadino police were so enraged at this murder of Chris Barber and Linda Bosteder that many of them worked overtime for months until five youths between seventeen and nineteen were finally arrested.

The youths were all on the dole, and had been driving around aimlessly all day, swigging from a bottle of vodka. Their crime produces an effect like a slap in the face; few people can doubt that the suffering they caused during the half-hour or so of the rape was 'evil'. But they were not demons or sadists; they were simply bored teenagers, probably from poor environments. Their evil lay in their stupidity, their blindness, their *lack of fellow feeling*. Colin Turnbull's book *The Mountain People* describes an African tribe called the Ik, whose traditional hunting grounds have been taken from them so that they live in conditions of poverty and total boredom; as a result, mothers will allow their children to starve to death; all fellow feeling has vanished. Poverty and hardship produces this effect – as we can see from Emile Zola's novel *Earth*.

In short, the evil we encounter on earth is a narrowing of our powers of vision, of our sensitivity and intelligence, by stupidity and laziness. And it seems to be a direct consequence of the fact that we possess physical bodies. We say 'The spirit is willing but

the flesh is weak', recognising that the two tend to pull in opposite
directions. When the flesh is tired or starved, then the mind's
powers are weakened. In order to experience the states of insight
in which Shelley wrote the 'Ode to the West Wind' or Beethoven
the Ninth Symphony, we need leisure and freedom from physical
discomfort; we also need to be in a state of mind of which the basic
characteristic is *interest*. In the days when I worked in a factory or
office, I found that my attention had been so exhausted by
boredom by the time I arrived home that I had lost the power of
concentration. This seems to have been the main factor in the case
of the five teenage rapists. So 'interest' is also partly dependent on
the state of the body.

Which seems to dispose of the notion of evil spirits or 'Dark
Gods'. Except that, if non-physical (or at least, non-fleshly) life-
forms are possible, then presumably they must be subject to their
own forms of limitation. Madame Blavatsky taught that our earth
is the lowest of seven possible 'planes', the most heavily weighted-
down with matter; yet that the very density of the matter in which
we are trapped also permits a far higher level of achievement than
on any other plane – just as it is possible to create greater statues in
marble than in cotton wool. Living creatures without dense
physical bodies might well experience their own forms of rage or
frustration. Which in turn suggests that they might be capable of
their own forms of mischief. . . . In short, as I have suggested
elsewhere, the 'spirits' that seem to spend so much time
manifesting themselves through mediums *may* be the crooks,
murderers and juvenile delinquents of the 'astral plane'.

All these are matters on which I prefer to keep an open mind. As
a matter of common sense, I am personally inclined to explain most
paranormal phenomena in terms of our 'hidden side of the mind'.
But it would be absurd flatly to exclude other possibilities.

The Dark Gods is a book about those other possibilities. Some
will strike you as far-fetched. But a few may cause you to become
thoughtful and speculative. In which case, the book will have
served its purpose.

1978

FIFTEEN

Writer in residence

When I arrived at the University of Washington, Seattle, as a 'Visiting professor', my only fellow countryman in the same position was the poet Venon Watkins. I had never met him, but always thought him one of the finest contemporary poets; and I looked forward to getting to know him. The evening before he was due to come to our house for supper, the Department Chairman called on us; he told us Vernon had just died of a heart attack while playing tennis. The poet's wife had apparently remarked: 'America seems to be a graveyard for poets. . . .' She was thinking of their friend Dylan Thomas.

It is surprising how widely this opinion is held – often by literary people who ought to know better. Rayner Heppenstall once pointed out that Thomas' death came pretty close to suicide; he should have known enough about drink to know that eighteen straight whiskies – and the American single is close to the English double – taken in 90 minutes would kill anybody. And if he did know, the blame for his death can hardly be put on 'America'.

For myself, I have found America a demoralisingly pleasant country to live in. For at least ten years, it has been something of a writer's paradise, and is becoming steadily more so. I shall be surprised if, by 1980, there are still any reputable writers living in England – or on the continent, for that matter.

Look at the figures. In England in this year, 1969, the average sale of a novel in hard covers is around 5,000 copies – (and I am speaking of novels by known writers with an established audience; the unknowns are lucky to sell a thousand). This means around £600 in royalties. As the author of several published novels, I have noticed the decline. My first novel, in 1960, sold 25,000 copies; my most recent, with better reviews, and an 'established' audience, has still to reach 5,000.

241

Paperback rights on the 'average novel' sell for anything between £750 and £2,000 – the latter would be an unusually high figure. The publisher of the hard-cover edition takes half of this. So on the English edition of his novel, the writer can hope to make a total of, say, £1,600 if he is lucky; less than £1,000 if there happens to be a credit squeeze. As to the paperback advance, he will receive half on signature, half on publication two years later. It is unusual for a paperback to make more than its advance.

What of American publication and foreign rights? My own experience is that my hardback sales in America have been approximately the same as in England, so that a novel may bring in between $1,500 and $2,500. But the American paperback market is harder to break into for the non-American writer. Most American novels get into paperback; probably less than one-tenth of English novels manage it in America. As to foreign rights, a book may bring an advance of £50; usually, that is all. Royalties seldom seem to follow. I suggest that the above figures hold good for most of the best-known English writers today – the ones whose names you would find in the chapter on 'The English Novel in the Fifties and Sixties' in some Pelican on modern literature. It is hard – almost impossible – to live by writing in England.

All of which explains why, when I set off on a lecture tour of the States in January 1966, I decided to investigate the possibilities of getting into the American academic racket. The opportunity came fairly quickly. On a freezing January day, in a small New Hampshire town, I met the writer Calder Willingham, author of *End as a Man*. I knew little about Willingham, except that his novel had made him a sudden and violent notoriety at about the time Mailer's *Naked and the Dead* appeared; for a while, Mailer and Willingham were cited as America's leading hopes for the future of the novel. Willingham is a thin, sandy-haired man with a charming southern accent and a flamboyant personality; you could not be in a room with him, no matter how large and crowded, without knowing he was there. When I met him, he was telling the story of how a nymphomaniac Hollywood agent had read his novel *Eternal Fire*, and told Willingham's agent – while the author listened over an extension – that the book should be burned and the author deprived of his manhood. The rest of the story – of how Willingham's agent was ravished at a restaurant table by the nymphomaniac – is unrepeatable here, but it had the crowd of professors' wives listening wide-eyed as they gulped their martinis.

Our host told me that Willingham had recently turned down a job as Writer in Residence at a girls' college. I mentioned this to Willingham, and within ten minutes, I had the job. He simply picked up the 'phone, got on to the college, and said: 'I've got an English writer here – Colin Wilson' . . . he put his hand over the 'phone and asked me 'Did you write *Hemlock and After?*' – then, back into the 'phone 'Yeah, he did. He wants to be Writer in Residence there. Shall I put you on to him?' I was handed the telephone. The professor on the other end asked: 'Are you married?' I said I was. 'Good. Do you expect to publish anything next year?' I said I had about four books in the works. 'Fine. Can you start in September? We pay $12,000 for the year and travelling expenses for you and your family, and you get a house on campus.' It was as simple as that.

I have to admit the prospect cheered me. I am a peaceful, domestic sort of character, and I hate leaving my family behind when I go abroad. Besides which, a three-month American lecture tour feels like three years after the first week or so. There seem to be a great many misconceptions about these tours – partly due to Dylan Thomas, partly to Malcolm Muggeridge's highly-coloured accounts which aim to make a TV impact and miss the lights and shades. It was Thomas who said that every time he held out his hand, someone put a whisky into it, and every time he took off his trousers, he found a girl in his bed. And while there is plenty of drink to be had if you want it, the latter part is downright untrue. You are moving in and out of places much too fast; you seldom make direct contact with the students; and American college girls are not all that promiscuous. They talk about sex and think about sex, but there is an odd sort of middle-class innocence about them. They are looking for Mr. Right and the house with a swimming pool; and while most of them sleep with their boy-friends, they would regard casual sex as close to prostitution.

The financial rewards on these lecture tours are pretty low – as anyone can see by consulting the appendix to Constantine

FitzGibbon's biography of Thomas. It *sounds* marvellous – to get between $500 and $750 per lecture, and do five lectures a week. Until you discover that your lecture agent takes half your earnings. And you pay your own fares across the Atlantic, and your own hotel bills. (The agent pays your fares around the States.) And American tax takes thirty per cent of your share. So in all probability, you emerge with less than $100 per lecture. And if, like me, you find it impossible to pass a book shop or a record shop, and you are so subject to homesickness that you call your family several times a week, the profits begin to look pretty miserable. You could actually make more money by staying in England and writing one article a week for any large circulation newspaper.

What is more, you work harder for this than you have ever worked in your life. On an average day, you place a call with the motel desk to wake you at 6 o'clock to catch an 8.30 'plane from an airport fifty miles away. Around 3.30 in the afternoon, after two or three changes of plane, you arrive at the small mid-western town, and are met by your host, the assistant head of the English department, who tells you that a creative writing class has been waiting for you since two thirty . . . however, it goes on until five, so there is still time. At 5.15, he takes you to your motel, where you can get a shower and collapse on the bed for half an hour. At six, your host picks you up again, and you go to his home for a cocktail hour with 'selected faculty members', which means that you are introduced to twenty people in succession, and tell each one how you like America, how long you have been here, where you've been so far and where you go to next. . . . At 7.15, to the house of the head of the English department for dinner with more selected faculty members. At 8.30, you lecture for an hour, rather hazy from food and drink, but aware that it doesn't matter what you say because they are listening to your English accent. (I have varying levels of accent, ranging from my natural Midland gutturals, up through BBC, and Oxford, and the John Osborne drawl, to strangulated Knightsbridge, and I turn it up or down depending on my degree of incoherence.) At 9.30, questions for half an hour or so. Then a group of students explain they are giving a party for you in somebody's downtown pad – only beer and California wine, but they'd love to go on discussing your ideas. You climb into bed finally around one thirty, and leave a call with the desk to get you up at six. . . .

Towards the middle of the sixth week, life begins to take on an odd, grey futility, and you find yourself wondering how Beckett could be so optimistic about human existence. Then a sort of blessed trance decends, and you march through the rest of the tour like a robot, amazed that your mouth goes on saying the right things. It takes about three months back in England for the numbness to wear off.

I wasn't sure how life as a 'visiting professor' would compare with this, but obviously, it could hardly be worse. And since the salary is tax free – due to a treaty – the pay is a great deal better.

We arrived at Hollins College in Virginia in early September: myself and wife, and two children, aged six and one. It looked too good to be true. The college is set in green, rolling countryside, with mountains in the background and the Blue Ridge Parkway – a mountain-top road that runs on for several hundreds of miles – close to the front door. The campus itself has an almost chocolate-box prettiness, all southern colonial architecture, white colonnades, emerald green lawns, immense trees. I suppose it could be described as a rich girl's college; the parents of its thousand students pay well over a million pounds (not dollars) a year to keep their girls there.

The house proved to be a roomy and pleasantly furnished bungalow on a hilltop overlooking the college buildings – part of 'Faculty Row'. My wife was excited about the kitchen, with a fridge large enough to stable a small horse, and a stove of a size you would only find in a hotel kitchen in England. William Golding had been a previous tenant – and Writer in Residence – and his year there had been a fortunate one. For some reason that no one – not even Golding himself – understands, his books quite suddenly caught on with American students during his year there. It must have been quite an experience – for a writer approaching fifty, with a highbrow reputation and small sales, to suddenly find himself up there with Salinger and Tolkien as the hero of the campuses. Opinions on Golding among the faculty varied from the warm to the curiously bitter; the latter may be due to an article on Hollins that Golding published in a mass circulation magazine, which paints the school as a quaint survival from pre-Civil War days, with rich, soft-voiced southern belles and the soothing swish of falling dollar bills.

I must admit that there was one thing that worried me from the time Louis Rubin (head of the English department) offered me the job. I am not more than averagely susceptible to women; but I couldn't help wondering whether being surrounded by so many specimens of teenage girlhood wouldn't prove wearing to the nerves. I expected to feel like Mr. Bloom among a thousand Gertie Macdowells. A brief visit paid on the earlier lecture tour had proved fairly disturbing, and Louis Rubin had mentioned that I could do anything I liked except have the girls. (I enjoyed telling an apocryphal version of this story in which I replied 'What, not *one*?', and he replied after reflection: 'Well, perhaps just *one*.') Besides, the mini-skirt had just arrived, and the Hollin version was minnier than anything I had ever seen.

In fact, the problem doesn't arise. A girl is never more attractive than when she is alone among a crowd of boys. Conversely, she is never less attractive than when she forms part of a crowd of girls in a sort of girls' barracks. She tends to dress in a canvas skirt, ankle socks and sensible shoes, and she obviously sees herself as a unit in a female menagerie, not as a woman doing her stuff to attract males. I found, to my surprise, that a crowd of girls is no more interesting than a crowd of boys. In fact, it is possible to form a sort of flirtatious relationship with your class on this under-standing – rather as you might flirt with the twelve-year-old daughter of a friend. My students used to take a certain pleasure in putting me off my lecturing stride by crossing and uncrossing their legs at crucial points, until they discovered that I tried to stare brazenly up their skirts. They then waited until I took drinks from a mug of water before crossing their knees; so I bought a mug with a glass bottom. (Actually, it was impossible to see anything but a blur through the water, but they didn't know that.)

I suspect all male lecturers have this problem, although few of them will admit it. No matter how paternal you feel about your students, it is hard to restrain the normal reflex of glancing up a skirt as the legs change position, even though you know most of the girls are wearing dreadful knee-length panties with the

consistency of armour plating. One colleague told me of a
dilemma in which this placed him. He was over-looking an exam,
and was idly glancing at uncrossed knees, when he realised that
one girl had a sheaf of papers tucked into the leg of her panty-
girdle, which she could examine by casually pulling back her skirt.
For half an hour, he struggled with his conscience, but ended by
deciding to let it go. 'There are times,' he said, 'when it is more
morally courageous to be a coward.'

The mini-skirt made me focus a realisation which, I suppose, is
obvious enough, but which had never struck me before. Teenage
girls are naturally sentimental creatures; sex is not a physical act
but a corollary of romance. They don't understand the male urge
to satisfy the *will* by the act of penetration; they want to be petted
and caressed, and perhaps rather adored as an incarnation of the
Ewig-weibliche. Logically, therefore, they should go in for
demureness and concealment and rosy blushes, so the male
understands that sex is a long way from their thoughts. The
emotion they want to arouse – particularly at seventeen – is a sort
of paternal tenderness. On the other hand, the male attention has
to be arrested to begin with – hence the mini-skirt. What the
mini-skirt does, of course, is to arouse a purely impersonal desire
to tear it off and perform an act of rape, and this should be obvious
to the dimmest female. But even the most intelligent ones prefer
not to face this. So they raise the hem line until it is an eighth of an
inch below the crotch, and then try to look as if they are posing for
a Pre-Raphaelite picture of the Lady of Shalott.

Personally, I am against mini-skirts on purely logical grounds. If
they don't want the bull to charge, they shouldn't wave the red
flag. And if they insist on waving the red flag, then males should
retaliate by wearing cod-pieces, or very tight trousers padded in
front with cushions, like ballet dancers. Anything for consistency.

The teaching load was incredibly light – about two hours a week. I
was also told that I should attend 'creative writing groups' two
evenings a week. I explained that I didn't believe that creative
writing could be taught. Louis Rubin said he didn't think so either;
it was purely a question of allowing the girls to gain experience by
reading their poetry aloud to a group. I said I thought the basic

principle of creativity was discouragement and survival of the fittest. Then the weak ones cease to write, and the strong ones survive by making an immense effort that turns them into good writers. Encouragement is like putting fertiliser on a garden full of weeds. I attended one of the creative writing seminars, and tried to put my principle into practice. After that, Louis Rubin requested that I stay away. So I went back to my two hours a week.

Although I had seen a great deal of America – travelling five thousand miles a week on lecture tours – I'd had no chance to get the feeling of the 'American way of life'. If pressed to generalise after one of these lecture tours, I would probably have agreed with the views expressed in Henry Miller's *Air Conditioned Nightmare*. But actually living in the same spot, with occasional trips to other parts of the country, allowed me to sink gently into the rhythm of American life, and I found it delightful. America has simply gone further in doing what all civilisation sets out to do: making life pleasant and convenient. At first, the sheer size of our Chevrolet station wagon (bought second-hand) worried us, until we got used to driving on excellent roads in a roomy car, and the children being able to stretch out and sleep in the back when they got tired. We drove down to Florida in November – the college didn't seem to worry if I took time off – and found American road-side cafés a revelation, after the English variety. We discovered it was not necessary to stop for lunch to get a decent meal. You went into a Howard Johnsons and asked for beef sandwiches 'to go'. The sandwiches – made with beef and gravy – came in a large box, together with plastic containers of potato salad, pickled gherkins, mustard, tomato ketchup and crisps, all thrown in free. There was also coffee in ingenious cups with a hole in the lid, so you could drink while the car was in motion without getting it up your nose. I also liked having a fridge large enough to keep several cans of beer and a couple of bottles of hock in. I liked the centrally-heated lavatory in which I could sink into a gentle state of meditation or read a chapter of *Tristram Shandy* (which I find quite unreadable off the lavatory).

It's not that I have a taste for luxury; on the contrary, I tend to be rather ascetic; and my asceticism consists in ignoring my surroundings and getting on with my work. And the more comfortable the surroundings, the easier they are to ignore.

Hollins was so comfortable that it produced a dream-like sensation. I got out of bed at a quarter to nine in the morning to drive my daughter to school – half-a-mile away. The sight of the campus in the morning never ceased to give me pleasure. Americans sometimes say that England is the greenest country in the world, but I have never seen so much continuous, luxuriant greenness as between Hollins and Washington D.C. And Hollins in the autumn is incredibly beautiful, with thousands of trees on the mountains turning every shade of red and brown. Back at home, I drank half-a-dozen cups of tea, then walked down to my office and did a couple of hours work on a novel. The moment of decision would always arrive around mid-afternoon, when I was tired of writing, for I had discovered the delights of the American supermarket. It was like having a kind of Disneyland on the doorstep. I could take the whole family, and leave my wife to wander blissfully through the drug store, grocer and delicatessen, while I wandered round the department store browsing through records, books, hardware and electrical equipment. I knew that anything we accumulated would have to be packed and sent back to England, but the hour of reckoning was a long way off. I am not comfortable unless surrounded by books, so within a few months, I had a bill for a thousand dollars at the college bookstore. I would suddenly feel nostalgia for some familiar favourite – *Seven Pillars of Wisdom* or the novels of Peacock or John Cowper Powys – and rush off searching for a copy. I could buy records with less conscience, for I could make sure I got different performances of my favourite works. It was interesting to note how I would feel a longing to hear some work that I thought I knew too well to ever want to hear it again – the Brahms symphonies, Tchaikovsky ballets, Monteverdi madrigals. I had taken a great pile of English music with me – Elgar, Delius, Warlock, Vaughan Williams, Gilbert and Sullivan – but it proved insufficient, and I bought every English record I could lay hands on. Although I was certainly not consciously homesick – I was finding Virginia too delightful for that – I think that perhaps an unconscious desire for continuity leads one to keep turning to the past and to one's own country.

Perhaps the most insidious thing was the greed for tools. I am not a particularly good mechanic or carpenter, but I enjoy messing about with electrical equipment and sawing bits of wood. Naturally, I had not bothered to take tools with me. I now developed a positive addiction to browsing around hardware stores and buying things like electric drills and soldering irons and hacksaws. The American ones were always so much cheaper and better than the ones I had left behind in England – for example, the soldering iron was shaped like a gun, and achieved soldering heat in three seconds by pressing a trigger. Every time my monthly pay cheque arrived, I evaded my wife's accusing eye, and made for the hardware store.

As far as teaching was concerned, I was given a completely free hand. There are certain theoretical restrictions; you are not supposed to actually preach communism, and I heard a story of a teacher who was dismissed for asking the girls in his class how many were still virgins. (Perhaps this was the one was who asked to fill in a form that asked: 'Do you wish to see the overthrow of the state by force or violence?', and he answered: 'Force'.) In fact, I found it necessary to give my students a solid grounding in *Das Kapital*, and nobody seemed to care. As to sex, I grasped the full extent of American academic liberalism when I finally read Calder Willingham's *Eternal Fire*. The nymphomaniac agent had been right about it. I don't think anyone nowadays can be shocked by the kind of violent obscenity to be found in De Sade or Burroughs – or *Ulysses* for that matter. But I find I can still be shocked by a 'dirty book' that is obviously written purely for money, with rapes carefully interspersed with sadistic violence, incest, and voyeurism. To do Calder Willingham justice, I am convinced he was rocking with laughter as he wrote it; its courtroom scene is actually one of the most brilliant pieces of comedy in modern fiction. But unlike some of his other books, *Eternal Fire* is not literature in any sense, even bad literature. I asked one of my colleagues what he thought would have happened if Willingham had become Writer in Residence, and some parent had read *Eternal Fire* – surely it would be like discovering that Harold Robbins or Mickey Spillane is the head of the creative writing department? He said casually, 'Oh, parents don't read.' But I am not sure this was the answer. I think a more likely explanation is that in America, writing it still regarded as a kind of sacred calling. To be a successful writer means you have followed your sacred calling successfully, and no one has a right to question your credentials, no matter what you write.

Certainly, my own complete lack of academic qualifications didn't seem to bother anybody. When I first took my daughter to school, I had to fill in a form with some details of myself. Under 'Educational Qualifications' I wrote '*High-school drop-out*'. Under 'Present Occupation', I wrote '*College professor*'. I also noticed that when I was introduced to lecture audiences, my sponsor seldom forgot to mention that I was a high-school drop-out, perhaps to encourage his duller students. In England, professors who introduce me carefully skirt the subject, obviously afraid of embarrassing me.

In spite of my enthusiasm for the American way of life, I was aware of its darker aspects. In the morning, as I drove Sally to school, I would switch on the car radio. The nearest town to Hollins is Roanoke, a pleasant little place with a population of less than 100,000 (which I have always associated with Delius, since he taught in the nearby Roanoke College, at Danville). And every other morning, the announcer would mention that there had been a robbery at some gas station or drug store during the night. One day, a woman's body was found in a field close to the college. She was a young Catholic, helping to take a census of co-religionists. Her killer had cut her body open and stuffed her with kerosene-soaked rags, which he then set alight. She was the third victim of similar crimes in the past two years.

I drove up to a girls' school fifty miles away to lecture. The town was peaceful and extremely pretty, the college delightful, and the students full of enthusiasm. (I am not a bad lecturer when I'm on form.) As we drove away, I said to Joy: 'This is the kind of place I'd like to settle in – peaceful, comfortable, with a low crime rate. . . .' She then told me that on the previous day, two youths had walked into an ice cream parlour in the town, taken the two girls behind the counter into the back room, and shot them both to death.

Later, in Seattle, the crime rate made Roanoke seem pastoral. On one single day I counted three murders mentioned in the local newspaper, and this was not unusual. There were armed robberies in our local supermarket – and the university quarter of the town was relatively 'respectable'. And shortly before I left Seattle, the police uncovered an immense conspiracy that involved dynamiting several police stations in the northern part of the town, and then robbing several banks in the central area while the police were occupied in the north. America seems to be in the middle of a permanent crime wave. With a population only four times as large as Britain's, its murder rate is sixty-six times as high.

Living on the picture-book campus at Hollins, it was hard to understand all this violence. But one day I took a walk around the Negro 'village' behind the campus. Most of its inhabitants work in the college as maintenance men, cleaning women, and so on. It was worse than any slum I have seen in London or Leicester. There was a school-like building, and every window in it was smashed. The houses were rickety wooden shacks, and one was literally leaning at an angle of forty-five degrees and propped up with poles. There was no glass in any window – only cardboard or linoleum. The stench was atrocious, but this may have been because a few of them kept pigs in their back-yards. The ditches were full of broken glass, rusty sheets of galvanised tin, discarded shoes, twisted bits of perambulators, dead animals (an enormous pregnant rat among them). A professor's wife who helped run a school for the Negro children told me – what I could have guessed – that there was little furniture in any of the houses, and that they were all overcrowded. The odd thing was that some of them had TV aerials, and a great yellow Cadillac stood outside one of them. (But this is largely due, of course, to the elaborate American credit system, which means you can run up immense bills and pay them off – at high interest rates – over years.)

I wondered how it must feel for some young Negress to take a domestic job with the college and compare the lives of the faculty children with those of her own children. Or what must be the reaction of a Negro youth to the southern belles with their horseback riding and expensive cars? Hollins does not think of itself as a rich girls' college – just as a comfortable, pleasant place with good academic standards – but from the Negro point of view, its girls must seem completely pampered and decadent. And the same, no doubt, goes for visiting English writers.

As I came back from my walk, the girls were making the most of the sun, stretched out all over the grassy slope below our house, a hundred or so sunburned bodies in bright bikinis. And very clearly, there was nothing wrong with that. The contrast was a symbol of America, Scott Fitzgerald's America and Booker T. Washington's, side by side – and, unfortunately breathing down one another's necks. The crime figures ceased to be puzzling.

One of the most unexpected things I discovered about America is that it is so like England, so completely un-foreign. Perhaps this is because we are brought up on American films and novels and magazines. But from the writer's point of view, no two countries could be less alike, simply because England must be very nearly the worst country in the world for writers, and America probably the best. There is still a romantic *cachet* attached to the idea of being a writer in the States. And while this certainly didn't help Poe and Melville, it is at last beginning to pay off. On the simplest level, America pays its writers more. For reasons I have never been able to understand, an American publisher may be willing to offer immense sums as advances – sums like $100,000, which he cannot possibly make back on hard-cover sales unless the book stays on the best-seller list for a year. I once asked Norman Mailer – who received more than that for *The American Dream* – how it was possible to do this, and he explained that the publisher hopes for a huge profit on the paperback edition. With a little hard pushing and a half-clad girl on the cover, the paperback can sell a million, which represents about a million dollars. The profit margin is huge, and he can afford to pass on a little to the author.

Journalism can also pay a lot more in the States. It is nothing for a mass-circulation magazine to pay two or three thousand dollars for an article. A writer could live comfortably on half a dozen of these a year.

The 'educational explosion', the tremendous increase in the number of colleges, offers another source of income. If a writer as unqualified as myself can be taken on as a full professor, a writer who also has a degree will obviously have no problem at all. The consequence is that some unknown poet who has published two thin volumes of verse can find himself a comfortable position as Poet in Residence on some mid-western campus, and have a level of comfort and security that would be impossible for his counterpart in England. He also gets asked to appear on TV programmes to express the Writer's views on Viet Nam and *LSD*, and attractive female students ask him if he would consider giving them private tuition in creative writing. I know two such poets, and they live the life of Riley.

There is another basic difference between the American literary scene and the English one: it is less centralised. If you live in London, and frequent the pubs around the BBC and Fleet Street, you will sooner or later meet every major writer, publisher and critic in England. In America, they are spread out from New York to Los Angeles. There are plenty of cliques, but their influence is necessarily small. If your novel is slaughtered in the *New York Review of Books*, it may reduce your sale with a certain audience, but you may be a best-seller in California because it was praised by the *Los Angeles Times*.

All this means the writer has a feeling of freedom of movement that he can never have in England, unless he is old and thoroughly respectable. James Drought, for example, publishes his own books. And without a single comment, adverse or otherwise, from the critical moguls, he is a best-seller on campuses. He couldn't last for a week in England.

Over here, there is a definite feeling that if a writer is serious, he cannot be successful, and if he is successful, he cannot be serious. In America, there seems to be a feeling that if a writer is serious, it is a national duty to see he makes money. So a writer who has never aimed at a large audience is likely to wake up any morning and find himself at the top of the best-seller list with Harold Robbins and James Michener. This has happened to Saul Bellow, Herbert Gold, Bernard Malamud, Katherine Anne Porter, Isaac Bashevis Singer. What is more, the critics who have made him successful do not seem to bear a grudge about it afterwards, as in England. The rare exceptions – like James Gould Cozzens – only emphasise the general rule.

I am not claiming that America is an ideal country for writers. There has always been plenty of back-biting and back-stabbing in the literary world, which makes it a nerve-racking existence wherever you happen to live. And academic life – where you might expect disinterestedness – is not all that much better.

However, the academic creative writer is a hybrid who gets the best of both worlds. His only problem is whether he is the kind of writer who thrives on security, or the kind who needs emotional – and financial – ups and downs. There is also the fact that the academic environment tends to sterilise and dehydrate, and a writer would be well advised to get out of it once he has stabilised his finances.

I can only say that my past two years in America have been a kind of holiday. I didn't realise how much I detested the English literary establishment until I got away from it. Culturally speaking, living in England is like living in a small village. And although you may carefully avoid reading the *New Statesman* or the posh Sunday papers, you gradually soak up the atmosphere. You feel 'known' in the way you are known to your friends and family. In America, it is possible to sink into a refreshing anonymity, to forget your own identity in its size. We drove from New York to Seattle, pulling a U-Haul trailer loaded with our books, records, and other junk. It was a strange sensation, to drive for eight hours, and then look at the map, and realise we had only moved half an inch across it. It induces the Whitman frame of mind – a quite impersonal pleasure in multiplicity, in being a unit among two hundred million people, all unaware of your existence.

The anonymity is, of course, optional. When we arrived in Seattle, there was a brief rash of offers to appear on TV or radio, requests for interviews, and so on. I steered clear of most of these, as of social invitations. The consequence was that after a month, everybody – except my students – had forgotten I was there. And since we now lived so far off campus that it was inconvenient for students to visit me, life was even quieter than at Hollins. I actually wrote more than I would usually write at home. And once again, a monthly pay-cheque produced an altogether unusual sense of security.

We came back by sea; it seemed the only practical way to transport the seven monstrous crates of accumulated household equipment. The customs were unexpectedly lenient – presumably because we had been away for two years – and let us through without paying duty. Then we came back to Cornwall, and a freezing, rainy English April, and the credit squeeze, and the domestic chaos that usually results from a long period of absence. But the old harness no longer feels so tight, since I know we could go back at any time. That is, unless all the other English writers rush there ahead of me and grab all the jobs.

1969

SIXTEEN

A memoir of the 'fifties

I was sitting on the wall in the courtyard of the British Museum, eating a tomato sandwich, when a young man approached me. He said: 'I see you're reading Kierkegaard. I wonder if you'd care to have a look at the thesis on Heidegger I'm studying?' It was actually pretty obvious that I was reading Kierkegaard. The Museum copy of the *Selected Writings* has gold letters an inch high down its spine, and I'd left it at the top of a pile of other books. All the same, his offer struck me as curious. There is not much fraternisation in the Reading Room (unlike the *Bibliothèque Nationale*, where you get the idea you've wandered into a club). However, I took it that he wanted to be friendly. So I told him I didn't read German, and that anyway, I wasn't particularly interested in German existentialism, which seemed to me an abortion. He sat down at the side of me and opened a flask of coffee, and we contemplated the American tourists who sat eating their sandwiches on the steps, unaware of the danger from the pigeons whose aim has an impressive accuracy. I liked his quiet, American voice; we talked about Descartes and Berkeley, on whom he was writing a thesis. Finally, he said:

'You know, I'm certain I've seen you somewhere apart from this place. You don't speak on Hyde Park Corner, do you?'

I admitted I did. At this time (the spring of 1953) I was a member of the Syndicalist Workers' Federation of North London. During the previous winter, I'd spoken for the London Anarchist Group, but they didn't like my heresies, and finally the group had separated into squabbling factions when Herbert Read accepted a knighthood. (Half the Anarchists were all for expelling him – a difficult matter since there is no official membership of the L.A.G. – while the other half felt that his name would be an even more valuable instrument of propaganda now that he had a title.) I had joined the anti-Read faction; not because I gave a

257

damn about the knighthood, but because most of my friends in the group opposed it. So a couple of us slouched off to the gloomy headquarters of the Syndicalist Workers – a damp room in a Paddington slum – and proposed to borrow their platform at weekends, and try for converts in the Charing Cross Road and in Hyde Park.

(I had no particular political convictions – anarchist, syndicalist, or otherwise. My sole bias was a certain pro-Wilson tendency; I spoke in Hyde Park because I was bored, frustrated, and had a vague feeling that something ought to be done about something. I also wanted to practise speaking in public, and would have been equally happy to discourse on Communism, Mormonism, or Nudism.)

We finished our sandwiches and wandered back into the Museum, while I gave him a sketch of the complicated inner-politics of the Anarchists. His interest flattered me. Finally, before we separated to go to our seats, he said: 'Look, why don't you come over and have a meal? I'd like you to meet a friend of mine.' I said O.K., and we arranged it for the following evening. It didn't strike me as particularly curious that he should take the trouble to make my acquaintance and invite me to supper. In the coffee-houses and wine-lodges where I spent my evenings, this kind of thing happened all the time; you were likely to become a bosom pal of a man you had never seen two days before and whom you wouldn't recognise in a month's time. Perhaps because human relationships help to insulate you from a sense of futility.

So I cycled over from the hospital in Fulham (where I was working as a porter) to the address in Berners Avenue, and the door was opened by the American boy. (He had introduced himself as John.) We tramped up two flights of stairs into a tiny room, lined with hundreds of books. An exotic cooking smell penetrated from the next room. A man wandered in, clutching a kitchen knife and a green pepper. John introduced us: 'George, this is Colin.'

I was surprised. I had expected him to be John's age. Instead, I found myself shaking hands with a plump, middle-aged man with a mid-European accent. He invited me to make myself comfortable, and went back to his cooking.

I felt instantly at home in the room. The shelves were full of Kafka, Mann, and Hesse, although some of the volumes that interested me most were in German or Hungarian. There were books on comparative religion, and a copy of Ballou's *Bible of the World*. Another case was full of record albums (all 78's; these were the days before LPs became popular) – I noticed some Beethoven quartets and the Mahler fourth symphony (the only one I knew). I had a premonition that I was going to like George a great deal.

In fact, this proved to be so. He was the first member I had met of a species that I have since come to know and like – the cultured, metaphysical mid-European. I wonder occasionally if it is a species that is becoming extinct. They are not numerous. Thomas Mann belonged to it; so (to judge by *Lolita*) does Vladimir Nabokov. I know only a few others: Erich Heller of Swansea, Heinrich Walz of Heidelberg. . . . I can count them on the fingers of one hand. For them, questions of human destiny and human freedom are of great importance; they know Dostoievsky's Legend of the Grand Inquisitor by heart.

The supper was excellent – a meat dish, cooked according to some Hungarian recipe, followed by guavas and cream. The conversation was vague and general – about Dostoievsky, Nietzsche, Tolstoy, Eliot. I had recently been studying Gurdjieff, and warmly recommended Kenneth Walker's book *Venture with Ideas* and Ouspensky's *In Search of the Miraculous*. After the meal, he insisted on playing me some Bruckner, with whom I was unfamiliar. Towards midnight I left, feeling well-fed, relaxed, and enormously pleased with my new acquaintance. Nothing had been said about Hyde Park or the Anarchists, and I had forgotten that this was supposed to be my reason for meeting George.

A few days later he contacted me and asked me over again for supper. This time, John was not present. We began by speaking of Gurdjieff. George had tried to read *All and Everything*, and had come to the conclusion that Gurdjieff was a fake. I got considerably excited, and tried to explain that *All and Everything* is the worst possible book to begin a study of Gurdjieff with, that he had written it deliberately in a prolix and repetitious style to discourage 'culture vultures'. To my dismay and irritation, George rejected this explanation, and declined to try Kenneth

Walker or Ouspensky. He told me stiffly: 'When I wish to make the acquaintance of a philosopher, I go direct to the fountainhead, not to some interpreter.'

This was the first of several discords. The next occurred when I talked about the Church and expressed my admiration for Pascal. George quoted some scathing epigram from Nietzsche. I countered by quoting Hulme, and asserting that if I thought the Church could ever regain the power she possessed in the Middle Ages, I'd enter a seminary immediately. George launched into a diatribe on Christianity, and referred to the clergy as 'crows in black' or something of the sort. This irritated me – not because I had any special feelings about the priesthood, but because he obviously expected to shock me. I had passed through the stage of total atheism and Rimbaudian blasphemy at thirteen; later I had re-created a religious attitude out of bits of Nietzsche, Eliot, Shaw, Dante, and the Bhagavad Gita. George's anti-religious attitude seemed to me incredibly naive, and his assumption that I was as shockable as some vicar's daughter struck me as an insult.

But later in the evening, we spoke of the anarchists, and I began to understand why I had been asked to supper. I left George to do the talking for about an hour, and an interesting story emerged. He had left Hungary in the 'thirties. During the war, he had been in the army and had worked for Intelligence. At the end of the war, he had been given the task of 'de-Nazifying' a particularly tough bunch of young Nazis. The authorities had little hope; their attempts at brain-washing had been met with total contempt and some physical violence. George was tried as a last resort.

He described his methods to me. He made no attempt to talk about politics but simply engaged them in discussion on neutral subjects. His young Nazis had that voracious appetite for intellectual discussion that I have noticed in German youth; they seem capable of going on for twenty-four hours at a stretch. So George played possum, and let them expound their ideas to him, shooting an occasional question. Besides, he endeared himself to them by making critical comments on the British and American way of life, and the corruptions nurtured by the democratic system. To everybody's surprise, it worked triumphantly. By using the Socratic method of asking questions and leaving his interlocutors to tie themselves in knots, he soon had them criticising their own beliefs. At this point, George would expound his own ideas – the need for tolerance and freedom, the evils inherent in all ideologies, the importance of refusing to be a member of the herd. (I wonder if the British Army would have been particularly happy if they'd realised what George was up to – that he was casting out seven devils of fascism with eight devils of total anti-authoritarianism? However, they never found out.)

When the former young Nazis returned to Germany, they kept in close contact with George, and formed a movement to propagate his ideas. One of his most enthusiastic converts was the young Baron von Altenburg, and his home near Kassel became one of the headquarters of the movement. They provided it with a name – *Die Brücke* (The Bridge) – and set about the work of proselytising. To begin with, they were fantastically successful. Germany was in the grip of post-war depression; a new idealism was needed. *Brücke* spread from Germany into France and the Scandinavian countries. George headed the movement in England, with von Altenburg as his chief lieutenant on the continent.

However, the depression passed, and the enthusiasm dwindled. Only a few faithful spirits remained by the time I met George.

But this was where I came in. George told me that he had gained his few Engish followers by speaking in Hyde Park. But he regarded himself as no orator; his manner was essentially intimate. He had gathered a few people around him, and talked with them standing on the ground, disliking the idea of a platform. But now, he declared, it was time *Bridge* made another effort to expand, and for this, platform oratory was a necessity. Soon, he intended to move out of the diminutive rooms in Berners Avenue, into a house. It would be my task to persuade idealistic young men to attend meetings at the new house.

Later that evening (it was a Saturday) we took a bus down to Hyde Park. George said: 'Well, go ahead – talk.' I protested that I had no platform. He pointed to a chair by the railings. So I stood on it and waved my arms and started to talk, and soon a crowd gathered. I forget what I talked about – probably syndicalism –

but it went well, and after half an hour the crowd was enormous, and I was exhausted. So I wound the meeting up (or handed it over to some gentleman who wanted to tell funny stories and take a collection) and we went off to Lyons for some tea. George was delighted. All I had to do now was to learn something about *Bridge*, and we were in partnership.

About a week later, I suddenly felt that I could bear no more of the Western Hospital, so I sold my books, dug out my passport, and went to Paris. Bill Hopkins joined me, and we lived precariously for a couple of months, working for a couple of English magazines. We were selling subscriptions on a commission basis, and the commissions were minute, so we were frequently forced to impound the subscriptions. I lived off chocolate; Bill, as far as I can remember, ate nothing but smoked hundreds of cigarettes. Finally we explained to the editors about the harsh economics of selling subscriptions, and came back to England on money borrowed from the British consulate. Immediately on arriving in London, I rang George and asked if he could put me up overnight. He answered with an invitation to come and stay in his new house for a few days.

Here, for the first time, I came into contact with *Bridge* members. Meetings were held on Tuesday evenings. I arrived on Saturday. So for three days I listened endlessly to Bruckner and Mahler, and involved George and John in discussions on Dostoievsky and the metaphysical nature of freedom. And on Tuesday evening, the 'disciples' turned up.

I was immensely disappointed. To begin with, there was only one pretty girl among them, and she was married to one of the *Bridge* members. And at first glance, the young men failed to strike me as promising material for an intellectual rebellion. They all looked honest and 'nice' enough, but dull.

Moreover, it soon transpired that the 'discussion' began with a long speech from George which seemed to be interminable. My memory of it is vague, but I believe it went something like this:

'Is *Bridge* an ideology? In order to answer this question, we must first define the word "ideology". [Then followed several examples of ideologies.] An ideology is a system of ideas about man or society. All ideologies start from the concept of man or society. They all believe in imposing their general notions upon individuals. But this is a denial of individual freedom. Therefore all ideologies are undesirable. . . .'

Then followed a demonstration that *Bridge* could not be an ideology, since it didn't want to impose anything on anybody. . . . This, George concluded, ended the series of discussions on what *Bridge* was *not*; at the next meeting they would begin a series of discussions on what *Bridge* is.

The young men then began tortuously following the various hares that George had loosed during the past half-hour. Again, it seemed to me that no one was asking the right questions. They all seemed to agree that Fscism and Communism were very wicked, and that Socialism is neither here nor there, that the important thing is freedom. Then somebody (probably George) raised the Kantian question of the greatest good of the greatest number, and they all lumbered after that like a football team on a cross-country run. Finally, in sheer exasperation, I broke in, quoting Nietzsche, and saying it was not a question of freedom *from* what, but of freedom *for* what? Never mind what they didn't want; what was it they wanted? Before the talk about freedom begins, we ought to consider the question of who is to be free. If we are talking about a crowd of fools, then freedom might do more harm than good.

I had hoped my irritation might stimulate the discussion, which had become unbearably turgid. But everyone seemed to be slightly cowed, with the exception of George. All eyes turned upon him as the defender of *Bridge*, and the evening turned into a duologue between us. Finally, round about ten, we had coffee, and listened to a movement of Bruckner's fourth symphony. Then everybody went home.

As soon as I was alone with George, I told him flatly that I considered he was wasting his time with his 'disciples'. They came to sit at his feet, but they would never learn to think for themselves in a million years. He told me gently that he thought I was being unreasonable, and that when I got older I would agree that he was right. This irritated me still more; the fact that I was twenty-two seemed to me to be irrelevant. The next morning, I hitch-hiked to Leicester and took a job in a big store over Christmas. It was about three or four months before I saw George again.

I was back in London, working in a laundry, and trying to finish the first version of *Ritual in the Dark*. George sent me an invitation to a party. Familiar with the excellence of his catering, I accepted with enthusiasm. I took Bill along with me, and discovered (to my surprise) that he and George had met several years before, when Bill had attended a few *Bridge* meetings. Bill's feelings had apparently been pretty close to my own.

The 'disciples' were more fun at a party than at a *Bridge* meeting. One of them played on a guitar and sang English folk-songs, another did a sort of Bernard Miles West-countryman act, while another young man was called upon to read from the poems of John Donne. The pretty girl got rather delightfully drunk and had to be carried upstairs. She was married to the young man who read Donne, and whose name was Stuart Holroyd. I saw Bill engaged in earnest conversation with Holroyd for about a quarter of an hour. But he finally edged over to me, reported that he thought they were all 'drips', and suggested we go back home. So we went.

Since I lived in North Finchley, I found it easy to cycle over to George's place in Mill Hill. We still got on capitally when we were alone; we played records and talked ideas without any violent disagreement. But the subject of *Bridge* usually started a bitter argument. In defending himself against my charge of wasting time, George had quoted Socrates with such frequency that I began to see Socrates as the key to his personality. Undoubtedly, George possessed the same, almost erotic charm attributed by Plato to his master. The quiet Hungarian voice, the curiously liquid-brown eyes, the serenity of manner which could become charmingly reproachful when I lost my temper, were all combined to give his interlocutor the impression that he was the only person in the world who mattered to George. This frequently had the effect of totally disarming me. He could, when he wanted, give an overwhelming impression of gentleness, love, and consideration. So long as we were alone, I found him immensely likeable. But as soon as the 'disciples' gathered around, his idealism became suspect, and it seemed to me that he was indulging a fantasy in which he played the part of The Teacher, a mixture of Christ and Socrates, for which an audience of admiring young men was essential.

At the *Bridge* meetings I attended, it became obvious to me that my annoyance was directed less at George than at the doctrines he was preaching. These seemed to me essentially inadequate, incomplete. *Of course* freedom is the only thing that really matters; of course totalitarianism is undesirable. Where do we go from there? In a sense, I found him annoying because, in over-emphasising freedom, he forced me to insist on the challenge-and-response mechanism, on the need for discipline, and on the stupidity of most human beings. In irritation at what seemed to me a wishy-washy and short-sighted anarchism, I found myself ranting like a convinced Fascist. And this annoyed hell out of me. In the opposition between spirit and necessity, freedom and authority, I found myself cheering for spirit and freedom. But if the dichotomy is reduced to a question of political freedom or leadership, 'culture' or vulgarity, I am carried away by irritation that these oppositions should be mistaken for extremes, and tend to say more than I mean. When George's 'disciples' got carried away by enthusiasm in condemning television or the *Daily Mirror* or 'Workers' Playtime', I would find myself going all thin-lipped like T.S. Eliot at a football match, and quoting T.E. Hulme in a rasping voice, or Yeats' *Mera*:

> Civilisation is hooped together, brought
> Under a rule, under the semblance of peace
> By manifold illusion; but man's life is thought,
> And he, despite his terror, cannot cease
> Ravening through century after century.
> Ravening, raging, and uprooting that he may come
> Into the desolation of reality. . . .

At these times I would be carried away until I sounded like Henry Irving playing Corporal Brewster.

It was after one such occasion that George requested me to come to no more *Bridge* meetings. I would, he explained, always be welcome at *Bridge* parties; but on the meetings themselves I acted only as a disruptive influence. He assured me that his feelings towards me were of the friendliest, but it would be many years before we would see eye to eye. One day I would become more mature and see that he was right. . . .

This kind of patronage infuriated me. It may have been shortly
after this that I spent a whole morning in the British Museum
writing him a long letter, a violent indictment of his ideas and of
himself personally. It seemed to me that the two were being
thoroughly mixed up, and he was making his ideas an excuse for
indulging a taste for playing Socrates. My main line of attack was
that, if he was serious about his ideas, he would look for some
more effective way of propagating them than lecturing to his
'disciples' – writing a book, for example. (In his younger days,
George had published poetry in Hungarian.) It seemed to me that,
in restricting himself to the Tuesday meetings, he was betraying
the same craving for immediate 'effect' that drove Dickens, in
later life, to give public readings from his novels. And in throwing
me out of the meetings, he was confirming my suspicions that they
were intended to be sessions of 'George-worship', conducted with
the decorum of a Church of England service.

The immediate effect of this letter was a kind of reconciliation.
I went to supper, and we settled down to a serious discussion of
ideas. I explained that, in my view, his weakness consisted in an
over-emphasis of 'sweetness and light'. Preaching universal
tolerance to a small crowd of not-very-bright young men seemed
to me a boring half-measure. I accused him of failing to
understand the forces of modern history or the forces that had
kept the Church in power for so many centuries. George
immediately asked me to explain my defence of the Church. At
this point, one of us used the term 'subconscious mind', and it
proved to be the magic pass-key. Provided I defended my belief in
the mystical and the irrational in terms of Freudian psychology, it
was O.K. We agreed that all that matters is for man to break
through to this enormous power-house that underlies consciousness; our disagreement lay only in the means. For me the answer
had to be subjective, to lie in a personal discipline. For George, it
was important to persuade these young men to think for
themselves, to appreciate music and poetry; he was not a writer by
vocation but a teacher. . . .

When John arrived home later, he was surprised to find us in
amicable agreement. But this was of short duration. Within a few
weeks, we were arguing as violently as ever. The discussion
tended to get personal. I was accused of 'confused thinking', of

not knowing what I 'really meant', of being irritated by George's 'maturity and serenity'; I countered with accusations of smugness and laziness. On some occasions I left him in a furious mood, determined never to see him again. But he was good-tempered and amiable, and always seemed glad to see me. And I was sleeping in the open in a waterproof sleeping-bag, and spending my days in the British Museum, so the evenings of Bruckner and Beethoven were a welcome diversion.

One day, George invited me round to a 'cultural evening'. There were readings from his favourite humanist philosophers and an hour or so of music. This gave me an idea. I proposed that *I* give a cultural evening, reading from my favourite poets and philosophers. He agreed readily. This delighted me. Since I was no longer allowed to state my objections to the *Bridge* group, I would spend a whole evening presenting my indictment in terms of poetry and philosophy.

At this time, my girl-friend was looking after my books for me. I spent an evening going through them, marking various passages for reading. (Many of these passages were subsequently included in *The Outsider*.) I chose deliberately to illustrate my feeling of the world's basic violence and irrationality. It was designed as an attack on sweetness and light, on political utopianism and scientific humanism. There were chunks from *The Seven Pillars of Wisdom*, from Hemingway and Blake, Newman and Hulme.

Half-way through my preparations, I decided I needed an accomplice. The only member of the *Bridge* group who seemed a tolerable reader was Stuart Holroyd. My difficulty lay in the fact that I was pretty sure he wouldn't abet an attack on George. So I approached him and asked him if he'd be willing to give some readings from the metaphysical poets; my aim, I explained, was to demonstrate the self-division produced by intellect in imaginative writing.

Up to this point, I had gained a distinct impression that Holroyd was vaguely hostile. He very seldom spoke at *Bridge* meetings, but his occasional comments had been in defence of George. I hoped my Machiavellianism would conceal my true intentions until it was too late. I was mistaken. Holroyd tumbled in no time at all. But to my enormous surprise, instead of refusing to have anything to do with it, he joined me with enthusiasm. I realised that his taciturnity at *Bridge* meetings had concealed a growing dissatisfaction with George. Now we spent several evenings discussing the reading, marking passages of William James, Dostoievsky, Nietzsche, and Hulme. Finally, on the evening of the reading, we staggered around to George's clutching about a hundred books between us.

The direction of the reading was pretty obvious from the word go. Using deliberate shock tactics, we opened by reading some of the most revolting bits from the *Seven Pillars*, and Hemingway's description of bodies hanging on a barbed-wire fence in *Natural History of the Dead*. In between readings, we expounded our theme: that in the face of a world capable of overpowering beauty and overpowering terror, simple rationalism is an inadequate reaction. And trusting emotional attitudes are completely out of place. The contradictions call for an agonised intellectual effort; the agony is a sign of awareness of reality. The belief in sweetness and light is mere self-deception or deliberate laziness.

Half-way through the reading, we stopped for coffee. The room was crowded, and everyone was looking a little bewildered; but Stuart and I were enjoying ourselves like mad. George murmured, 'You are twisting a knife in my stomach.'

The main item in the second half of the reading was a long section from the Night-town scene of *Ulysses*, complete with blasphemy, delirium, and Anglo-Saxon profanities. This again was a deliberate shock-tactic. At the end of the reading, everybody looked dazed. There was no discussion. Only a Catholic friend we had taken along said that, after all that, he had decided he agreed with George, and would renounce Catholicism. (He wasn't joking – he actually ceased to be a Catholic.)

In a sense, this meeting was the end of my association with George. I still saw him occasionally, but it was understood that we were irreconcilably opposed. Instead, I saw a great deal of Stuart Holroyd, and we began pacing one another on critical books: he began *Emergence from Chaos* and I *The Outsider*. Besides, George always returned to his comments about my age, and the assurance that I'd feel differently when I'd had more experience of 'life'. This enraged me, and made me determined not to renew our acquaintance until he could have no further excuse for this kind of patronage. When *The Outsider* was accepted, I lent him the manuscript, but he returned it months later, still unread.

I saw nothing of him for several years.

We met again recently for lunch. It was obvious within the first five minutes that the same total failure to communicate still exists. The personal element has become too strong; we react uncontrollably, like chemical compounds. The difference of temperaments makes any real discussion of ideas impossible. This is a pity, since I feel that, in many ways, he was right. I *have* changed in the six years since I first met him, although not entirely in the way he predicted. I no longer regard the Church as the necessary antithesis of modern materialism, and political freedom seems no longer so irrelevant to the question of man's absolute freedom. But the basic differences remain. I would not like to try the experiment of attending another *Bridge* meeting. George, no doubt, feels the same about me.

I was amused by a story he told me about one of the 'disciples'. When *The Outsider* was published, a young man who had been particularly opposed to me approached George carrying a newspaper. 'You misled us about Colin. A journalist here says he's a genius. Why didn't you tell us?' George assured him gravely that the journalist was probably exaggerating. Eighteen months later, when my *Religion and the Rebel* was published, the same young man brought a copy of one of the posh weeklies to the *Bridge* meeting. 'You were right about Colin. This man here says he's not a genius. I apologise for doubting your word.' It is to George's credit that he pointed out that a critic in a posh weekly may be as fallible as a penny-a-liner in a low-brow daily. I hope the lesson has taught the disciple to think for himself.

1959

Notes and references

CHAPTER ONE

1. *New Pathways in Psychology: Maslow and the Post-Freudian Revolution*, Taplinger, 1972.
2. In this last speech, the playwright's leader dots.
3. *Poetry and Mysticism*, Eighth Edition (1970).
4. See also the symposium *Beyond Reductionism*, edited by Koestler.

CHAPTER TWO

AUDEN, W.H. *Poems*. London: Faber, 1933.

HUSSERL, E. *Ideas*. London: G. Allen, 1912.

JOHNSON, S. *Rasselas: Prince of Abissinia*, 1759.

MASLOW, A.H. *Toward a psychology of being*. Princeton, N.J.: Van Nostrand, 1962.

RYLE, G. *The concept of mind*. London: Hutchinson, 1949.

SARTRE, J.-P. *The transcendence of the ego*. New York: Noonday Press, 1936.

SARTRE, J.-P. *Nausea*. London: John Lehmann, 1938.

SHAW, G.B. *Back to Methueselah: As far as thought can reach*. Fair Lawn, N.J.: Oxford University Press, 1947.

STRINDBERG, J.A. *Legends: Autobiographical sketches*. London: Melrose, 1912.

TEILHARD DE CHARDIN, P. *Le phenomene humaine*. Paris: Editions de Seuil, 1955.

VERNON, J.A. *Inside the black room*. London: Souvenir Press, 1963.

WELLS, H.G. *Experiment in autobiography*. London: Golancz, 1934.

WITTGENSTEIN, L. *Philosophical investigations*. Fair Lawn, N.J.: Oxford University Press, 1953.

YEATS, W.B. Under Ben Bulben. In *Last poems and two plays*. Dublin: Cuala Press, 1939.

CHAPTER THREE

1. Recent evidence suggests that these stones could have been brought to Salisbury Plain by glaciers. However, considering the sheer engineering skill and patience required to erect Stonehenge, I feel my example remains valid.

CHAPTER FIVE

1. *The Autobiography of Bertrand Russell* (London, 1968), II, p. 87.
2. *Memories and Studies* (New York, 1912), pp. 237–238.
3. *Ibid.*, p. 239.
4. See E.H. Visiak, J.B. Pick and myself, *The Strange Genius of David Lindsay* (London: John Baker, 1969).

CHAPTER SIX

1. I am not denying the importance of these fine novels; only commenting on a black, gloomy atmosphere that reminds me of certain Russian novels of the nineteenth century.

CHAPTER SEVEN

1. I might add that Graves once accused me of putting too much personal bitterness and malice into *The Outsider*, a remark that has always baffled me. I wonder how far he was again playing the strange trick of reading his own characteristics into someone else's work? I hasten to add that I do not consider Graves in general an envious or malicious man.
2. I cannot resist adding here that Eliot has constantly reprinted a similar blooper in his essay *Tradition and the Individual Talent*. Explaining the metaphor of a catalyst, he remarks that when oxygen and sulphur dioxide are passed over platinised asbestos, the result is sulphurous acid. In fact, of course, the result is sulphur trioxide gas, which must be dissolved in dilute sulphuric acid to make concentrated sulphuric acid. I suggest that both Eliot and Graves need a short course in chemistry.

CHAPTER THIRTEEN

1. Interested readers could make a start with: *Towards a Psychology of Being* by A.H. Maslow (Insight Books, New York, 1962; Van Nostrand, London, 1962), *Explorations in Transactional Psychology*, ed. by F.D. Kilpatrick, and *Existence, A New Dimension in Psychiatry*, ed. by Rollo May (Basic Books, New York). All are obtainable through any good bookshop.